Contents

KU-549-657

1 Illicit drugs and their effects

Edited from: *The Essential Guide to Drugs and Alcohol*, Harry Shapiro, DrugScope, 2007

The use of drugs (including alcohol, tobacco and coffee) for non-medical purposes is an often misunderstood aspect of human behaviour. The most extensive and solid scientific work on drugs focuses on their chemical compositions and effects on laboratory animals. We also know something about the characteristics of people who use large amounts, seek help or get into some kind of trouble with drugs because they are the ones most likely to come to the attention of, for example, doctors, drug agencies and the police, and therefore most accessible to researchers.

But information derived from these areas of research doesn't necessarily help much in understanding the 'everyday' use and misuse of drugs, nor how social and psychological processes influence the outcome of drug-taking behaviour. Instead, it can only offer a very rough guide to whether the consequences will be beneficial or harmful in any individual case.

Drug effects are strongly influenced by the amount taken, how much has been taken before, what the user wants and expects to happen, the surroundings in which they are taken, and the reactions of other people. All these influences are themselves tied up with social and cultural attitudes to, and beliefs about, drugs, as well as more general social conditions. Even the same person will react differently at different times. So it is usually misleading to make simple cause-and-effect statements about drugs, such as 'drug X always causes condition Y'.

The drug-by-drug method of presentation may give the impression that drug users themselves fall into these categories. This is not necessarily the case. While there must be many people who restrict their drug use to alcohol, tobacco, caffeine or cannabis, others (especially compulsive users) will switch drugs depending on availability, or use drugs in combination or one after another.

> No nation so ancient but had its narcotic soother from the most distant times; none so remote and isolated but has found within its own border a pain-allayer and care-dispeller of native growth; none so savage which instinct has not led to seek for, and successfully to employ, this form of physiological indulgence. The craving for such indulgence and the habit

of gratifying it, are little less universal than the desire for ... consuming our common food.

James Johnson, *Chemistry of Common Life,* 1854

Drug-taking and risk-taking

The majority of people who use drugs come to no physical or psychological harm, and many will feel that they have benefited (and may well have done so) from the relaxation, diversion or temporarily improved social, intellectual or physical performance that can be afforded by some drugs. But there are very serious risks, and a large part of this publication is about these and how they arise. Some of the most important points to be made about the risks of drug-taking apply to all or most of the drugs in this publication. To an extent, these represent rules of thumb about what not to do with drugs in general, though each drug has its own array of potential risks. It should not be assumed that the extent to which a drug is legally restricted is much of a guide to how harmful it can be.

Overdoing it

The adage about moderation applies to drugs in two different ways. First, taking too much in one go risks an experience that gets out of control and causes distress or even a fatal overdose. Obviously the more taken, the greater the risk of accidents due to intoxication, including choking on vomit while unconscious.

Second, anyone taking a psychoactive drug frequently, in high doses, and for a long time, is likely to experience a distortion in their perception of and response to their environment, such that normal functioning and normal development are impaired. Social relationships may narrow down to a small group of people with similar habits, and finding or keeping work and housing may be difficult. As tolerance/ dependence develops, the problems of financing drug purchases can add to the deterioration of diet, housing and lifestyle, and may result in revenue-raising crimes. Normal desires for say food and sex, and reactions to discomfort and pain, may be dulled by the drug, and the resultant self-neglect can damage health. Indirect damage – arising from the lifestyle associated with heavy, and especially, illegal drug use, rather than a direct effect of the drug on the body – is often the most significant, but can sometimes be minimised even if drug use continues. Obviously, heavy use is most likely if someone becomes dependent on the drug, when they will find it hard to stop, despite their health being affected.

Wrong time, wrong place

Even in moderate doses most of the drugs (except the stimulants) impair motor control, reaction time and the ability to maintain attention. These effects can last several hours. No matter how the person feels, they are not as capable as before, and activities such as driving, operating machinery and crossing roads become more hazardous to themselves and to others. They will also be less effective at their job.

Even stimulants may impair delicate skills and the learning of new skills, and in high doses will impair performance of tasks they previously enhanced.

Also many drugs amplify mood, such that if someone is feeling – or is in a situation that makes them feel – depressed, anxious or aggressive, the drugs could make things a lot worse. Even drugs (like alcohol and tranquillisers) we think of as calming people down, can also release aggressive impulses because they weaken the grip of social and personal inhibitions.

Individual differences

Statements about drug effects are often statements about what might happen in extreme cases, or alternatively about what usually happens with most people. But not everyone is 'usual'. For instance, some people develop a toxic reaction to a single cup of coffee, and the normally insignificant elevation of heart rate caused by cannabis can be painful for people suffering from angina pectoris. Glaucoma patients, on the other hand, may find cannabis beneficial, but three strong cups of coffee will aggravate the condition. Individuals with pre-existing psychotic tendencies may be 'pushed over the brink' by their experiences under the influence of powerful hallucinogens like LSD.

Also, the extent to which a drug affects the body tends to vary with body weight, so, in general, less heavy people will get greater effects and consequently greater dangers from the same drug dose than heavier people will. Sex differences in response to psychoactive drugs are poorly researched, but, for instance, it is known that women alcoholics are more susceptible to liver disease than men, due to physiological differences. Individual differences in the degree of response to the same amount of a drug mean that dose levels for a given effect quoted in this publication can only be generalisations.

Pregnancy

There are several ways in which drugs might damage the foetus. First, heavy use may affect the mother's health either indirectly or through self-neglect and poor nutrition. Second, drugs may indirectly affect the foetus through the mother's bloodstream. Very rarely do they cause malformations; this risk is at its greatest in the first three months of pregnancy.

More significantly, some of the drugs listed in this publication affect the foetus in the same way as they affect adults, and the baby's immature body is less able to cope. Thus, drugs like alcohol, opiates, sedatives and tranquillisers, which depress the adult's respiration and other body functions, will also depress these functions in the foetus and in the newborn.

There is also the possibility that babies born to mothers dependent on opiates, sedatives, tranquillisers or alcohol will need medical care to avoid withdrawal symptoms.

These risks are by no means the same for all drugs, and are best established for drugs with depressant effects. But, in general, heavy drug use in pregnancy is associated − probably for a variety of reasons − with premature birth and low birthweight, and an increased risk of losing the baby around the time of birth. On the other hand, the evidence on the effects of moderate drug use during pregnancy is generally inconclusive, and many heavy drug users give birth to perfectly healthy babies. But this is an under-researched area, and doctors generally advise pregnant women not to take any drugs if it can be avoided.

Injection

Injection of drugs is less widespread than other ways of using them, but also the most hazardous. Drugs that are injected are mainly of three kinds: opiates, sedatives and tranquillisers, and stimulants (amphetamines and cocaine). These may well be mixed to combine their different effects.

When injected into a vein, all the drug enters the bloodstream and some is carried directly to the brain, producing a noticeable effect within seconds. For these reasons, the onset of the drug's effects (the 'rush') is quicker and more striking after injection. In general, the short-term effects of injected drugs are along the lines of those taken by mouth, but more intense. Opiates, for instance, produce a sensation of warmth and relief from physical and mental discomfort, but when injected these effects can be magnified into a short-lived burst of intensely pleasurable sensations. Drugs can also be injected under the skin or into muscles, when the effect is more delayed and less intense than with intravenous injection.

The major dangers of injecting are: overdose; infection from non-sterile injection methods (including hepatitis, HIV/AIDS and other diseases transmitted by more than one injector sharing the same needle); abscesses and gangrene caused by missing the vein when injecting; and damage from using crushed-up tablets and other dosage forms not meant to be injected.

For a few people, the injection may become as important as the effect of the drug, and if no drugs are available almost anything will be injected. Nevertheless, dependence is not inevitable and will take time to develop.

These are just a few examples. But, in general, it cannot be guaranteed that the effects a drug has on an individual will match those cited in publications like this, especially if that person is particularly vulnerable due to illness or because of their psychological make-up.

Adulteration and mistaken identity

Drugs offered on the illicit market are not always what they are claimed to be, and if illicitly manufactured they are likely to contain any one of a range of impurities or adulterants. Also, the buyer can rarely be sure how strong the substance is. And even if they did know, they wouldn't necessarily know how much to take.

These factors add greatly to the unpredictability of the effects of, and damage from, the use of drugs obtained without the safeguards of medical supervision or the quality control imposed on licit manufacturers. (See also **What's in a drug?** below.)

Doubling up

People who attempt suicide using large amounts of benzodiazepine tranquillisers almost invariably wake up unharmed. But the same dose on top of a large dose of alcohol could easily prove fatal. This example illustrates the point that effects of drugs which individually depress body functions (alcohol, solvents, sedatives, hypnotics, opiates, tranquillisers) will add up if they are taken together, so that much lower doses of each will be fatally depressant than would normally be the case. Since drugs remain effective for varying periods, often many hours, the two substances don't even have to be taken at the same time.

Doubling up on depressant drugs is probably the most dangerous, but complex interactions can occur between other drugs. Doctors and experienced drug-takers make use of these to 'fine-tune' drug effects, but for most people loading one drug on top of another multiplies the risk of a harmful outcome.

Drug laws

Even the police would agree that most drug offences are never discovered. But to help enforce drug laws police have very wide powers. They can stop and search people in the street on suspicion, search homes on a warrant and remove property, and have successfully used undercover police officers.

The laws themselves are very wide-ranging. An occupier who allows someone to grow cannabis in their house, even if they had nothing more to do with it, has committed a very serious offence. Just planning together to commit a drug offence renders people liable to the same maximum sentence they might have got if they had actually done it.

So even with drugs where the medical dangers seem slight, the legal dangers remain. First-time possession offences rarely attract a prison sentence, but being arrested, prosecuted and convicted can be enough in themselves to cause great distress and to affect the offender's education or career.

While legal prohibitions help minimise the number of people who take prohibited drugs, the same laws can increase certain risks for those who do take them. Risks associated with adulteration, uncertain purity, poor hygiene, high costs, inadequate or misleading information, possible added delay in seeking medical or social assistance, all these are closely related to the illegality of certain drug-taking behaviours.

Drug terms

Addiction implies that a drug dependency has developed to such an extent that it has serious detrimental effects on the user. They may be chronically intoxicated, have great difficulty stopping the drug use, and be determined to obtain the drug by almost any means. The term addiction is inextricably linked to society's reaction to the user, and so medical experts try to avoid using it, preferring the term dependence instead.

Addict is a drug user whose use causes serious physical, social or psychological problems. As it is a much-abused term, many people prefer to talk of dependent, problem or chronic drug users instead.

Analgesic is a painkiller.

Benzodiazepines are the most commonly prescribed minor tranquillisers (for daytime anxiety relief) and hypnotics (to promote sleep). They include products such as Valium and Temazepam.

Chaotic use is when an individual is regarded as taking a drug or drugs in a spontaneous way that tends not to follow any typical drug-using pattern. It is generally associated with problematic bouts of heavy use that may cause the user harm.

Controlled drugs in the UK are preparations subject to the Misuse of Drugs Regulations 1985. These drugs are divided into five schedules covering import, export, production, supply, possession, prescribing and appropriate record keeping. The first schedule deals with drugs such as LSD and ecstasy for which medical prescription is not available. The strictest schedules for prescribed drugs are two and three and these include opioids and stimulants.

Come down is the hangover or after-effect of taking a drug. Reflecting the low feeling experienced after the high of taking a drug, come down is mostly associated with the after-effects of stimulant taking, in particular ecstasy, which can last anything up to four days.

Dependence describes a compulsion to continue taking a drug in order to feel good or to avoid feeling bad. When this is done to avoid physical discomfort or withdrawal, it is known as **physical dependence**; when it has a psychological aspect (the need for stimulation or pleasure, or to escape reality) then it is known as **psychological dependence**.

Depressant is a drug that acts on the central nervous system to suppress neural activity in the brain. Opioids and sedatives are both classes of depressants.

Designer drugs is a term coined in the 1980s to describe drugs specifically synthesised to circumvent regulations on controlled substances. Ecstasy is often cited as a designer drug, but this is incorrect. As an analogue of amphetamine, there was no need for new legislation to control its use when it became popular. In the US, Fentanyl, a painkilling drug many more times potent than morphine, induced Parkinson's Disease in some users who sampled it. More recently, the anabolic steroid tetrahydrogestrinone (THG) is another example of a designer drug – in this case 'designed' to avoid detection.

Detoxification is the process by which a user withdraws from the effects of a drug. It usually refers to withdrawal in a safe environment (a detoxification/detox centre), with help on hand to minimise the unpleasant symptoms.

Drug use/ misuse/ abuse. Drug use is an easy term to understand. Misuse and abuse are more difficult to pin down, as they are highly subjective. In most circles, misuse means using in a socially unacceptable way. However, the definition currently being adopted defines misuse as using drugs in a way that results in experience of social, psychological, physical or legal problems related to intoxication and/or regular consumption. Many regard the term abuse as too judgemental, as it suggests impropriety regardless of how the drug is being used. In general, abuse means using drugs in a harmful way. As abuse and misuse can be morally 'loaded' terms, many people prefer to talk of drug-taking, or of harmful or problematic use instead, when appropriate.

Flashbacks are hallucinations that occur a long time after a drug (often LSD) has been used.

Hallucinogenic is a drug which induces hallucinations and alters perceptions (eg LSD, magic mushrooms). (See **Psychedelic** below.)

Hard drugs usually refer to drugs which are seen to be more dangerous and more likely to cause dependency, such as heroin and crack cocaine, than those designated as 'soft', such as cannabis and LSD. Obviously there is an element of truth in the distinction, but it is generally a value judgement used for propaganda purposes by both pro- and anti-drug lobbies and so is best avoided. The terms 'hard' and 'soft' when applied to drugs have no legal or pharmacological validity.

Harm reduction is a term that covers activities and services that acknowledge the continued drug use of individuals, but seek to minimise the harm that such behaviour causes.

Legal highs are drugs that do not fall under the Misuse of Drugs Act, although they may be controlled under the Medicines Act. Most are herbal (also called herbal highs) such as ephedrine, yohimbine and salvia, but some, such as poppers, are synthetic or processed. Many are sold as legal and safe alternatives to illegal drugs, but are usually retailed without a licence, and are not without their own risks to health.

Narcotics are commonly used to mean any illicit drug, especially in the US. However, the term technically refers to chemicals that induce stupor, coma or insensibility to pain, such as **opiates** or **opioids**.

Opiates are derived from the opium poppy (eg morphine, codeine, heroin).

Opioids include both opiates and their synthetic analogues (eg methadone, pethidine).

Over-the-counter drugs are those which are available from chemists without a prescription (eg Benylin, Nurofen).

Overdose is the use of any drug in such quantities that acute adverse physical or mental effects occur. It can be deliberate or accidental; lethal or non-lethal.

Paraphernalia is the equipment for drug-taking (eg silver foil, spoon).

Pharmaceutical drugs are those drugs available from chemists, either on a prescription or **over the counter**.

Polydrug use is the use of more than one drug, often with the intention of enhancing or countering the effects of another drug. Polydrug use, however, may simply occur because the user's preferred drug is unavailable (or too expensive) at the time.

Prescribed drugs are those drugs obtained on a prescription, and may refer to methadone and other **opioids** or to **tranquillisers** and **anti-depressants**.

Problem drug use tends to refer to drug use which could be either dependent or recreational. In other words, it is not necessarily the frequency of drug use which is the primary 'problem', but the effects that drug-taking have on the user's life (ie they may experience social, financial, psychological, physical or legal problems as a result of their drug use).

Psychedelic was coined in 1956 by the LSD researcher Humphrey Osmond, and literally means 'soul manifesting' – an activation of consciousness. Although virtually synonymous with **hallucinogenic**, psychedelic implies that the drug or experience acts as a catalyst to further feelings and thoughts, and is not merely hallucinatory.

Psychoactive or psychotropic are perhaps the most all-encompassing ways of describing mood-altering drugs in general, though they are more often used to describe LSD and similar hallucinogenic drugs.

Recreational drug use is the use of drugs for pleasure or leisure. The term is often used to denote the use of ecstasy and other 'dance drugs', and implies that drug use has become part of someone's lifestyle (even though they may only take drugs occasionally).

Sedative is a **depressant** which acts on the central nervous system to relieve anxiety and induce calmness/sleep (eg **benzodiazepines**).

Stimulant is a drug which acts on the central nervous system to increase neural activity in the brain (eg amphetamine, cocaine, caffeine, and – if used in high quantities – **anti-depressants** and certain **opioids**).

Tolerance refers to the way the body gets used to the repeated presence of a drug, meaning that higher doses are needed to maintain the same effect.

Tranquillisers are calming drugs used to manage various mental disorders. They can be differentiated from **sedatives** in that (unless used in high doses) they do not interfere with thought processes or send the user to sleep.

Volatile substances refers to all solvents and inhalants (not, as is sometimes thought, to aerosols only).

Withdrawal is the body's reaction to the sudden absence of a drug to which it has adapted. The effects can be stopped either by taking more of the drug, or by 'cold turkey' – which may last for up to a week.

What's in a drug?

Impure street drugs can be dangerous but these dangers are sometimes exaggerated. There is a degree of urban mythology about street drugs – the main one being that drugs are cut with substances such as rat poison, strychnine and brick dust. Such contamination is rare. Unless a dealer has some score to settle, it is not in their best interests to have customers dropping dead from deliberately contaminated drugs.

There is no comprehensive list of what has been added to street drugs. Most drug testing is done for police and Customs who only need to identify what (if any) controlled drugs are present. As testing is an expensive business, laboratories are rarely asked for detailed information about other substances.

Batch to batch variation

Drugs are often cut simply to improve profit margins. But there are a number of other reasons why they may not be as advertised or may vary in content. For example, this week's batch of Mitsubishis (an ecstasy 'brand name') may be of a particular strength or composition; next week's may be entirely different. This could be because there was a supply problem with one or more of the chemicals used to produce the drug ('precursors') so substitutes were used. It could instead (or as well) be due to some error in the manufacturing process, or just that the Mitsubishis of one week have entirely separate origins from next week's batch.

Drug content guidelines

The following is a very rough guide to average purities of street drugs and what they contain. To repeat the warning already given, *this should not be relied on to determine the content of substances actually circulating in your area.*

Amphetamines By a long way, the most impure drug on the market. Typical purity is around 5%, with samples as low as 1% seen recently. The main cutting agents are sugars, followed by caffeine and ephedrine.

Cocaine Anything between 30–60%, but averages out around 35%, with the rest mainly made up of sugars.

Crack Typically around 50% pure cocaine freebase. Sophisticated production techniques – mainly 'washing' with solvent before or after heating – mean that a high-purity drug can be produced from only moderately pure cocaine powder.

Heroin Typically 30–80% pure, averaging around 40%. The main adulterant is paracetamol, along with other opiate alkaloids and sometimes methaqualone and diazepam. Sugars, too, are sometimes used to bulk out the product. There is no evidence that heroin is diluted following importation. The average purity of heroin seized by the police is nearly the same as that seized by Customs and has been for several years. The reason is that heroin has travelled a long way from the countries of origin and most if not all the cutting has been done en route.

Ecstasy Most samples contain MDMA; other related drugs such as MDEA or MDA are now uncommon. Fake ecstasy tablets may contain other substances such as ketamine or amphetamine, although again this is not that common. The average amount of MDMA in a genuine tablet is 70–80 milligrams, but occasionally much larger amounts may be present.

LSD Now rarely seen by police or Customs. Usually sold as small paper squares cut from a larger sheet which has been soaked in the drug. Mostly the genuine article, though completely inert fakes are not unknown. Dosage can vary significantly depending, for example, on how the paper sheets have been prepared.

Anabolic steroids Most steroids bought in gymnasia are either fakes or counterfeits. Fakes contain little or no steroid (though sometimes they do contain drugs other than steroid) or a different steroid from that cited on the label. Counterfeits are illicitly manufactured products sold as the genuine pharmaceutical drug.

How can you tell what it is?

Is there any way the drug user can test the drug they have bought or that parents or professionals can get drugs they have found tested?

Field testing kits are available, but they contain dangerous substances like acids. As long as they do so without delay, a parent or worker can take a sample to the police and ask for it to be tested. Some laboratories will test substances at a price, but if the substance *is* a controlled drug then, under certain circumstances, the person who took the drug to the laboratory, and the laboratory analysts, may open themselves up to a successful prosecution for unauthorised possession of the drug.

A note on terminology

Words such as 'adulterant' and 'impurities' are used interchangeably to denote that something other than the pure drug is being sold. There are two main types of impurity: first, substances which are psychoactive but are not the ones the buyer was expecting; second, substances which are virtually or completely inert. However, these words do have more specific meanings, as follows:

Impurity Substance or substances present in the drug as a natural result of the manufacturing process rather than deliberately added, eg opiate alkaloids from the process of refining opium into heroin or the by-products of manufacturing amphetamine.

Adulterants Psychoactive drugs deliberately added to 'mimic' the effects of the drug being offered. This would include the stimulants caffeine and ephedrine that make up much of what is passed off as amphetamine. Invariably this is done to increase profits.

Diluents Inert substances such as sugars (glucose, lactose or mannitol) added both to bulk out the deal and assist the process of dilution for injection.

Excipients Mainly relates to tablet/pill manufacture; the starch or gums used to bind the drug together in tablet form.

The drugs

Please note this is only meant to be indicative of the range of illegal drugs available in the UK. For a more comprehensive overview, please refer to *The Essential Guide to Drugs and Alcohol* and also DrugSearch on the DrugScope website at www.drugscope.org.uk/resources/drugsearch/drugsearch.htm

Amphetamines

Speed, uppers, whizz, Billy, Dexedrine, dexies, Ritalin

Amphetamines are stimulants in the form of synthetic powders available as a variety of tablets, capsules, etc – sometimes in combination with other drugs. These have a medical use and in the 1950s and 1960s they were widely prescribed for depression or to suppress appetite. They are now only recommended for the treatment of pathological sleepiness and (paradoxically) hyperactivity in children. Amphetamines may be swallowed in tablet form, or sniffed, smoked or injected as a powder. A crystalline form of the drug methamphetamine known as 'ice' has currently low-level presence on the UK drug scene.

What does the law say?

Amphetamines are controlled under the Misuse of Drugs Act as a Class B drug, but as Class A if prepared for injection. Methamphetamine has been re-classified as a Class A drug in any form.

What are the short-term effects?

Amphetamines arouse and activate the user in much the same way as the body's natural adrenaline does. Breathing and heart rate speed up, the pupils widen and appetite lessens. The user feels more energetic, confident and cheerful. Because of these effects, there is a risk of psychological dependence.

As the body's energy stores become depleted, the predominant feelings may become anxiety, irritability and restlessness. High doses – especially if frequently repeated over several days – can produce delirium, panic, hallucinations and feelings of persecution.

The effects of a single dose last about three to four hours and leave the user feeling tired, but often unable to sleep due to the residual stimulant effect of the drug. It can take a couple of days for the body to fully recover.

What are the long-term effects?

To maintain the desired effects, the regular user has to take increasing doses, often many times the normal dose. When they eventually stop, they are likely to feel depressed, lethargic and ravenously hungry. Amphetamines merely postpone fatigue and hunger and do not satisfy the need for rest and nourishment. Heavy use risks damaged blood vessels or heart failure, especially for people with high blood pressure or pulse rates and those who take strenuous exercise (eg athletes) while using the drug.

Regular high-dosage users are liable to develop delusions, hallucinations and paranoia. Sometimes these develop into a psychotic state, from which it can take several months to fully recover. Heavy use also debilitates the user due to lack of sleep and food and lowers resistance to disease, all of which can have serious effects on health.

Cannabis

Hash, spliff, blow, draw, toke, grass, weed, marijuana, skunk

Cannabis derives from *Cannabis sativa* (although other strains exist), a bushy plant easily cultivated in Britain. It is generally used as a relaxant and a mild intoxicant. The most important active ingredients, tetrahydrocannabinol (THC) and cannabinoids, are concentrated in the resin at the top of the plant. Hashish or hash is resin scraped from the plant and compressed into blocks. For many years, imported resin was the most used form of the drug in the UK, but increasingly the market for commercially home-grown herbal cannabis has been developing rapidly

What does the law say?

Cannabis is controlled under the Misuse of Drugs Act as a Class C drug, but this is currently under review.

What are the short-term effects?

The effects of cannabis depend largely on the expectations, motivations and mood of the user, the amount used and the situation. Most people do not experience very much at first and have to learn which effects to look out for.

The most common, and most sought-after, effects are talkativeness, bouts of hilarity, relaxation and greater appreciation of sound and colour. While intoxicated, the cannabis smoker will be less able to perform tasks requiring concentration or intellectual or manual dexterity. Some of these effects can be reduced with sufficient application and concentration, however.

There may be perceptual distortion with higher doses. People who use the drug when anxious or depressed, may find that their unpleasant feelings are magnified, and can sometimes experience short-term panic. The same is true of inexperienced people using high doses. There is virtually no danger of fatal overdose.

The effects generally start a few minutes after smoking, and may last up to one hour with low doses and for several hours with high doses. There is no hangover of the type associated with alcohol, although some may feel tired, light headed and possibly edgy the next day.

What are the long-term effects?

There is no conclusive evidence that long-term cannabis use causes lasting damage to physical or mental health in the vast majority of users. However, as with tobacco, cannabis smoke probably causes bronchitis and other respiratory disorders if frequently inhaled, and may cause lung cancer. Cannabis may therefore cause special risks for people with lung, respiratory or heart disorders. Heavy use in people with disturbed personalities can precipitate a temporary psychiatric disorder and there are concerns about longer-term mental health problems for those who might be psychiatrically vulnerable.

Cannabis does not seem to produce physical dependence. Regular users can, however, come to feel a psychological need for the drug or may rely on it as a social lubricant. As with other sedating drugs, people chronically intoxicated on cannabis may appear apathetic, sluggish and neglect their appearance, but there is no evidence of a special cannabis amotivational syndrome, where users become chronically lethargic and unmotivated.

Cocaine and crack

Coke, Charlie, snow, 'C', crack, rocks

Cocaine is a white powder derived from the leaves of the Andean coca shrub, with powerful stimulant properties similar to those of amphetamine. It is commonly sniffed or snorted up the nose through a tube and absorbed into the blood supply via the nasal membranes. It is also injected and smoked, the smokable variety being known as crack.

What does the law say?

Cocaine, its various salts and the leaves of the coca plant are controlled under Class A of the Misuse of Drugs Act.

What are the short-term effects?

Like amphetamine, cocaine produces physiological arousal accompanied by exhilaration, decreased hunger, indifference to pain and fatigue, and feelings of physical strength and mental capacity. Sometimes these desired effects are replaced by anxiety or panic. When sniffed, the psychological effects peak after about 15 to 30 minutes and then diminish. This means the dose may have to be repeated every 20 minutes to maintain the effect. When smoked, the effects are felt more immediately and wear off more quickly.

Large doses, or a spree of quickly repeated doses, can lead to an extreme state of agitation, anxiety, paranoia and, perhaps, hallucination. These effects generally fade as the drug is eliminated from the body. The after-effects of cocaine include fatigue and depression, though in comparison to amphetamines and ecstasy, these effects are less profound. Excessive doses can cause death from respiratory or heart failure, but these are rare.

What are the long-term effects?

There are no clear-cut tolerance effects with cocaine. Nor are there withdrawal effects of the kind that require the user to continue taking the drug to avoid feeling ill. However, cocaine users may develop a strong psychological dependence on the feelings of physical and mental well-being it affords and are often tempted to step up the dose. After discontinuing, the user will feel fatigued, sleepy and depressed, all of which reinforce the temptation to repeat the dose.

With heavy and frequent use, increasingly unpleasant symptoms develop. Euphoria is replaced by an uncomfortable state of restlessness, hyper-excitability, nausea, insomnia and weight loss. These generally persuade people to cut down or stop for a while. Continued use may lead to a state of mind similar to paranoid psychosis. Regular users may appear chronically nervous, excitable and paranoid. All these effects generally clear up once use is discontinued. Repeated sniffing can damage the membranes lining the nose and may also damage the structure separating the nostrils. Prolonged smoking may cause a number of respiratory problems.

Ecstasy

'E', MDMA

Ecstasy, or MDMA (methylenedioxyamphetamine), is classed as a hallucinogenic amphetamine, a group of drugs with effects roughly combining those of amphetamines and LSD. Although developed in 1912, ecstasy did not become widely used until the emergence of the 'acid house' scene in the late 1980s, and has been associated with dance music and parties ever since. The drug comes mainly in pill form, but powder MDMA is also available

What does the law say?

Ecstasy is a Class A drug.

What are the short-term effects?

MDMA is effective at the moderate single dose level of 75–100mg. Effects are experienced after 20–60 minutes and can last several hours. Pupils become dilated, the jaw tightens and there can be brief nausea, sweating, dry mouth and throat, a rise in blood pressure and pulse rates, and loss of appetite. There can be some difficulty with bodily co-ordination, making it dangerous to drive or operate machinery. At doses above 200mg, or if the drug is being used repeatedly over a few days, all these effects may be experienced more acutely. Once the drug has worn off, there may be some residual effects similar to those experienced by amphetamine users, including fatigue and depression, which can last for several days.

As with LSD, whether the experience is bad or good often depends on the mood and expectations of the user. With moderate levels of use, most users report a mild euphoric rush followed by feelings of serenity and calmness, and the dissipation of anger and hostility. Most bad experiences with the drug have been reported by those using higher doses over a period of time. Effects include anxiety, panic, confusion, insomnia, psychosis, and visual and auditory hallucinations. These generally die down once the drug is stopped, but can leave the user in a weakened mental and physical condition for a while. Some of these effects have been experienced by those who have tried the drug for self-therapy and have then been unable to deal with the emotions that using MDMA has brought to the surface.

So far around 80 deaths directly associated with the effects of taking ecstasy have been recorded in otherwise apparently healthy young people. Most of these young people collapsed at raves or shortly afterwards and all exhibited symptoms associated with severe heatstroke. The current best guess is that these users have succumbed to the cumulative effects of taking MDMA while dancing for long periods in a very hot, humid atmosphere.

What are the long-term effects?

There is evidence from research carried out by the National Poisons Unit of an association between ecstasy use and liver damage. Tolerance to the effects of MDMA develops, but there is no physical dependence, no heroin-like withdrawal symptoms nor any evidence that MDMA is used compulsively for years.

Overall, the literature suggests that people should not take MDMA if they suffer from heart disease, high blood pressure, glaucoma, epilepsy or are in poor physical or mental condition. Women with a history of genito-urinary tract infection should not use the drug. There is no evidence that the drug has any effect on the foetus or causes problems in the newborn.

Increasing documentation is emerging on the effect of ecstasy on brain cells and brain function. A number of studies on animals (mainly rats, monkeys and squirrels) have shown that MDMA can cause permanent neurotoxic damage to serotonin-producing parts of the brain – serotonin, a neurotransmitter, is involved in the enhancement of mood and memory. While animal studies may say little about human behaviour, some human studies suggest that MDMA is similarly neurotoxic in humans. One such study has shown that self-reporting ecstasy users had possible damage to serotonin-producing areas (decreased serotonin transporter binding sites). Although these results are significant, they must be interpreted with caution. Not only does the measure for ecstasy use rely on self-reporting, which may be incorrect or omit the use of other substances, there is also concern that the researchers failed to fully control for pre-existing serotonin function abnormalities, which could be a cause or caused by ecstasy use. Nor do we know the exact functional effects of the apparently damaged areas, and so can say little about what behavioural effect, if any, this will produce.

Heroin and other opiates

'H', brown, skag, smack, junk, methadone, meth, Diconal, dikes, codeine

Opiates are drugs derived from the opium poppy. Opium is the dried milk of the poppy and contains morphine and codeine. From morphine it is not difficult to produce heroin, which is, in pure form, a white powder more than twice as potent as morphine. Opiates have medical uses as painkillers, cough suppressants and anti-diarrhoea treatments. A number of synthetic opiates are manufactured as painkillers. These include pethidine, dipipanone (Diconal), dextropropoxyphene

(Distalgesic) and methadone (Physeptone), a drug often prescribed for opiate addiction. Opiate powders can be swallowed, or dissolved in water and injected. Heroin can be sniffed up the nose like cocaine, or smoked by heating it and inhaling the fumes; this is known as 'chasing the dragon'.

What does the law say?

All opiates including heroin and methadone are controlled under the Misuse of Drugs Act as Class A drugs.

What are the short-term effects?

Moderate doses of pure opiates produce a range of generally mild physical effects (although the painkilling effect will be marked even at moderate doses). They depress the nervous system, including reflex functions such as coughing, respiration and heart rate. They also dilate blood vessels (giving a feeling of warmth) and depress bowel activity, resulting in constipation.

Low doses produce euphoria. Higher doses produce sedation and the chance of overdose, where the user can go into a coma and possibly die from respiratory failure. Overdose is more likely if other depressant drugs, like alcohol, are used at the same time, and there can be fatal reactions to injected adulterants.

Opiates induce a relaxed detachment from pain, desires and anxiety. They make people feel drowsy, warm and content, and relieve stress and discomfort. However, among people who have developed physical dependence and tolerance, positive pleasure is replaced by the need to obtain opiates in order to stay normal.

Along with, or instead of, these reactions, first use (especially injection) often causes nausea and vomiting. These unpleasant reactions quickly disappear with repeated doses. The effect of sniffing heroin is slower and less intense than that of intravenous injecting. The effects of heroin are felt as quickly after smoking as after intravenous injecting, but are not so intense. Heroin can be addictive no matter how the drug is taken, including smoking, eating and sniffing.

What are the long-term effects?

As tolerance develops, regular users increase the dose to achieve repeated euphoria. Sudden withdrawal after several weeks on high doses results in varying degrees of discomfort, comparable to flu. The effects start 8–24 hours after the last dose and include aches, tremor, sweating, chills, sneezing, yawning and muscular spasms. They generally fade in seven to ten days, but feelings of weakness and loss of well-being last for several months. People can overdose when they take their usual fix (the amount taken) after a break during which tolerance has faded.

Physical dependence is not as significant as the strong psychological dependence developed by some long-term users. Dependence of any kind is not inevitable and many people use heroin on an occasional basis without experiencing problems.

The physiological effects of long-term opiate use are rarely serious in themselves. But physical damage, associated largely with repeated, often unhygienic, injecting and with the injection of adulterants, is common among long-term users. Injectors also run the risk of HIV infection unless they always use sterile equipment. Repeated heroin sniffing can damage the membranes lining the nose. Decreased appetite and apathy can contribute to illness caused by poor nutrition and self-neglect. As tolerance and dependence develop, financial difficulties can also contribute to self-neglect and a diminished quality of life.

Ketamine

Special K, 'K', Ketalar

Ketamine is an anaesthetic with analgesic and psychedelic properties chemically related to phencyclidine (PCP, or angel dust). Like PCP, ketamine is a dissociative anaesthetic – ie patients feel detached and remote from their immediate environment. Ketamine comes in a variety of forms, ranging from its liquid pharmaceutical state, for injecting, through to pills to be taken orally. Powders are sniffed up the nose or sometimes smoked.

What does the law say?

Ketamine is a Class C drug under the Misuse of Drugs Act.

What are the short-term effects?

Ketamine takes effect over varying time periods depending on the route of administration (from 30 seconds for intravenous injection to 20 minutes if taken orally), and the effects can last up to three hours. The normal dose for sniffing ketamine is about 100–200mg. Used intravenously or intramuscularly, a sub-anaesthetic dose would be around 1–2mg per kg of body weight. Ketamine effects are dose-specific, with roughly 100mg sniffed resulting in a stimulant effect, and 200mg and above causing more hallucinatory and out-of-body experiences.

Reported physical effects include an initial cocaine-like rush, vomiting and nausea, slurring of speech and vision, numbness and ataxia (irregular muscle co-ordination). Many users report a temporary paralysis and a feeling of being out of the body.

Aside from the risks from injecting common to all drugs, it is ketamine's anaesthetic properties which pose the main physical dangers. Under its influence, users are less likely to feel pain and, combined with the fact that some might not realise they are hallucinating (because they believe what is happening is real), there is the potential for serious injury.

As with any anaesthetic, eating or drinking in the hours prior to use could cause vomiting; because of the risks of choking, this could be particularly dangerous if too much is taken and the user falls unconscious. If the dose exceeds the standard surgical dose, then there is the risk of respiratory collapse or heart failure. However, ketamine deaths appear to be rare; only one case is cited anecdotally in the literature, with no precise reference given.

Users report that although ketamine's psychological effects come on and recede faster than with LSD, these effects are similar – including hallucinations, synaesthesia ('seeing' sounds and 'hearing' colours), euphoria, de-personalisation and confusion, plus the powerful dissociative or out-of-body (flying or floating) sensations, which appear specific to ketamine. Different from the LSD experience, however, are the reported feelings of aggression and stimulation. And, unusually for a drug with hallucinogenic properties, ketamine has a high potential for addiction primarily because of the powerful detachment and heightened visual and potentially spiritual experiences which occur.

What are the long-term effects?

The literature on the consequences of long-term ketamine use is sparse, and the following observations are invariably based on single case studies. Flashbacks (short-lived recurrences of the drug experience) similar to that experienced by some LSD users are possible. One clinical report suggests there may be memory, attention and vision impairment from long-term use, which in this case did not return to normal once use was reduced.

Physical dependence and withdrawal are not a feature of ketamine use, although as stated, the psychological power and detachment can make it an addictive drug for some users. Tolerance develops quickly. Stimulant-like weight loss and loss of appetite can occur during periods of heavy use.

One authority has concluded that frequent and prolonged use of ketamine could cause the same problems as PCP, including psychological dependence, psychosis and gradual loss of contact with the real world.

Hallucinogenic mushrooms

Several species of mushrooms can have hallucinogenic effects when eaten. About a dozen of these grow wild in the UK, notably the liberty cap or 'magic mushroom'. The liberty cap contains the hallucinogenic chemicals psilocybin and psilocin. It may be eaten fresh, cooked or brewed into a tea, and can be preserved by drying. Due to variations in potency, it is impossible to say how many mushrooms are required for a hallucinogenic experience; 20 to 30 is a general amount, but much fewer may suffice.

Distinguishing hallucinogenic from poisonous (and possibly deadly) mushrooms is a complex skill, requiring knowledge of botany and expertise in mushroom classification.

What does the law say?

Prior to 2005, it was not illegal to pick and eat magic mushrooms so long as nothing was done to the mushroom (like drying or infusing in a hot drink) which could be deemed as attempting to extract the active ingredient psilocybin, which is a Class A drug. However, since 2005, it has been illegal simply to possess the mushrooms themselves. This does not apply to other forms of hallucinogenic mushrooms such as Fly Agaric.

What are the short-term effects?

The effects of psilocybin- and psilocin-containing mushrooms are similar to a mild LSD experience. However, the effects come on more quickly and last for a shorter time. At low doses, euphoria and detachment predominate. At higher doses, visual distortions progress to vivid hallucinations. Commonly, there are feelings of nausea, vomiting and stomach pains. Bad trips can occur and may develop into a psychotic episode. These are most common after repeated or unusually high doses, or if the user is inexperienced, anxious or unhappy. They can usually be dealt with by friendly reassurance.

There have been reports of longer-lasting disturbances, such as anxiety attacks and flashbacks to the original experience, but these almost invariably fade. By far the greatest danger is the possibility of picking a poisonous mushroom by mistake.

What are the long-term effects?

Like LSD, tolerance rapidly develops – eg twice as many liberty caps may be needed on a subsequent day to repeat an experience of the day before. This discourages frequent use. There are no significant withdrawal symptoms or physical dependence. Individuals may, however, feel a desire to repeat their experiences. No serious effects of long-term hallucinogenic mushroom use have been reported, but no studies have been undertaken to assess the effects of extended frequent use.

Further reading

Online

BNF.org – the British National Formulary is *the* reference book for medical drugs: http://www.bnf.org/bnf/ (free registration required)

DrugSearch – DrugScope's online encyclopedia: http://www.drugscope.org.uk/druginfo/drugsearch/home2.asp

Re-Solv – provides information on glue-sniffing and other volatile substance use: http://www.re-solv.org/default.asp

Books

Grilly D M, *Drugs and human behaviour*, 5th edn, US: Allyn & Bacon, 2006, ISBN 0205443621
As well as describing basic pharmacological principles, this text discusses the general factors behind drug tolerance, dependence and abuse. Available from: http://www.ablongman.com

McGavock H, *How drugs work: basic pharmacology for healthcare professionals*, 2nd edn, Oxford: Radcliffe, 2005, ISBN 1857756916
Aimed at a medical audience, this book explains the effects of drugs to equip

readers with clear concepts to inform their prescribing decisions. It is also useful for anyone with an interest in drugs generally or therapeutic drugs in particular.

Shapiro H, *Recreational drugs: a directory*, London: Collins & Brown, 2004, ISBN 1843402440
Each entry in this reference work includes a physical description of the drug, discussion of its origin, its street name and chemical name, method of use, likely effects on the body, brain and emotions, and the latent health risks. Available from: http://www.chrysalisbooks.co.uk

Spratto G R and Woods A L, *PDR nurse's drug handbook: the information standard for prescription drugs and nursing considerations*, 2006 edn, US: Thomson Delmar, 2006, ISBN 1418001325
Contains information on drug action, dosage, interactions and contraindications for the most common FDA-approved drugs. Available from: http://www.delmarlearning.com

Wills S, *Drugs of abuse*, 2nd edn, London: Pharmaceutical, 2005, ISBN 0853695822
Each chapter of this book covers a particular drug group. It also covers the prevalence of drug use, a detailed assessment of side effects, and interactions between illicit drugs and conventional medicines. Available from: http://www.pharmpress.co.uk

2 Why people use drugs

Martin Plant

Professor of Addiction Studies, Alcohol & Health Research Unit, University of the West of England, Martin.Plant@uwe.ac.uk

Abridged and updated (2007) from *Drugs in perspective*, M Plant, Hodder and Stoughton, 1987

A daunting number of suggestions have been put forward to explain why people use drugs and why some users become dependent on them. Many of these theories are speculative and anecdotal, stemming from personal experiences and observation of a few drugtakers rather than from rigorous research. Most theories about the *causes* of drug use or drug dependence rely upon descriptions of *established* drugtakers. There is very little information about the characteristics of these individuals before they become involved in drugs. For this reason, there has been frequent confusion between the *causes* of drug use and its apparent *correlates* or even *consequences.*

Many British studies of drug users have been confined to highly selective groups such as students or people in treatment institutions. The significant differences noted between different groups such as heroin dependants in a clinic or cannabis smokers in a college have been largely responsible for the different causal theories put forward. Virtually every writer on the subject of drug use has ventured some opinion, but most have highlighted themes that are relevant to *their* particular study group of drugtakers and which may have little relevance to others. While a perplexing number of equally plausible and useful theories co-exist, few people would suggest that either drug use in general or drug dependence are caused by any single factor. It seems that drug use in general is the outcome of interactions between the drug, the personal characteristics of the individual and the individual's environment. It is clear then that drug use stems from many causes and is the subject of many research interests. It is equally clear that it would be unrealistic to conclude that research in any single field has all the answers.

That said, three general types of theory have been suggested. These are constitutional, individual and environmental.

Constitutional (or biological) approaches

These are concerned with either biological predispositions or with the relationship between a drug and the body.

It has been suggested that depressant drugs such as alcohol, barbiturates and tranquillisers might appeal to those in need of relaxation while stimulants, such as cocaine and amphetamines, might appeal to extroverts who are predisposed to hyperactivity. Animal research has shown that sometimes there does exist a genetic predisposition to use specific drugs. There is a growing body of evidence that inherited factors can predispose some people to develop alcohol-related problems. Such factors obviously interact with availability, social context and other important influences on drug use.

In recent years, considerable interest has been aroused by the discovery that the body produces opiate-like substances. It had been known for over 20 years that the human brain has specific receptors for opiates. It now appears that these receptors, in addition to responding to externally produced opiates such as morphine and heroin, respond to a group of internally produced peptides. Some of these substances, called endorphins (literally 'the body's own morphine'), closely resemble opiates. The receptors excited by such substances are concentrated in the pathways of the brain that are concerned with the perception of pain. In consequence, it is an important and intriguing possibility that the development of opiate dependence by some people, or even the general use of certain drugs, may be explained by the ability of some substances to modify the perception of profound experiences such as pleasure and pain.

Individual approaches

Individual approaches are largely concerned with either unusual personality traits (in the case of drug-dependent individuals) or far more general factors such as extroversion which may explain a willingness to experiment with cannabis or indulge in other forms of drug use.

Personality characteristics

It is a commonplace belief that drug dependence is at least partly attributable to personality abnormalities, and many studies have supported this conclusion. Even so, the evidence for this view is confusing to say the least, because it is based upon a comparison of 'drugtakers' with 'others'. It does appear that opiate users are probably more neurotic than 'normal' people, but this is not a universal conclusion. And although some institutionalised drugtakers have been noted to exhibit higher than average 'hostility scores', they are not unique in so doing. There are, after all, plenty of neurotic, hostile non-drug users. More generally, it has been noted that if any kind of drug is widely acceptable, as is alcohol, then there is no reason at all why users should have unusual personalities.

Intelligence

Evidence shows that drugtakers are of average or above-average intelligence. This conclusion is supported by studies of drugtakers in treatment, educational and penal institutions and in the general population. It is clear that drugtakers vary a great deal in many respects, and there is little support for the view that drug use is caused by lack of intelligence.

General psychiatric state

It is evident that drug dependants in treatment institutions are often psychiatrically disturbed. Sometimes this could be the result of drug misuse, but there is also evidence that sometimes individuals displayed signs of disturbance before becoming drugtakers. Case history data are often cited to support the view that drug-taking satisfies a variety of psychological needs and that sometimes drug dependence is secondary to a clearly defined psychiatric illness. However, it is possible of course that both psychiatric disturbance and drug-taking may be caused by some other factor. It cannot necessarily be assumed that they invariably lead to one another.

Gender

Men appear far more likely than women to use psychoactive drugs (tranquillisers and depressants excepted) and to be heavy users or dependent upon such substances. There may be many explanations for this. Biological or personality differences between the sexes may predispose men to be drugtakers. Certainly social pressures have traditionally inhibited women even from using legal and socially approved drugs (although these inhibitions are waning – eg there is evidence to suggest that young women are now more likely to smoke than young men).

Age

Most users of illegal drugs are young, as are most of those who experience
alcohol-related problems. There has been much speculation about whether or not
age affects drug dependence. It is probable that youthful anxieties and sexual
uncertainties may encourage the use of certain drugs. Also, the menopause in
women and old age in general may often generate pressures that make drug
use attractive. On the other hand, if drug use is attributable to personality
predispositions, there is no reason why it should be especially prevalent among
certain age groups.

Drug use as self-medication

Most drugs have clearly defined effects. It is possible that people who have high
anxiety levels or other psychological needs use drugs specifically for this reason
– that is, to adjust their 'unsatisfactory' mental state to a more acceptable level.
Many drug users certainly report that they use drugs 'to get high', 'to feel relaxed'
or 'for the experience'. People who are drug dependent also frequently account for
their reliance upon drugs in similar terms – eg 'I use drugs to stop being depressed.'

It is difficult to assess how truthful or perceptive such accounts are. Precise
motivation for complex acts are hard to pin down accurately. The main problem is
that one cannot guess what would have happened if drugs had not been used. That
depression and anxiety are commonplace among drug addicts is not reason enough
to conclude that they adopted drug use as a calculated means of countering such
conditions.

Hedonism

Drugs can be fun. They offer an accessible and often reliable means of obtaining
enjoyable experiences. Anyone who doubts this should remember that most adults
use drugs (alcohol, tobacco, coffee) and appear to accept uncritically that such
use is valuable. By their own admission, drug users make it abundantly clear that
they take drugs for the most part because they like it. By definition, drugs alter
the user's mental state – slowing, speeding or distorting perceptions – and many
autobiographical accounts of drug use emphasise the appeal of these effects.

A basic human need?

Psychoactive drug use is virtually universal in some form or other. It has been suggested that this may be so because there is a basic human need to experience an altered state of consciousness. This is compatible with the fact that most people use drugs and most people are clearly not psychologically disturbed. This is really a philosophical theory but it merits consideration in the face of the willingness of such huge numbers of people to use drugs in whatever way and for whatever effect.

Curiosity

Numerous studies of drug use in social settings report that curiosity is often stated to be the reason for initial drug use. This is as true of alcohol and tobacco as it is of cannabis, LSD, solvents, cocaine or opiates. This view, propounded by drugtakers themselves, may, however, be partisan. Even if curiosity does account for initial drug use, it does not explain why some users become dependent while others do not.

Self-destruction/risk-taking

The obvious dangers of unwise or excessive drug use have led to speculation that sometimes drug-taking is prompted by self-destructive impulses. Alcohol dependence, for example, has been called 'chronic suicide'. This theory is compatible with the fact that many institutionalised drugtakers appear to have poor self-images and sometimes have quite strong feelings of hostility directed at themselves. It is also consistent with the fact that some drugtakers, for whatever reasons, do overdose on psychoactive substances. Another theory is that drug use is a form of risk-taking. But there is little evidence that drugtakers are particularly predisposed to take risks. Even so, it does appear that some individuals probably choose drugs which produce effects compatible with their personalities or emotional needs.

Resolution of personal problems

Clinical studies indicate that many drug-dependent people have serious personal problems. In addition, youthful illegal drug use is often a symbolic gesture of defiance against parental or authority values. It is also possible that adopting the lifestyle of the drugtaker (or the 'regular' at the local) provides some people with friendship and social support. There is little doubt that strong social pressures exist, encouraging individuals to conform to certain patterns of drug use as part of more general lifestyles. As ever though, it is difficult to 'work backwards' and deduce whether an individual's current drug use is attributable to pre-existing poor social relationships.

Environmental approaches

Environmental approaches relate drug use to wider social and cultural factors. Many studies have examined the life experiences of drugtakers, emphasising issues such as broken homes, delinquency, educational and occupational disadvantages. It has also been suggested that social changes or deprivation sometimes precipitate or foster drug use. The following section examines some of these environmental factors.

Family disturbance

Much attention has been focused on the family background of drugtakers, especially of drug-dependent individuals in treatment institutions. Many studies of such clinic populations have noted that a high proportion have come from abnormal or disturbed homes and that excessive drug use or drug dependence does sometimes appear to have been aggravated by a family problem of some sort.

The suggested link between drug misuse and parental separation or other family disruptions becomes far less clear-cut when drugtakers are compared to other people. There is no clear evidence that drugtakers *do* differ in this respect from non-drugtakers. In addition, surveys provide abundant evidence that the majority of casual or experimental drug users do not come from disturbed homes.

There is evidence, however, that many institutionalised drug dependants (including problem drinkers) report having parents who were themselves alcohol or drug misusers or who were otherwise unhappy or disturbed. It is widely noted that institutionalised drug dependants often come from 'loveless homes' or have been 'excessively protected'. A result of this appears to be the limited abilities of some of these individuals to form satisfactory relationships or to communicate with other people. There is little doubt that very often one generation will imitate the drug use of their predecessors. Parents who use drugs excessively may well produce children who do the same, even if they do so with substances of which their parents strongly disapprove, such as cannabis or heroin.

Unemployment, education and work problems

There is abundant and convincing evidence that many institutionalised young drugtakers exhibit signs of educational disturbance, particularly truancy. In addition, many drop out of further or higher education or have had very poor employment records. In fact, a growing body of evidence suggests that illegal drug use in the United Kingdom is associated with unemployment. In contrast, tobacco use has clearly declined as unemployment has risen. Young unemployed people appear to be particularly susceptible to illegal drugs, but the relationship between drugs and unemployment is complex and requires further research.

Social class

Drug-taking and drug dependence occur at all social levels. Illegal drug use in the United States has often been connected with severe social deprivation, for example among poor urban ghetto dwellers. A similar picture has developed in some deprived areas of Britain. Despite this, drug users are drawn from all social classes – in fact, one national survey found that the higher socio-economic groups were the most prominent in drug usage (Ramsay and Partridge 1999).

The youthfulness of many drugtakers implies that few will have attained their final occupational level. Even so, many surveys have shown that experimental drug use is quite common among students (who are predominantly from non-manual backgrounds). Social class also appears to influence patterns of drug use. It has been suggested that drug users from working-class backgrounds are more likely to be heavy or excessive users of a wide range of drugs. Those from middle-class families are generally more restrained and selective.

Peer pressure

One of the most commonly given reasons for initial drug use is peer pressure – being goaded into it by friends and acquaintances – and a very large number of studies support this view. This appears to be as applicable to heroin injectors as to cannabis smokers. Some young people appear to be especially likely to be subject to social pressures to indulge in drug use. These include the unemployed, people whose jobs encourage drinking or students and others living away from their parental homes. All are likely to be exposed to, if not influenced by, the fashions and enthusiasms of their peers. Sometimes this pressure will generate strong social endorsement for using cannabis, LSD or heroin.

There is plentiful evidence to support the view that peer pressure is often a potent reason for beginning or continuing drug use. This conclusion rests largely upon self-reporting by drug users who may be reluctant to concede that their use was motivated by any 'abnormal' causes. It is also possible that disturbed or impressionable individuals may be particularly susceptible to peer pressure. This is consistent with the frequently expressed criticism that drug use is sometimes due to 'falling into bad company'. The fact is that from the drug user's point of view the company is often very good. It is clear that people will normally only be influenced by those who they like and by whom they wish to be accepted. There is very little evidence to support the view, beloved of certain tabloid newspapers, that innocent children are lured on to the rocks of addiction by commercially motivated pushers lurking outside the nursery.

Ideology

Some types of drug use are much more widely accepted and indulged in than others. Alcohol and tobacco are generally seen as symbols of maturity and sociability. Medically prescribed tranquillisers and sleeping pills are not seen in this way, and their use is much less discussed or publicly paraded. And finally, illegal drugs carry a whole 'belief system' with them, often regarded as being indicative of protest against or rejection of conventional attitudes and values.

During the 1960s, drug use, especially that of cannabis and LSD, was widely linked with the emergence of a distinctive 'teenage culture' associated in the public mind with permissiveness and hedonism. 'Turn on, tune in, drop out' and other slogans clearly linked drugs with the hippy movement and with a variety of 'new' religious cults.

There is a clear relationship between religious ideology and the use of illegal drugs. Self-reports by young drugtakers, especially those deeply involved with drug use, showed that during the 1960s and 1970s most regarded themselves as not sharing their parents' religious views. It could be that the very illegality of drugs frightens off people with conventional and orthodox beliefs. It certainly seems that strong religious views may 'insulate' young people from experimenting with illegal drugs. Religion certainly appears to influence alcohol use and is often a reason why people choose not to drink at all. This applies not only to Islamic countries but also to parts of Scotland and to large areas of the United States.

Delinquency

Many institutionalised drug dependants have criminal records preceding their drug use. This is also true of institutionalised problem drinkers. As noted above, any type of unusual or antisocial behaviour may predispose those indulging in it to break other social conventions. For this reason, people who have a criminal history may be more prepared to begin using illegal drugs than would others. In addition, some of the factors which foster illegal drug use may be the same as those prompting other types of crime. In spite of this, the overwhelming majority of those using illegal drugs are not otherwise delinquent.

Occupation

Some professions certainly expose people to distinctive social pressures and other stresses. Those in medical, nursing and associated occupations have long been known to be at high risk of becoming drug dependent. Until the post-war boom of youthful heroin use, virtually the only people known to be dependent on opiates in Britain were those in professions which gave them ready access to drugs (usually morphine) or individuals who had become drug dependent while undergoing medical treatment. Doctors have also widely been reported to have high rates of alcohol problems. It is important to remember that the medical profession is relatively well informed about the effects of drugs – calling into question the view that drug problems arise from a lack of knowledge.

Availability

To a large extent, specific drugs are used because they are available. Most social groups use whatever substances they have ready access to. Many young drug users, particularly those in treatment institutions, appear to be willing to use whatever is to hand. Not everyone is so catholic in their drug tastes. Even so, it has often been noted that when, for any reason, large amounts of a drug are available at a reasonable price from whatever source, their use and misuse will invariably increase. The extent of alcohol and tobacco use, for instance, is certainly related to their high levels of availability. There is also abundant evidence that the consumption of any drug, be it heroin or alcohol, is influenced by its price relative to other drugs.

Studies of drug users show that whatever their previous characteristics and inclinations, the availability of drugs in conducive surroundings is an important reason for initial use. The upsurge in drug use which began in the 1960s has been attributed in large measure to the introduction of new drug types, either because they had just been 'invented' or because they were being imported from other countries. The fashion for using amphetamines recreationally was certainly encouraged by the vast quantities available either through thefts or through prescription. In addition, the upsurge in heroin use in the 1960s and 1970s was clearly exacerbated by casual prescribing so that 'spare' supplies could be passed on to others eager to experiment.

As the above should have hinted, the National Health Service is one of the major suppliers of drugs in Britain. Prescribed drugs have certainly been re-sold, stolen or just left around for others to take. Some of those receiving prescriptions have accidentally become 'therapeutically dependent' upon opiates, barbiturates, tranquillisers and other substances. It is clear that even drugs which are considered to be relatively 'safe', such as Ativan, Librium and Valium, will be misused provided they are available in sufficient quantities.

The medical profession has frequently tried to deal with this 'leakage'. The famous 'Ipswich Experiment', when doctors voluntarily curtailed amphetamine prescribing, proved beyond doubt that controlling the supply of drugs may sometimes drastically reduce their misuse. Such restrictions will, of course, only work if the demand for such drugs is comparatively low and if no alternative sources of supply exist. The classic Western example of an attempt to control the availability of a drug was Prohibition in the United States (1920–33). During this period, while 'conventional' alcohol-related problems such as liver cirrhosis declined dramatically, others emerged in the form of bootlegging and gangsterism. Even in Britain today it is clear that curtailing a wide range of drug use requires considerable Customs, police, court and penal resources. In addition, restricting the legitimate supply of any drug creates the risk that illicit supplies may be sought instead. These may be poorly manufactured, adulterated or impure. Furthermore, infringements on civil liberties and the imposition of harsh penalties may cause more harm than the drugs themselves would otherwise do.

Historical reasons

There has been considerable discussion about why certain types of drug use, especially recreational drug use, blossom when they do. Very often the explanations are clear cut – the introduction of tobacco to Britain by Sir Walter Raleigh or the production of new drugs by the pharmaceutical industry. More often than not though, explanations are hard to pin down – the emergence of a distinctive youth drug culture during the 1950s and 1960s occurred for a myriad of reasons, many of which remain only partly understood.

It has been noted that even during the 1940s and earlier, a certain amount of drug trafficking was carried out by sailors. Cannabis use also received a boost from American musicians and 'beat' poets. Even so, there is little to suggest that either of these influences went much beyond the dockyard gates or the fringes of the avant-garde. The arrival of West Indian immigrants to Britain during the 1950s certainly introduced for the first time fairly large numbers of people used to smoking cannabis. Some of these immigrants certainly continued their cannabis smoking, but it is difficult to see them actively influencing the host community. That said, while immigrant cannabis use was probably fairly self-contained, it may have contributed to the general spread of the recreational use of 'new' drugs. It is also probable that, like many other fashions from wearing jeans to break-dancing, certain types of drug use were adopted due to American influence.

The whole lifestyle of young adults changed during the 1960s. Pop music, 'permissiveness' and 'hippy culture' arrived, and drugs were legitimised by cult figures and the new generation of millionaire rock superstars in the 1970s. Youth culture was established with a heavy emphasis on rebellion against established norms. Invariably the drugs used complemented the musical preferences of the user, which was often explicitly drug-oriented. Amphetamines fuelled the Northern soul circuit, helping dancers stay awake all night, while cannabis soothed the strains of softer sounds and LSD helped the listener appreciate Pink Floyd. With the demise of the hippy, came the nihilism of punk with its glue and heroin. More recently, dance has made a comeback, with the rave introducing a raft of new 'feel-good' drugs such as ecstasy.

Many people (politicians and newspaper editors among them) make the simplistic assumption that drug use is caused by the activities of traffickers and dealers. In fact, most studies conclude that initial drug use is largely attributable to encouragement by friends. The direct influence of commercially motivated suppliers has almost certainly been over-emphasised. In more general terms, there is a great deal of evidence supporting the view that young people's drug use largely spreads in a friendly and hospitable way, reflecting much wider social changes. That said, drug use is fostered by both demand and supply and, as noted by Freemantle

(1985), the international drug trade is a massive and relentlessly expanding industry.

The increase in officially recorded drug dependence may be a logical corollary of the growing acceptance of all forms of drug use. Because relatively large numbers of people were prepared to experiment with substances such as cannabis and LSD in the 1960s, a minority may have been encouraged to use opiates. Even so, such a conclusion is by no means certain and the great majority of illegal drug users appear to confine themselves to casual experimentation.

Sociological theories

Several sociological theories have been applied to the post-war spread of drugs in Britain. Probably the most important view is that drug use reflects an increase in *alienation* or *anomie*. Such theories attribute drug use to new social pressures, such as competition for jobs, housing and education. Those whose needs are left unmet by the mainstream of society simply opt out, turning instead to the supportive 'alternative' lifestyle of the drug scene. This provides status and companionship without the demands of the mundane, workaday world. Instead of having to accept the constraints of 'straight' society, with its long-term planning and deferment of gratification, the drug scene permits instant enjoyment. Because of its free and easy values, the scene allows people to 'do their own thing' and becomes a haven for individuals who, for whatever reasons, cannot or will not fit into the rat race of the broader society. This view certainly makes some sense of the commitment to drug-taking. It is also consistent with the fact that many drug-dependent people have psychological problems or are socially deprived. In particular, this approach has the merit of linking drug use with the structure of society.

Another sociological view is that once a 'deviant' behaviour, such as drug-taking, becomes evident society attempts to control it, and inadvertently makes it worse. The logic of this theory is that as drug-taking is labelled and legislated against, those who indulge in it become more secretive and more cut off – ie their deviance is 'amplified'. Consequently, the social controls against this 'growing' problem are increased which, in turn, ratchets the deviants into further isolation and so on. This theory provides a useful insight into the possible effects of identifying and attempting to curb a newly defined social problem. There is much truth in this view and some drugtakers certainly appear to enjoy the drama conferred upon their activities by legislation and by their battles against those who enforce it.

Conclusion

As this chapter has attempted to show, many plausible theories have been put forward to explain why people use drugs and why some become dependent upon them. Each of these theories is consistent with the characteristics of some drugtakers, but it is clear that no single theory can account for all types of drug use. Drug-taking and drug dependence appear to be influenced by a great number of factors, whether constitutional, individual or environmental. Probably different reasons account for different types of drug use. The casual or experimental use of drugs is probably due largely to social pressures combined with availability. Dependence upon drugs may well be attributable to much more profound factors such as social deprivation or psychological disturbance. And finally, other factors may account for the way some people remain dependent while others do not. It should be emphasised that illicit drug use is firmly established and widespread in the UK (Hibell et al 2004). Morever, those who use illicit drugs are also often heavy drinkers and smokers who may also engage in other forms of risky behaviour (Plant and Plant 1992).

References

Freemantle B (1985) *The fix*, London: Michael Joseph

Hibell B, Andersson B, Bjarnasson T, Ahlström S, Balakireva O, Kokkevi A and Morgan M with Plant M et al (2004) *The 2003 ESPAD report: alcohol and other drug use among students in 30 European countries*, Stockholm: Swedish Council for Information on Alcohol and other Drugs

Plant M A and Plant M L (1992) *Risktakers: alcohol, drugs and youth*, London: Tavistock

Ramsay M and Partridge S (1999) *Drug misuse declared in 1998: results from the British Crime Survey*, London: Home Office

3 How many drug users are there?

John M Corkery

Senior Research Fellow in Drug Epidemiology, International Centre for Drug Policy, St George's, University of London, jcorkery@sgul.ac.uk

This chapter answers questions most often asked about illegal drugs: how many people use drugs and how many are hurt by drugs. Statistics on the prevalence of drug use and the number of people seeking help for their drug use are described, and an attempt is made to explain what these figures say, and more importantly, what they do not say.

What do the statistics say?

DrugScope deals daily with enquiries on the prevalence, or the extent, of drug use in the UK. The answer, unfortunately, is never straightforward. The most accurate statistics are taken from a number of population samples. The statistics are based on a number of important assumptions, however, and these must be fully acknowledged before any figures are used.

Proportionately representative of population

Who the researchers select for surveying is important. Two factors must be considered. The sample questioned:
- must be representative of the general population as a whole
- must be chosen with an equal likelihood of selection, either randomly or matched to the population.

The main concern for researchers is whether the results are applicable to everyday conditions without the research context, ie how generalisable are the survey's findings to similar situations which have not been studied. For example, if, out of a group of 1,000 adults from a wide range of ages, ethnic groups, religions, gender, social classes, etc (the list can go on), 200 say they have used a drug at least once, we could predict that, with all things equal, this figure could be applied to the rest of the general population with similar characteristics. We would therefore say that 20% of the adult population has tried a drug at least once.

However, because the use of illicit drugs is socially unacceptable and therefore clandestine in nature, it is difficult to survey accurately. (Drug use per se is not illegal in the UK, although unlawful possession, trafficking, etc in illegal drugs is against the law.) Users are often marginalised and difficult to reach. Most large-scale surveys, such as the British Crime Survey, select households using the Postcode Address File (a postcode database), thereby omitting large numbers of people who do not live in homes or have recognised addresse for example those living in hotels, in university halls of residence, in care, hospital or prison, in temporary accommodation or on the streets – ie the 'roofless'. Such surveys, therefore, run the risk of underestimating the overall level of drug use by excluding people who are, possibly, more likely to use drugs. Another example would be school surveys: depending on the age eligibility criteria, those who have left school would be missed; those who truant or have been excluded would also be left out, research has shown that these groups are at greater risk of using drugs. In any event, even if the heaviest or most problematic drug users are living in households, they are likely to be the most difficult to contact and the most unwilling to admit their drug use. It may also be the case that general population surveys of drug use will over-estimate the prevalence rate of groups with lower usage rates, eg members of the Armed Forces.

Robustness (validity and reliability, bias)

Scientific analyses are underpinned by a number of assumptions (implicit or explicit). The extent to which these assumptions are altered affects the validity of the results or their robustness. For figures to be robust they must be:

- valid – that is, we are measuring what we are supposed to be measuring, eg the results of a questionnaire designed to elicit information on drug use match the results of urinalysis of the same subjects
- reliable – that is, the figures are accurately and consistently measured, eg the same instrument tested under the same conditions by different administrators and scoring the same produces the same results
- unbiased – that is, the measurements are not consistently higher or lower than the true value.

Robustness can be affected by two main factors: how people are questioned, and human nature.

Household surveys of self-reported drug misuse cannot give exact figures for the number of people in the general population who are, or have been, misusing drugs. Since only a sample of the population is covered by a survey, estimates of any particular behaviour will be faced by the problem of sampling error. This type of error is liable to be great in respect of estimates when rare or infrequent behaviours are being examined. However, it can be reduced by selecting a large sample and using efficient sample designs and estimation techniques.

Non-response leads to attrition of the sample. Some potential respondents will have doubts about confidentiality, or may lack the time or inclination to participate, and will therefore refuse to take part. Not all the questions may be answered by those who agreed to take part in the survey.

How people are questioned

An important consideration is who, how and when people are questioned. A teacher asking children at school about their drug use may get a very different answer than if an unknown researcher at the local youth club asks them the same question. The way in which a question is worded or presented may also affect the response. Researchers must consider literacy when using questionnaires: if a respondent cannot read or write, or finds it difficult, the chances are they will not fill in a questionnaire.

Human nature

People often lie, particularly about behaviour which is either frowned upon or given prestige (ie from which they derive 'street cred' or kudos). Parents, teachers and managers, for example, may be inclined to deny they have used a drug, whereas a student may be eager to admit using drugs if it is regarded as fashionable at their educational institution or among their peers. Under-reporting is more likely to affect recent use and use by younger respondents.

Apart from deliberately concealing or exaggerating both the frequency and type of their drug use, respondents may have memory recall difficulties. The two main problems here are: (a) recall delay – the tendency to forget events that happened long ago; and (b) forward telescoping – the tendency to say an event occurred more recently than it did in reality. Others may not know for certain what substances they have taken, eg a dealer sells them an 'ecstasy' tablet which, in reality, contains no MDMA but does contain amphetamine and caffeine.

How can we test robustness?

There are ways of gauging whether a respondent is answering accurately and reliably. One way is to repeat a question, but in a different way. Another is to ask a question to which you know the answer. If the question is answered wrongly, a respondent's accuracy can be tested and even measured. Some questionnaires, for example, add a bogus drug to the list of drugs being surveyed – eg the non-existent 'Semeron' was included in the British Crime Survey. The number of responses stating 'yes' they have used this bogus drug can indicate the level of accuracy among respondents. Another validation method is to administer the same questionnaire to the same subjects a few weeks later. Another way is to carry out drug tests, which can establish fairly accurately the existence of a drug in someone's body. Again, this can be used to establish how accurately an individual has responded to questioning or to measure rates of (recent) drug use – as is done by the arrestee survey (Bennett 1998, 2000; Bennett et al 2001).

Advantages of surveys

The disadvantages or limitations of surveys outlined above can be more than outweighed by their benefits. Self-report surveys provide the most practical and efficient means of collecting information on the extent of drug use. When repeated over time, using the sampling techniques, questions and methods, surveys of nationally representative samples can be used to monitor trends in drugs most commonly misused, and the extent of their misuse. Furthermore, surveys facilitate the customising of data collection on key research issues that are not captured by other indicators of drug use, eg initiation, experimentation and accessibility.

What the surveys say

The best source of data on drug use by young people (16–24-year-olds) are the British Crime Survey, which covers England and Wales, and the parallel Scottish and Northern Irish Crime Surveys. Although their differing methodologies do not allow for direct comparisons or for merging, this often occurs. The following section is a summary of these and other important UK drug prevalence studies.

The British Crime Survey

The British Crime Survey (BCS) is the largest household survey in England and Wales on experiences of crime, including the use of drugs. Because of its size, the rigour of its methodology and the fact that it has been running since 1982, using the same methodology on a consistent basis since 1996, it is regarded as the most reliable drug prevalence survey in the UK and hence sets the recognised baseline figures for drug prevalence. For more information on its development, see Ramsay and Percy (1997). Technical information can be obtained from the website of the Economic and Social Research Council (ESRC 2007).

Coverage

Contrary to what the name suggests, the BCS does not cover all of Britain or the United Kingdom, nor because of its size and scope does it break down in any detail the behaviour of minorities or specific groups, eg problematic drug users who lead chaotic lifestyles or are seldom at home. It does not cover all the substances that might be misused. This is because some will be very rarely used, and the longer the list, the greater the cost of the survey.

Sample

The sample is derived from the Postcode Address File, which selects households for surveying. The sample ranges in age from 16 to 59 years. Many parts of the survey report on the main age group of drug users in the UK, ie young people (16–24-year-olds), often highlighting otherwise hidden patterns in drug-using aetiology. In 2006/07 a sample of about 47,200, including a boost of non-white adults and youths aged 16–24, was used for the drug misuse component. Respondents are drawn from all regions of England as well as from Wales.

How often is it done?

Although initially the BCS was carried out biennially, allowing trends to be monitored every two years, from 2001 data started to be collected on a continual basis. Patterns in use are now reported annually.

Methodology

Individuals aged 16–59 years old are questioned using Computer Assisted Personal Interviewing, where respondents key their answers into a laptop computer. This has been shown to make answering easier and to encourage honest responses (see *British Crime Survey 1994* for an explanation (Ramsay and Percy 1996)).

What does it report?

The BCS is useful in providing breakdowns of drug use according to age group, gender, geographical region, ethnicity, educational level, lifestyle, socio-economic status, drug type and levels of use according to three recall periods – use in last month, last year and ever (lifetime).

How useful are recall periods?

Different drug use recall periods are useful for ascertaining which drugs are currently being used. The categorisation can also be used to help differentiate between regular and experimental use. An individual who has used a drug in the last month is likely to be a current user – though not always. It is important, therefore, to recognise that the number of people who have ever tried a drug, or indeed have taken a drug recently, is not an indicator of current use. Most people who try a drug, do just that – try it and then stop.

The BCS main findings

In 2006/07, a total of 29,144 individuals aged 16–59 years were questioned. There was an additional booster sample of 2,089 aged 16–24, providing a sample for this age group of 5,786.

Overall prevalence

Since they began, nearly all the BCS surveys have shown a steady increase in overall drug use, particularly in the category of 'lifetime' use or 'ever tried' a drug. The 2006/07 sweep of the BCS reported around one in three (35.5%) adults ever having used a drug, 10% within the last year and 5.9% within the last month. Table 3.1 shows the steady increase in all three of these rates from 1996 to peaks in 2002/03 or 2003/04 followed by subsequent declines – although there was a slight increase in lifetime use in 2006/07.

Table 3.1 Prevalence (%) for 16–59-year-olds, 1996 to 2006/07

Recall period	1996	1998	2000	2001/ 02	2002/ 03	2003/ 04	2004/ 05	2005/ 06	2006/ 07
Ever tried	30.5	33.6	35.7	34.0	35.7	35.6	34.5	34.9	35.5
Last year	11.1	12.1	11.9	11.9	12.2	12.3	11.3	10.5	10.0
Last month	6.7	7.1	7.2	7.4	7.4	7.5	6.7	6.3	5.9

Source: Murphy and Roe 2007

Who is using?

The years around the end of compulsory schooling at 16 years and early adulthood are consistently found to be times of greatest drug consumption, with peak years particularly among 16–24-year-olds. The 2006/07 sweep of the BCS reported around 45% of this age group ever having used a drug, 24% within the last year and 14% within the last month. Table 3.2 shows the steady decrease in all three of these rates from 1998 onwards.

Table 3.2 Prevalence (%) for 16–24-year-olds, 1996 to 2006/07

Recall period	1996	1998	2000	2001/ 02	2002/ 03	2003/ 04	2004/ 05	2005/ 06	2006/ 07
Ever tried	48.6	53.7	52.0	49.1	48.2	47.5	46.0	45.1	44.7
Last year	29.7	31.8	29.9	30.0	28.5	28.3	26.5	25.2	24.1
Last month	19.2	20.8	19.0	19.3	18.1	17.5	16.4	15.1	14.3

Source: Murphy and Roe 2007

Of the adults surveyed by the BCS in 2006/07, the highest lifetime use rates (at 50.8%) were among 25–29-year-olds. This is closely followed by the 20–24-year-olds (50.7%) and the 30–34 age group (46.2%). Therefore, roughly half of the under-30s in the survey have at some point in their lives tried an illicit substance.

As Figure 3.1 shows, the trend for lifetime use has been fairly stable for all ages since 2000, whereas the rate for 16–24-year-olds has declined in every year since 1998. Among the under-30s as a whole, drug use prevalence tends to outstrip that of the older generation by about 1.5:1 (46% of 16–29-year-olds, for example, have tried a drug, compared with 31% of 30–59-year-olds). This becomes more pronounced when prevalence rates for regular use are looked at (13% compared to 3% having used any drug within the last month respectively).

Figure 3.1 Lifetime use for 16–24 and 16–59-year-olds, 1996 to 2006/07

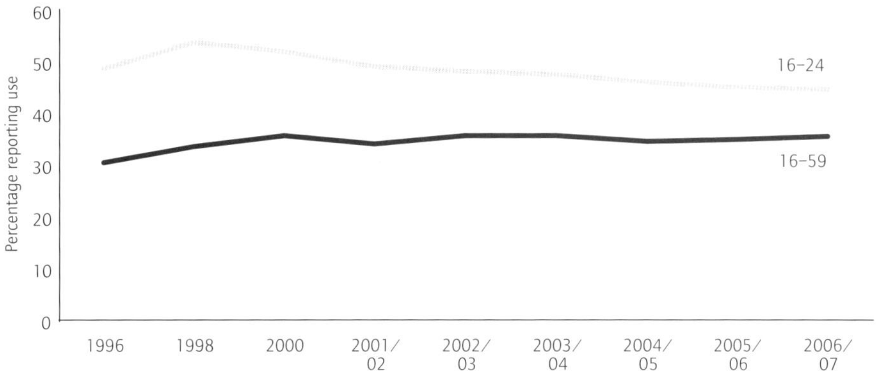

Where do they use?

The prevalence figures from the BCS apply only to England and Wales. A regional breakdown is given where obvious trends emerge, but figures are not detailed for each drug nor are all recall periods and ages given. Figures focus on 16–24-year-olds, who are more inclined to use drugs and so more likely to reveal significant trends.

In the past, prevalence rates were highest in South-East England and in London, but spreading elsewhere. Although waning, London still has a high rate of drug use. However, the latest BCS sweep shows that in 2006/07 the highest rate of use in the last year was in the South-West (11.1%), compared to 9.1% in the East; 9.2% in the West Midlands; 9.5% in Yorkshire & Humberside, the South-East, and Wales; 10% in the East Midlands (the national average); 10.4% in London; 10.8% in the North-East; and 11% in the North-West. However, care should be taken with these figures, as drug use tends to be localised. A number of good regional surveys show a large degree of variation across regions and within them.

What drugs do people use?

The BCS provides data on who is using which type of drug and when. This is very useful for understanding which drugs are moving in or out of fashion.

Cannabis is the most commonly used illegal drug, with roughly 30% of the whole survey, and 47% of 25–29-year-olds, reporting having ever taken it. Amphetamines, poppers and hallucinogens are next in order. What is interesting is the relative popularity these drugs have among what is often termed the clubbing generation, ie the 20–24-year-olds. Of these, roughly one in seven have used amphetamine and ecstasy. However, rates for all three drugs are higher in the 25–29 age group. The fact that the rates for use in the last month is one-third to one-half that of lifetime use indicates that a very large proportion is using less regularly.

The BCS is a poor indicator of the prevalence patterns of the so-called hard drugs. With only 1% of the BCS sample reporting use of heroin or crack, the dataset is too small to reveal any significant changes in patterns of use. On the other hand, cocaine use, at 8% of the whole sample and about 15% of those in their 20s ever having used, has shown a steady increase since 1992, initially among the under-30s in London and then throughout England and Wales.

How many people use drugs in England and Wales?

It is possible to derive estimates of the number of individuals in the general population of England and Wales using drugs from the BCS. The 'best' estimates from the 2006/07 sweep are given in Tables 3.3 and 3.4 for ages 16–59 years and 16–24 years respectively.

Table 3.3 Best estimates of numbers (000s) of users aged 16–59 years, 2006/07 BCS

Drug by class	Lifetime	Last year	Last month
Class A			
Cocaine	2,398	828	396
Crack	303	58	33
Ecstasy	2,315	567	255
LSD	1,706	77	28
Magic mushrooms	2,268	201	48
Heroin	227	41	31
Methadone	114	37	25
Class A/ B			
Amphetamines	3,790	421	159
Class B/ C			
Tranquillisers	936	136	67
Class C			
Anabolic steroids	197	32	14
Cannabis	9,595	2,616	1,526
Amyl nitrite/'poppers'	2,883	440	173
Solvents	764	61	29
Any Class A drug	4,389	1,074	538
Any drug	11,298	3,186	1,891

Source: Murphy and Roe 2007

Table 3.4 Best estimates of numbers (000s) of users aged 16–24 years, 2006/07 BCS

Drug by class	Lifetime	Last year	Last month
Class A			
Cocaine	671	373	190
Crack	83	25	13
Ecstasy	659	272	124
LSD	233	57	15
Magic mushrooms	523	190	46
Heroin	34	11	4
Methadone	25	5	5
Class A/B			
Amphetamines	714	207	102
Class B/C			
Tranquillisers	163	45	23
Class C			
Anabolic steroids	43	18	9
Cannabis	2,536	1,357	821
Amyl nitrite/'poppers'	766	245	103
Solvents	225	29	13
Any Class A drug	1,071	533	255
Any drug	2,851	1,597	954

Source: Murphy and Roe 2007

What does the BCS not cover?

As mentioned above, the BCS does not cover Scotland or Northern Ireland. It also omits those under 16 or over 60 years of age. Furthermore, because it is a household survey, the BCS omits those not living in recognised household accommodation – ie those in residential institutions such as hospitals, hostels and prisons as well as the homeless and 'roofless'. These populations are more likely to be problematic substance users, of alcohol and solvents as well as illegal drugs. Since levels of use of some drugs (such as heroin, cocaine, crack and methamphetamine) are much lower than other substances used by the general population, it is probable the rates given for such substances in the BCS are much lower than is the actual case. As a crime survey carried out by the Home Office, the BCS is likely to receive under-reporting of drug use. Unlike reporting a crime that has happened to the respondent, the drugs questionnaire asks respondents to reveal illegal activities they themselves have perpetrated. The longer recall periods, although useful, are not a reliable indicator of regular or current use; however, last month use is commonly used to measure current use. These factors would suggest that the BCS is liable to underestimate drug use among certain sub-populations of users and, therefore, overall use.

Other important surveys

Scottish Crime and Victimisation Survey (SCVS)

The SCVS used different methods of research from those used by the BCS prior to the latest sweep in 2006, making direct comparisons difficult for previous years. The SCVS moved from being a paper-based survey to using Computer Assisted Personal Interviewing (CAPI). This change in methodology has resulted in higher reported levels of drug use in the 2006 survey compared with previous sweeps. Because of these methodological changes it is difficult to make meaningful comparisons between the 2006 SCVS, and drug use reported in previous years.

Table 3.5 Lifetime drug use (%), Scotland 1993–2006

Age group	1993	1996	2000	2003	2004	2006
16–19	29	39	29	37	34	46
20–24	35	46	44	46	36	58
25–29	23	34	35	47	42	57
30–34				32	33	55
35–39				22	21	39
40–59				15	13	20
16–59	18	23	19	27	24	37
30+	13	15	13	19	18	15
Sample size	3,196	2,997	2,886	3,135	2,955	3,158

Sources: Fraser 2002; McVie et al 2004; Murray and Harkins 2006; Brown and
Bolling 2007

Lifetime use varied from year to year during the period 1993–2004, with the hint
of a drop between 2003 and 2004 across most age groups (Table 3.5). Similar
patterns are evident for last year use (Table 3.6). Historically, Scottish surveys
generally reveal that young adults (aged 16–30) are more likely to have used a
drug than their English or Welsh counterparts, while the over-30s are less inclined.

The 2006 SCVS found that 37% of 16–59-year-olds had taken one or more illicit
drugs in their lifetime, while 17% had ever taken one or more Class A drugs. Levels
of current drug use were lower, with 13% of respondents having taken one or
more drugs in the last year and 8% having taken one or more drugs in the last
month. Use of one or more Class A drug in the last year was reported by 5% of
respondents, while 3% reported use of Class A drugs in the last month. Although
reported levels of lifetime drug use in Scotland were broadly similar to those
reported in England and Wales by the 2005/06 BCS, levels of current drug use
were higher in Scotland.

Table 3.6 Last year drug use (%), Scotland 1993–2006

Age group	1993	1996	2000	2003	2004	2006
16–19	20	23	18	24	22	35
20–24	25	29	18	28	17	28
25–29	9	13	14	15	16	22
30–34				10	9	13
35–39				5	5	12
40–59				3	2	3
16–59	7	9	7	9	8	13
30+	2	4	3	5	4	6
Sample size	3,196	2,997	2,886	3,135	2,955	3,158

Sources: Fraser 2002; McVie et al 2004; Murray and Harkins 2006;
Brown and Bolling 2007

One-third (33%) of respondents had used cannabis at some point in their lives; 11% in the last year and 7% in the last month. Cocaine and ecstasy were the second most commonly used drugs in the last year – having been taken by 4% and 3% of respondents respectively. Only 0.5% had used heroin in the last year and only 0.4% crack cocaine. Use of Class A drugs was more common among respondents who were not currently in work (including students) and among those who had never worked.

Northern Ireland Crime Survey

In 1998, a report on adults' knowledge and awareness of illicit drugs was published, using information from the Northern Ireland Omnibus Survey of 969 people carried out in February 1997. The main findings indicated that approximately 24% of those aged 16 to 59 years reported that they had ever taken an illicit drug, slightly less than the figure of 28% for 1996 (NIO 1998).

Data from the last three sweeps of the Northern Ireland Crime Survey show that last year use among 16–59-year-olds has generally fallen (McMullan and Ruddy 2006). Lifetime use rose slightly from 26% in 2001 to 27.4% in 2003/04 before returning to 26.2% in 2005. Last year use of any drug fell from 11% in 2001 to 8.2% in 2005. Last year use of cannabis fell from 7.3% to 5.8%; use of cocaine powder rose during this period from 0.5% to 1%. The overall level of prevalence is lower than in England and Wales but exhibits similar patterns and trends.

Who is using what – more detailed analyses

The crime surveys are useful because they give a baseline figure of use among the general adult population. However, drug use differs greatly across the population, often localised and specific to certain ages, ethnicity and religion, class or lifestyles – something a large, generic survey fails to pick up. The following section looks at surveys conducted among specific groups of users.

Schoolchildren

The principal surveys of school-age children in terms of size and availability of trend data are two-fold: (a) those carried out by the independent Schools Health Education Unit; and (b) those commissioned by government departments. Surveys reported in the previous edition of this publication have not been repeated in recent years; for example, the Health Behaviour in School-age Children (HBSC) survey has not been conducted since 2001/02.

Schools Health Education Unit

The longest-running and largest survey in the UK of drug taking by school children is conducted by John Balding of the Schools Health Education Unit (SHEU) in Exeter. The SHEU databases contain data from a large number of independent surveys carried out across the country mainly by health authorities, using the SHEU survey methods and in collaboration with other local partners. These partnerships are responsible for the timing and sampling procedures, although there is a strong incentive to make the sample representative of their own area. The sampling is therefore not random nor fully representative. School teachers known to the class collect data in these surveys. The SHEU believes, rightly or wrongly, that this promotes a conducive atmosphere in the classroom, and with the support of classroom assistants the completion rate of pupils with special educational needs is increased.

It is estimated that on any given day about 10% of pupils are absent from school. Although drug users may be more likely to play truant, absent pupils may also include groups like those who are often ill and those frightened to go to school, who may be less likely to use drugs than the rest of the class. The effect of absentees on the assessment of prevalence rates is not known. That said, the survey results are remarkably similar to those generated by studies with more rigorous sampling methods. The size of the samples and availability of data stretching back for over two decades make the Balding studies a uniquely useful source. For the purposes of this chapter, we will make use of the 1987–2004 overview (SHEU 2005) and the 2006 report (SHEU 2006).

When looking at the figures from 1987 to 2004, it was found that, when compared with figures from earlier years, young people in recent years were more likely to: have been offered drugs (up to 53% of 14–15-year-olds in 2002); have been offered cannabis (up to 48% of 14–15-year-old males in 2002, up to 42% of females in 2004); have taken drugs (up to 33% of 14–15-year-olds in 1996); have taken cannabis (up to 29% of 14–15-year-olds); think that amphetamines are 'always unsafe' and – as pupils get older – fewer think that cannabis is 'always unsafe'. Young people in recent years were less likely to (a) know (personally) a drug user (up to 70% of older pupils in the mid-1990s; in 2006, up to 57% of the 14–15-year-olds were 'fairly sure' or 'certain' they knew a drug user); and (b) worry about drugs (between 1993–1999 declining numbers reported worrying 'quite a lot/a lot' about drugs). The older they get, pupils think drugs are 'always unsafe', except cannabis, which is considered to be 'always unsafe' by a smaller percentage of the older groups.

In some years, over 50% more young people reported being offered drugs compared to those reporting taking them. If taken at face value, this suggests that young people are both willing and able to refuse unwelcome offers of drugs. There was a rising trend for those who were offered drugs other than cannabis. Experimentation with other drugs stabilised at below 20% between 1999–2004. Over the years, around 30% of 12–13-year-olds, and up to 70% of older pupils in the 1990s, have reported knowing personally a drug user. For the older group, this has declined to around 60% in recent years.

Figures from 10–11-year-olds for 2006 show that around 20%, and up to 27%, report knowing a drug user. More younger males than females consistently report higher percentages. About one in five pupils in Year 10 – four times as many as in Year 8 – have tried at least one drug. Cannabis is by far the most likely drug to have been tried, with up to 24% of 14–15-year-olds, and up to 6% of 12–13-year-olds reporting having taken it. Up to 17% of 14–15-year-olds have mixed drugs and alcohol 'on the same occasion'.

Surveys for government departments

Over the last decade, government departments have started to commission large-scale annual or biennial surveys of school-age children. Increasingly, the sampling and surveying techniques are becoming standardised, thereby allowing cross-national comparisons. There is no national survey as yet for Wales.

ENGLAND

The longest-running of these, although evolving over time, is that for England – commissioned by the Department of Health. *Smoking, drinking and drug use among young people in England* (Fuller 2007) and its predecessor surveys now cover the period 1998 to 2006. The 2006 sweep (which focuses on smoking and drinking) is the most recent survey in a series that began in 1982. Each survey since 1998 has included a core section of questions on smoking, drinking and drug use and, since 2000, the remainder of the questionnaire has focused in alternate years on smoking and drinking or on drug-taking.

The key findings emerging from the 2006 sweep, which covered 8,200 secondary school pupils aged 11 to 15 pupils in 288 schools, are:
- 35% of pupils reported they had ever been offered drugs, a decrease from 42% in 2001
- 24% had ever used drugs, 17% in the last year (20% in 2001), 9% in the last month (12% in 2001)
- the proportion who took Class A drugs in the last year was 4%, unchanged since 2001
- pupils were most likely to have taken cannabis; 10% in the last year (13% in 2001)
- 5% of pupils had sniffed glue or other volatile substances in the last year and 4% had taken poppers; other drugs had been taken by less than 2%.

The proportions of pupils who had taken drugs increased with age. Although boys and girls were equally likely to have taken drugs in the last year, boys (10%) were more likely than girls (8%) to have taken drugs recently (in the last month). Black pupils and those of mixed ethnicity were more likely than white pupils to have taken drugs recently. Recent drug use was associated with regular smoking and recent drinking. Pupils who had been excluded also had an increased risk of recent drug use compared with pupils who had not, and the same was true of pupils who had truanted from school compared with those who had not. The proportions of pupils who took drugs at least once a month (4%) was lower than in recent years. Older pupils were more likely to say they usually took drugs at least once a month; 8% of 15-year-olds said this, compared with 1% of 11–12-year-olds.

SCOTLAND

The Scottish school survey of 11–15-year-olds for 2000 (Boreham and Shaw 2001) found that lifetime use among this age group was higher (at 17%) than in England (16%) but last year use was the same (14%). By the age of 15, one-third had ever used drugs, 30% in the last year, and 22% in the last month. Boys (19%) were more likely than girls (14%) to have ever tried drugs, and had higher last-year and last-month rates. Last-year use of cannabis was slightly higher (at 13%) than in England (12%). As was the case south of the border, the rate for no other single drug exceeded 3%. The highest rate of 3% was for 'gas', followed by 2% for ecstasy and magic mushrooms. Overall, the rates reported for 2000 were marginally lower than those recorded in 1998, but the changes were not statistically significant. Drug use had a slightly higher prevalence among those in receipt of free school meals, those from manual social classes and those from low-income groups. Pupils who smoked or drank alcohol were more likely to take drugs in the last month. The first factor was particularly important. Thus, 58% of regular smokers had used drugs in the last month compared to 39% of regular drinkers, and 1% of those who had neither ever smoked nor ever drunk. Older and male regular smokers were more likely to have used drugs in the last month, whereas there was no gender difference among regular drinkers.

The Scottish Schools Adolescent Lifestyle and Substance Use Survey (SALSUS) continued on from the previous survey and has now completed three sweeps of secondary school children. SALSUS was established by the Scottish Executive to provide a broad-based approach to the monitoring of substance use in the context of other lifestyle, health and social factors. The 2006 survey was undertaken by

BMRB Social Research, commissioned by ISD Scotland on behalf of the Scottish Executive. SALSUS was carried out in 2002 and 2004 by the Child and Adolescent Health Research Unit (CAHRU) at the University of Edinburgh. As in 2002, the survey in 2006 was designed to allow reporting at local as well as national level. In 2006 a total of 23,180 pupils from secondary school years 2 and 4 took part in the survey between August and December (Maxwell et al 2007). The main drug findings for 2006 SALSUS are as follows.

Over a quarter (27%) of 15-year-olds and 9% of 13-year-olds reported ever using drugs. Slightly lower proportions (23% and 7% respectively in these age groups) had used drugs in the last year; 14% of 15-year-olds and 4% of 13-year-olds had used drugs in the last month. In 2006, there were no significant differences between boys and girls in reported drug use. Between 2004 and 2006, last-month use fell among 15-year-old boys from 21% to 14%, and among 15-year-old girls from 20% to 12%. Similarly, among 13-year-olds there was a fall in last-month drug use: from 7% to 4% among boys, and among girls a fall from 6% to 3%.

Cannabis was the most frequently reported drug used in the last month, in the last year or ever. Eleven percent of 15-year-olds and 2% of 13-year-olds reported using cannabis in the last month. Very few pupils reported using any other drug. Six percent of 15-year-olds compared to 1% of 13-year-olds reported using cannabis and no other drugs in the last month. Fewer pupils reported using cannabis and other drugs (4% of all 15-year-olds and 1% of 13-year-olds), and 2% of 13- and 15-year-olds had used other drugs but not used cannabis in the last month. Ten percent of all 15-year-olds and 4% of 13-year-olds said they had only taken drugs once. A total of 8% of all 15-year-olds and 2% of all 13-year-olds said they used drugs once a month or more frequently.

NORTHERN IRELAND

To link up with the launch of the Northern Ireland Drug Strategy in 1998, the Young People's Behaviour and Attitudes Survey (the YPBA Survey) and an adjunct to the Northern Ireland Omnibus Survey (duplicating most of the questions in the YPBA Survey) were commissioned. The fieldwork for the YPBA Survey took place in October/November 2000 with a sample of young people in the secondary school system, achieving interviews with 6,297 students aged 11 to 16. The Omnibus Survey targeted all young people aged between 16 and 25 in households sampled by the Omnibus Survey in October/November 2000 and March 2001 and achieved a sample of 640. The analysed results of these two surveys were subsequently published (Miller and Dowds 2002).

The extent of drug use reported in the YPBA Survey, both in terms of having ever used an illicit drug and current drug use, were broadly comparable to figures reported in other contemporary high-quality self-report surveys of young people's drug use. The amounts reported were also sufficiently higher than other surveys to indicate that drug use among young people was continuing to rise. One-third (32.9%) of YPBA respondents reported having been offered drugs and 24.5% tried or used at least one illicit drug at least once. One-sixth (16.5%) of these 12–16-year-olds stated they were currently using at least one drug and 6.8% claimed to be using drugs frequently. Among the older (16–25) Omnibus Survey respondents, the equivalent figures were: 59.5% had been offered drugs; 37.3% had used a drug at least once; 23.1% reported current use; and 5.2% claimed frequent use.

After alcohol and tobacco, the most commonly used drugs in the YPBA sample were solvents (9% using solvents currently) and cannabis (9.5%) with the age profile of cannabis users tending to be older than that for solvent abusers. In the Omnibus sample, the most commonly used drugs were cannabis (21.2% current use) and ecstasy (6.6%). Considerably smaller degrees of use were reported for all other drugs covered by the two surveys. Multiple drug use was relatively uncommon. Among the YPBA respondents, only 10% reported using more than one drug in their lifetime and only 6.3% were currently using more than one drug. The equivalent figures for the older Omnibus respondents were 22.6% and 8.1%.

There are significant differences between the extent of drug use reported by different groups. In the YPBA Survey, boys, older pupils, students in secondary schools, those located in the Belfast and South Eastern Education and Library Boards, and pupils receiving free school meals all reported higher rates of drug use. In the Omnibus Survey, males and the unemployed or those in part-time work reported higher rates of drug use. Exposure to and first use of drugs, ease of access to drugs, current use of drugs and offering drugs to others are all strongly linked with age in the YPBA sample. For example, while 5.4% of 12-year-olds had used drugs (including solvents), this figure rose to 32.8% for 16-year-olds.

Use begins at 14

Even among school-age children there is a very strong variation in drug-using behaviour. While small proportions of those questioned by a range of surveys report being offered and/or using drugs at very early ages – ten, eleven or even younger, the modal time for first exposure and first drug use appears in mid-adolescence. Surveys carried out on school-age populations reveal a watershed around the age of 13 to 14 years of age. Those under that age are unlikely to have tried drugs, those above likely. For example, the age most often reported by the older YPBA respondents for both the first time they were offered drugs and the first time they used drugs is 14. Among the Northern Ireland Omnibus sample, the equivalent ages are somewhat higher – the modal age that respondents report being first offered or first using a drug is 16 (Miller and Dowds 2002). There is a clear trend that both exposure to drugs and drug use increase with age.

In the YPBA Survey, alcohol was the most commonly used drug, with the proportion of young people drinking alcohol rising steadily with increasing age – from almost 80% of 12-year-olds saying they have never drunk alcohol to only just over 20% of 16-year-olds saying they have never drunk. There is an age-related pattern for first cigarette similar to that for first drink, reflecting the gradually increasing proportion of youth who try cigarettes. After alcohol and tobacco, the most commonly used drug category reported by the pupils in the YPBA Survey was that of solvents, with first use tending to occur earlier than that for any other drug type (Miller and Dowds 2002).

There is a clear relationship between the age at which secondary school pupils first tried drugs and the type of drug taken at that age (Fuller 2006). Volatile substances tended to be used by those who first took drugs at a young age, while those who first used drugs when older were more likely to try cannabis. Of those pupils who first used drugs at the age of 11 or younger, 75% used volatile substances, compared with 15% who tried cannabis. However, pupils who first took drugs at the age of 13 were more likely to take cannabis (60%), than to sniff volatile substances (33%), and among pupils who first tried drugs at the age of 15, 79% took cannabis at that age, with only 13% trying volatile substances. Among pupils who had first tried drugs at the age of 11 or younger, 3% had sniffed poppers compared with the 75% who had sniffed volatile substances. The relative use of these drugs changed with age, so that among pupils who had first tried drugs at the age of 15, 20% had sniffed poppers and 13% sniffed volatile substances at that age. Generally, pupils only tried one drug at the age when they first tried drugs and this tended to either be volatile substances (41%) or cannabis (33%). Only 10% of pupils took a Class A drug at the age they first tried drugs.

The 2006 SCVS found that the most common age for first trying any drug was between the ages of 16 and 19, with over half (51%) of lifetime drug users having first tried any drug between these ages (Brown and Bolling 2007). Almost a quarter (26%) of lifetime drug users had first tried drugs when they were less than 16 years old. Cannabis was the first drug tried by three-quarters of lifetime drug takers (76%).

Table 3.7 Average age of first use of drugs by *Mixmag* readers, 2000

Drug	Years	Months
Cannabis	15	11
Poppers	17	10
LSD/speed	18	1
Magic mushrooms	18	4
Ecstasy/benzodiazepines	19	6
Herbal highs	19	8
Cocaine	20	7
Heroin	20	10
Ketamine	21	4
Crack	21	8
Crystal methylamphetamine ('ice')	21	10
GHB	22	6
2CB/Viagra	24	7

Source: Craske et al 2001, p 62

Some insight into the use of drugs on the club scene can be gained by looking at the results of postal surveys of readers conducted by *Mixmag* magazine (Craske et al 2001; French 2003). Although the results may not be generalisable to all clubbers, they are suggestive of what some individuals consume and their drug careers. The average age at which respondents to the *Mixmag* survey first tried different types of drugs indicates that cannabis is experienced initially at around 16 years, stimulants and hallucinogens are tried in the late teens. Hard drugs such as heroin, cocaine and crack are usually tried around the age of 20–22, followed by GHB, 2CB and Viagra (Table 3.7). McCambridge et al (2005) found that over the period 1999–2003 the mean age of first use of stimulants among *Mixmag* survey respondents remained stable for the most part, although there was a slight decrease for cocaine powder and base amphetamine and a small increase for methylamphetamine use. In 2003, the average ages for initiating use of stimulants were: amphetamines 18.5 years; 4-MTA 18.6; base amphetamine 19.1; ecstasy 19.5; cocaine 20.4; crack 21.2; and methylamphetamine 22 years.

The Offending Crime and Justice Survey of 2004 reported that the median age at which people reported first using drugs was 16 years (range 8 to 24 years). Almost half of those who had used drugs (48%) said they had first used a drug between the ages of 10 and 15. The drugs generally used first by young people were solvents and then cannabis. The age of first use for 'harder' drugs was generally higher with a median of 17 years for both amphetamines and any Class A drugs (Budd et al 2005). The type of substance used by median age is as follows: 14 years, solvents; 15, amyl nitrite, cannabis; 17, amphetamines, hallucinogens; 18, ecstasy, heroin; 19, cocaine, crack.

Class and lifestyle

Until recently there was a strongly held view that socio-economic status is in some way related to drug use. This view, however, has been challenged. The BCS has consistently found that people living in households where the head was in a non-manual occupation had higher levels of lifetime use than those living in manual households. However, while those with household incomes of over £30,000 tended to have high lifetime use, those with incomes of under £5,000 had the highest lifetime use. Of the young unemployed, 40% had used a drug in the last year, compared with 25% of those in employment.

Leisure drug use and the social life associated with it are often the preserve of those who can afford to do so. The 1998 BCS (Ramsay and Partridge 1999) found that those living in 'rising' areas, according to the ACORN[1] classification, are roughly twice as likely to have used a drug in the last year and month than people from most other categories. Rising areas are characterised by young employed, urban dwellers – the group most likely to go to pubs and clubs (CACI 1993).

The 2005/06 BCS found that use of cocaine powder was higher among those who had been to a nightclub or disco at least once in the last month compared to those who had not (Roe and Man 2006). Higher levels were also reported by those who had been to a pub or wine bar in the evening more than three times a week during the last month compared to those who had been less frequently or not at all. Unemployed respondents reported higher levels of cocaine powder use in the previous year compared to both those in employment and those who were economically inactive (eg those on disability benefit). Respondents living in areas of urban prosperity reported the highest levels of cocaine powder use.

Problematic or heavy use

Problematic or heavy drug users tend to be long-term economically inactive, living with their parents or partner, and living in urban or suburban areas (as the Scottish Drug Misuse Database reveals). However, research in England has shown that the use of heroin, often associated with problematic use, is spreading into more mainstream groups of young people (Parker et al 1998). Heroin is not only becoming cheaper but is also being sold in smaller, smokable quantities to young people in rural and urban areas, the majority of whom are in full- or part-time employment and successful relationships. The 2005/06 and other recent sweeps of the BCS have shown increasing use of cocaine powder (Roe and Man 2006). Between 1998 and 2005/06 use of cocaine powder increased, while use of amphetamines decreased and the use of other stimulant drugs (crack cocaine, ecstasy and amyl nitrite) remained stable. During this period, overall use of any stimulant has remained stable, supporting the proposal that cocaine powder has replaced other substances as the drug of choice for stimulant users.

---

1 ACORN – A Classification Of Residential Neighbourhoods – grades households according to the demographic, employment and housing features of the immediate locality; the BCS uses six categories: thriving, expanding, rising, settling, aspiring and striving.

Clubbing

Lifestyle is a very high predictor of drug use in some circumstances. Studies by Release (1997) and the London School of Hygiene and Tropical Medicine (Branigan et al 1997) have revealed the close link between drug use and clubbing. Some of the highest prevalence rates for any group have been found among clubbers, with 99% of 200 clubbers reporting having ever used a drug, and 93% planning to use that night. Different drugs are specific to particular dance events and music. For example, while 73% of the sample attending a Techno night were planning to take ecstasy, only 40% of those at a Garage night were planning to do so.

Table 3.8 compares use last month in 1999, 2000 and 2002 for respondents to the *Mixmag* survey (Craske et al 2000; French 2003). These figures reinforce the findings of the earlier surveys. What is noticeable are the increases in the use of poppers, ketamine, GHB, methadone, benzodiazepines, crack, etc in 2000. Many of these substances are prescribed medicaments. However, by 2002 there were falls for ketamine, GHB and crack. Prevalence increases for psilocybin, ketamine, GHB and nitrates use have been detected using this survey, with a sharp recent rise in psilocybin use in 2002/03 contrasting with more gradual and comprehensive evidence of increased ketamine use throughout the period 1999–2003. The declining prevalence of LSD use in general population surveys is replicated in this sentinel population study (McCambridge et al 2007). These researchers also found broad stability in patterns of frequency of stimulant use among ongoing users. Despite an apparent reduction in the current prevalence of ecstasy use, the proportion of heavy users (usually > 4 pills per session) more than doubled between 1999 and 2003 (McCambridge et al 2005).

A Home Office study of recreational drug use among clubbers in the south-east of England found that 79% of the clubbers had taken drugs at some time in their life, compared with 50% of 16–29-year-olds surveyed for the 2000 BCS. Levels and patterns of drug use varied greatly – from 9% at a leisure park event to 70% at an established dance/gay club (Deehan and Saville 2003). Ecstasy was by far the most commonly used drug while clubbing, followed by cannabis and cocaine. Current drug users were experimenting with a wider range of substances, including synthetic drugs such as ketamine and GHB, than were lapsed drug users. Despite such high levels of drug use, less than half of the current drug users felt that taking drugs was an integral part of their social life. Most of the club-goers had drunk alcohol on the night of the interview and two-thirds of these were classified as hazardous drinkers. A third of the overall sample was using both drugs and alcohol on the night of the survey.

Table 3.8 Drugs used by Mixmag readers, 1999, 2000 and 2002 (%)

Drug	1999	2000	2002	Drug	1999	2000	2002
Ecstasy	85.6	84.7	71.2	Steroids	–	20.0	–
Cannabis	73.1	79.9	71.6	Acid	10.0	17.5	3.0
Cocaine	45.6	39.6	35.5	Viagra	0.7	17.5	–
Poppers	21.5	39.1	–	Crack	2.1	17.4	1.2
Ketamine	3.9	29.7	12.6	Mushrooms	–	17.3	2.6
Speed	39.4	29.2	26.0	Crystal methamphe- tamine ('ice')	–	16.7	–
GHB	3.4	25.8	4.1	2CB	1.0	11.1	–
Paste	–	24.4	–	Herbal highs	1.7	9.3	–
Methadone	–	22.6	–	Heroin	1.3	8.2	0.06
Benzodia- zepines	8.3	21.6	–	Flatliners	0.8	4.5	–

Sources: Craske et al 2000; French 2003

Homeless people

Homeless people are difficult to survey, mainly because they are difficult to contact using conventional methods. Rates can vary across types of accommodation provided for the homeless and varying client profiles. Surveys that fail to include groups such as the homeless, particularly if they are local surveys in an area with many homeless people, will underestimate the level of drug use.

While there is a large body of literature on drugs misuse, only a small number of British pieces focus on the homeless in this context. The OPCS National Psychiatric

Morbidity Survey (Great Britain) found that substance-related disorders are some of the commonest disorders in the community, with 5% of the household sample alcohol dependent, 7% alcohol dependent in the institutional sample and over 21% alcohol dependent in the homeless sample. Tobacco, alcohol and other drug use and dependence were dramatically higher in the homeless sample than in either of the other two samples (Farrell et al 2003). The prevalence of psychosis was estimated to be 2% among residents of private sector leased accommodation (PSLA), and 8% among hostel residents (Gill et al 2003). The lowest level of alcohol dependence (3%) was among the PSLA sample, a group that has a large proportion of women, many of whom were pregnant or had young children. While 16% of hostel residents had alcohol dependency, the proportions among night shelter residents (44%) and day centre visitors (50%) were considerably greater. The prevalence of dependence on non-cannabinoid drugs rose from 2% and 6% among PSLA and hostel residents respectively to 13% among those using day centres and 22% of those living in night shelters.

A survey of 200 homeless people carried out by the Office for National Statistics (ONS) in 1999 on behalf of the Greater Glasgow Health Board found that, overall, one-quarter showed evidence of some form of drug dependence, with 18% being heroin-dependent (Kershaw et al 2003). Drug use was particularly widespread among the younger age groups. Among 25–34-year-olds, 51% were heroin-dependent and 34% had injected in the past month. Hazardous alcohol consumption was common in all age groups; over half (54%) of all respondents reported such consumption. It was especially prevalent among older age groups, with 63% of those aged over 54 years admitting to such behaviour. Males (60%) were more likely to show hazardous drinking patterns than females (16%). Forty-four per cent were assessed as having at least one other psychological disorder, compared to 14% of adults in private households across Great Britain.

Little research has been conducted on the drug use of those who sleep rough (on the streets) in the UK. An estimated 80% of rough sleepers have drug problems (SEU 2001); this contrasts with an interim evaluation of the Rough Sleepers Initiative (RSI) in Scotland, which estimated that 34% of RSI clients had difficulties with drugs (Yanetta et al 1999). Owen and Henry's (2001) study of rough sleepers in Edinburgh found that more than half were regularly using illicit drugs, and two-thirds of those were aged below 26 years of age. High levels of drug use among young homeless people have been repeatedly reported (Carlen 1996; Hammersley and Pearl 1997; Wincup et al 2003). Since the late 1990s, the prevalence of drug misuse has markedly increased among homeless people (Owen 2002).

Of the homeless population they studied, Goulden and Sondhi (2001) found that one-third had injected heroin and one-fifth crack. Furthermore, over 10% were likely to have used someone else's syringe or passed on their own syringe in the last month. Wincup et al (2003) found that among 160 young homeless people aged 25 years and under in England and Wales, 43% were currently taking heroin and 38% crack.

Homeless drug users have a tendency towards polydrug use, ie they use more than one drug, even though this is more hazardous than using one substance (Wright 2002). Commonly used drugs are: (i) opiates, such as heroin, methadone and morphine; (ii) stimulants, such as amphetamines, crack and cocaine; (iii) cannabis; and (iv) benzodiazepines, such as diazepam, lorazepam, Librium and Temazepam (Fountain and Howes 2002).

There has been little research conducted on young rough sleepers, but what little there is suggests 80% of those who have ever slept rough have tried an illicit drug, compared to 53% of those who have never slept rough. Klee and Reid (1998) highlighted the link in the late 1990s, followed a few years later by Goulden and Sondhi (2001), who reported over 80% of persistent runaways have tried illicit drugs compared to 42% of young people who have never run away.

Truants and excludees

Individuals who truant or are excluded from school are more susceptible to heavy drug use. The 2005/06 BCS reported the highest levels of drug use among those who had ever truanted and had ever been excluded followed by those who had only ever truanted and then those who had only ever been excluded. Young people who had neither truanted nor been excluded from school reported the lowest levels of drug use (Roe and Man 2006).

Drug use in custody

There is a strongly documented link between drug-taking and acquisitive crime. In an attempt to understand this link and, where possible, break it, the government has undertaken a number of initiatives, two of which try to ascertain levels of drug use among arrestees and detainees. The first, a large-scale survey known as

NEW-ADAM, screens arrestees for drug use using questionnaires and drug tests. The second, known as Mandatory Drug Testing (MDT), randomly and routinely tests prisoners while in detention. Because of their size and use of drug tests, these surveys offer a very reliable and valid estimate of drug use among these groups, provided inmates do not find ways of cheating the tests – which many have.

Again, the data should be analysed carefully. While a test may show the presence of a drug in a detainee's blood, it reveals nothing of how often the user takes that drug, how much, nor, in the case of cannabis (which can stay in the body for up to a month) how long ago it was used (see Chapter 11).

Arrestees

On the whole, drug use has been found to be very high among inmates – particularly on entry into the criminal justice system. Urine testing, undertaken as part of the NEW-ADAM research, showed that 61% of arrestees in five English cities had recently taken at least one illegal drug in 1997 (Bennett 1998). Two years later, a further study of four cities (including two of those visited in 1997) found a level of 69% (Bennett 2000). Not surprisingly, cannabis was most often found, with 46% testing positive for it in 1997. Those who tested positive for this drug alone were not heavily involved in acquisitive crime.

The link between offending and drug use is very clearly demonstrated by the results of Bennett's research (1998) on arrestees during 1997. Nearly half of those taking drugs believed their drug use was associated with their criminal behaviour, particularly the need for money to buy drugs. Relatively high proportions of arrestees had used cocaine/crack and heroin/opiates (18% and 10% respectively). Property offenders were more likely to be drug-takers than were offenders against the person, alcohol/drug offenders or disorderly offenders. A comparatively high proportion of property offenders in 1997 tested positive for opiates (23%) and cocaine (14%) compared with the other offender groups (in the ranges 8 to 17% and 2 to 7% respectively). Almost half of the shoplifters tested positive for opiates and three in ten for cocaine, indicating that heavy or problematic drug use is linked to crime rather than drug use per se (see Chapter 5 for a discussion of drugs and crime).

Arrestees used more risky methods of taking drugs than the general population: 14% reported injecting in the last year, and 3% had shared a needle during 1997. Both Nottingham and Sunderland reported increased rates of injecting between 1997 and 1999; for heroin the rates roughly doubled. High levels of drug dependency were reported in 1997: 45% at some point in their lives, 30% currently. Cannabis was most commonly reported (15%), followed by heroin (11%), with much lower rates for cocaine (2%) and crack (3%).

The NEW-ADAM methodology used in England was piloted in Scotland during the second half of 1999, in the Fife and Strathclyde regions (McKeganey et al 2000). Positive results were obtained from 71% of those providing urine samples. This is a higher level than for English sites. There were also higher levels reported of cannabis (52%) and opiate (31%) use. One-third of those arrested used benzodiazepines, 12% methadone and 3% cocaine. Female arrestees (51%) were twice as likely as males (26%) to test positive for opiates. Injecting was at a higher level in Scotland than in England, at 32% in Strathclyde and 20% in Fife. Levels of sharing injecting equipment were also considerably higher than in England: a third of injecting arrestees had passed on injecting equipment in the last 12 months, 43% of these in the last three days. Not unsurprisingly, arrestees reported comparatively higher levels of dependence – 52% ever and 40% recently. There was a clear and consistent relationship between the offending behaviour of an arrestee and their level of drug use. For example, whereas 87% of current injectors had shoplifted, a lower proportion (57%) of non-injecting drug users had committed this offence. A quarter of arrestees said they had been in receipt of illegal income within the last 30 days.

Arrest referral schemes

Data on arrest referral schemes from October 2000 to September 2001 show that those who seek help from treatment services are broadly similar to problematic users presenting for treatment (Sondhi et al 2002). Males accounted for 81% of those screened. The average age was 27 years (range 10–66); 90% were white. The percentage reporting use in the last month were, in descending order: heroin 56; cannabis 34; alcohol 27; crack 22; benzodiazepines 14; methadone 11; cocaine, amphetamines and ecstasy each 6. Nearly half (47%) had injected in the last month. All these rates were considerably higher among those referred to treatment services or seeking treatment. For example, in the latter category, heroin use rose to 81%, crack to 28% and benzodiazepines to 18% but alcohol and cannabis use were lower. Injecting rates were 59%. Mean weekly expenditure on drugs was £219 for those screened but £292 for those demanding treatment.

In the second year of operation of the arrest referral scheme, the number of individuals screened fell from 48,810 to 41,312 (O'Shea et al 2003). The proportion of males was similar (82%) as was the mean age (27.6 years). There was a wider age range (11–75) but a lower proportion aged under 17 (3% compared to 6% in the previous year). The majority of arrestees were white 88%, with other ethnic groups in similar proportions to the first year: black 6%, Asian 3%, mixed race 2%, other 1%. The most noticeable difference between the two years in terms of recent drug use was an increase in crack use from 22% to 30%. There was a slight increase for heroin, and small drops in methadone, cannabis and benzodiazepine use. As in the first year, the majority of people referred to drug treatment services had recently used heroin (72%), crack (40%), cannabis (29%) or alcohol (25%). Average weekly expenditure on drugs in the second year was £324 for those screened and £387 for those referred. Sixty-one per cent of those referred to services had received previous drug treatment. The figure for the previous reporting cycle was 54%.

Mandatory Drug Testing (MDT) in prisons

Contrary to common belief, drug use, particularly of cocaine and heroin, drops once the user is in detention. Mandatory Drug Testing shows that roughly one in eight inmates, when tested randomly, tested positive for drugs in 2001/02; this has now fallen to one in 12. Not surprisingly, cannabis accounts for nearly all positive results, with opiates occurring at about half that level. Benzodiazepines are found in small but significant quantities, particularly among women.

By the end of March 1996, MDT had been introduced into all penal establishments in England and Wales. Results for these countries show that there was an overall decrease in the proportion of inmates testing positive. The overall proportion of positive tests fell from 24.4% in 1996/07 to 12.4% in 2000/01, to 11.6% in 2001/02, rose to 11.7% in 2002/03, rose further to 12.3% in 2003/04, and then fell to 11.6% in 2004/05, 10.3% in 2005/06, and 8.6% in 2006/07 (HMPS 2001 p 10, 2002 p 10, 2003 p 9, 2005 p 110, 2006 p 88, 2007 p 89). The highest rates were in male local and open establishments.

The proportion of inmates testing positive for cannabis fell from 10.2% in 1999/2000 to 6.8% in 2001/2; there were rises in the use of opiates and benzodiazepines (Home Office 2001, 2003). The proportion for opiates rose from 4.3% to 4.7%, and that for benzodiazepines from 1.1% to 1.3% in 2000/01 although this fell slightly in 2001/02. Of note is that 1.5% of inmates in some establishments in north-east England tested positive in 2000/01 (and 1.2% in 2001/02) for buprenorphine, which is becoming more widely used in the treatment of opiate dependence. The Prison Service Annual Reports do not contain breakdowns by drug type. Such information was provided in the Annual Prison Statistics volumes only until 2002.

A survey of over 2,200 prisoners, male and female, remanded and sentenced, from a representative sample of prisons in England and Wales was carried out in two waves between September 2001 and January 2002 (Singleton et al 2005). It aimed to gather information on episodes of drug use in prisons, prisoners' experience of drug use prevention measures in prison, and the impact of these on attitudes and behaviours in relation to drug use. A pilot study was conducted in four prisons during July 2001. For the main survey, 11 establishments or clusters of smaller establishments (out of the 130 prisons in England and Wales) were selected to take part. A stratified random sampling approach was used to ensure the sample was representative.

About two in five prisoners (39%) had used some illicit drug at some time in their current prison, one in four (25%) said they had used drugs in the past month and about one in six (16%) in the past week. When use *in the past week* is considered (an indicator of the relative frequency of drug use), the highest prevalence was found in training prisons (21%) and local/remand prisons (16%), while significantly lower rates were found in other types of establishments. There is very little injecting drug use in English and Welsh prisons: only 1% of prisoners (14) reported having injected in the current prison. Cannabis and opiates (mostly heroin) were the drugs most often reported as having been used by prisoners. About a third had used cannabis and about a fifth opiates at some time in their current prison, while about one in ten prisoners reported using each of these types of drug in the past week. When the number of episodes of drug use within a week are considered, opiates are used slightly more frequently than cannabis in the prison system as a whole (25 compared with 21 episodes per 100 inmates per week) but the difference is not statistically significant. In local prisons, open prisons and young offender institutions (YOIs) more people reported using cannabis than opiates in the past month. In YOIs, there was very little use of opiates at all. In training prisons, use of cannabis and heroin was reported about equally, while in women's prisons and dispersal prisons opiate use was reported by a larger proportion of inmates than cannabis use in the month prior to interview.

Levels of drug use in prison need to be considered in the context of prisoners' levels of use outside prison. The proportion of inmates who reported using drugs in the year before coming to prison was 70%, and 66% reported using drugs in the month before prison. Cannabis was the most commonly reported drug, used by just over half the sample, while about a third used opiates, mainly heroin. Crack cocaine had been used by almost a quarter of prisoners in the month before coming to prison. Poly-drug use was very common. For example, over 90% of opiate users in the year before coming to prison also used at least one other type of drug. Therefore, it is clear that entry into prison is associated with a very significant reduction in drug consumption of all types. The route of administration also changes, as there is a reduction in injecting drug use. A small proportion of inmates (2%) started (or re-started) using drugs while in prison. There is also evidence that a proportion of inmates change the types of drugs used, as 5% of inmates were classed as new users/re-starters of cannabis and 4% as new users or re-starters of opiates. Although the proportion of prisoners starting to use drugs, particularly opiates, in prison or changing to opiates from other drugs is quite small, the size of the population means that this represents quite a substantial number of people and must be a cause for concern.

MDT results for Scotland show that the proportion of positive tests for any drug fell from 36% in 1996/07 to 21% in 2000/01 before rising to 23% in 2002/03 (ISD 2002 p 152, 2003 p 165). The rate then increased to 35% in 2003/04 and 37% in 2004/05; this increase was essentially due to illicit methadone which accounted for 9% in the 2003/04 and 15% in 2004/05 (ISD 2005 p 141). Over the period 1996/07–2001/02, the rates for cannabis and opiates fell most from 29% to 9% and from 16% to 11% respectively, before rising to 15% and 14% respectively in 2004/05. The rate for benzodiazepines fell from 9% to 4% before rising again to 8%. The rate of detection for buprenorphine has ranged between 1% and 3%. The results for the Addictions Testing Measure in 2005/06 were similar to the MDT results for 2004/05 (ISD 2006 p 153).

The levels of drug use among prisoners at reception increased in Scotland from 73% in 1998/99 to 77% in 2001, but fell to 75% in 2001/02 (ISD 2003 p 164). The use of cannabis rose from 49% to 63% in 2001 but fell to 45% in 2001/02 as well as benzodiazepines (from 43 to 52%). Methadone use increased from 8% to 12% in 1998/99 before falling to 10% in 2001/02, probably reflecting its wider use in treatment of dependence. Opiate use varied between 34% and 44%

during this period, and amphetamines between 2% and 4%. Cocaine use rose from 4% to 9% over the period 1998/99 to 2001/02.

These results relate mainly to the prison establishments in Aberdeen and Perth. A study in October 2000 found there were substantial geographical differences in the use of all types of drug (ISD 2002 p 151). For example, cannabis use ranged from 29% in Inverness to 93% in Perth; opiates from 11% in Polmont to 61% in Cornton Vale (a female establishment); and benzodiazepines from 12% in Dumfries to 84% in Aberdeen.

Prison surveys

Other, more conventional, surveys have shown a higher proportion of drug use than testing appears to reveal. This adds some credence to concerns that prisoners are findings ways to avoid testing positive, such as switching from cannabis, with its long residual retention, to drugs which are excreted much more quickly from the body – eg heroin. The surveys mentioned below provide details on levels of use, injecting and measures of drug use problems in prisons.

The Office for Population Censuses and Surveys (now the Office for National Statistics) carried out a survey of inmates in English and Welsh prisons during 1997 (Singleton et al 1998). It revealed that nearly half of sentenced males and a third of females reported using drugs during their current prison term. Cannabis use was reported by 46% of male and 31% of female sentenced prisoners. However, women were just as likely as men to report use of heroin. Around two-fifths of both male (43%) and female (41%) inmates reported dependence on drugs, somewhat lower than the rates for remand prisoners – 51% and 54% of males and females respectively. Females reported higher levels of dependence on heroin and non-prescribed methadone.

A survey of Scottish prisoners conducted in 1998 found that 44% of prisoners had used drugs while in prison during the previous six months (Wozniak et al 1998). Nearly two-fifths (39%) had used cannabis; the rates for other drugs were heroin 31%, diazepam 16%, dihydrocodeine 14%, ecstasy 9%, amphetamines 8%, methadone 4% and other opiate-based drugs, eg Temgesic (buprenorphine), 23%. There was a significant increase in the use of heroin between 1994 and 1998, from 9% to 31%. Levels of drug use reported by inmates varied from 11% in Peterhead to 59% in Glenochil. Drug use was more likely among young offenders, especially males. On average, 5% reported injecting drugs in prison; again this varied from prison to prison, reaching 19% in Aberdeen. About four-fifths (82%) of injectors reported sharing injecting equipment. Remand prisoners and long-term prisoners nearing the end of their sentences are less likely to have these practices.

The 2001 sweep of this survey found that 38% reported having used drugs in prison in the previous month (Scottish Prison Service 2001). Of these, opiates were reported by 76%, cannabis 70%. Four percent of this drug-using group reported injecting, and of these 77% had shared their 'works'. Drug use ever in prison was reported by 58%, of whom 43% had received help such as counselling or prescriptions while in prison. Three-quarters said their drug use had changed during their current period inside: for 80% use had decreased, but 12% reported more use, and 8% had used different drugs.

Table 3.9 Drug use (%) in previous month in Scottish prisons, 2001 and 2006

Drug	2001	2006
Opiates (eg heroin, codeine)	76	–
Heroin	–	72
Cannabis	70	70
Benzodiazepines (eg Valium)	28	43
Temazepam	–	13
Buprenorphine	35	–
Other opiates (eg buprenorphine, dihydrocodeine)	–	27
Amphetamines	14	7
Ecstasy	14	10
Cocaine	14	19
Methadone	9	18

Sources: Scottish Prison Service 2001; ISD 2006 p 155

The latest sweep (ISD 2006 p 155) indicates that while the use of opiates, buprenorphine and amphetamine-type substances has fallen since 2001, there have been increases in the use of a range of other drugs, eg cocaine, benzodiazepines and methadone (see Table 3.9). These changes have been accompanied by a reduction to 3% in the proportion reporting injecting drugs, and a lower proportion of these sharing (71%). Other patterns remained similar to 2001.

Young offenders

Less is known about drug use among young offenders. The Offending Crime and Justice Survey of 2004 found that just over half (52%) of those who had taken a drug in the last year had committed an offence, compared with 19% who had not taken a drug (Budd et al 2005). Frequent drug takers are more likely than others to have committed crimes in the last year. Nearly two-thirds (62%) of those who reported that they used drugs frequently had committed an offence in the last year. These figures demonstrate an association between drugs and crime but make no claim regarding causality. Over a quarter (28%) of those who had taken a drug had committed an acquisitive crime in the last year, while just under a quarter (24%) had committed a serious crime. Similar patterns were seen for those respondents who had taken a Class A drug. Those most likely to have committed an acquisitive or serious crime in the last year were frequent users of drugs (32% and 31% respectively). In addition, a third of frequent drug users were frequent offenders. Those young people who did not take drugs in the last year were significantly less likely than their drug-taking counterparts to have committed an offence. This was the case for all offence types.

A survey of 293 clients of 11 young offender institutions across England and Wales looked at substance use, self-reported offending and related risk and lifestyle factors, using an extensive structured questionnaire (Hammersley et al 2003). The cohort comprised predominantly white males age 15 and 16, although females were represented proportionally to their appearance as YOT clients, and black and Asian ethnicities were deliberately over-represented. The self-reported prevalence of all drugs exceeded that reported in the Youth Lifestyles Survey and in the British Crime Survey 16 to 30 cohort. However, the cohort contained relatively few heroin or crack cocaine users and use of these drugs was not generally that frequent. Instead, the cohort tended to use alcohol, cannabis and tobacco extensively, along with other drugs less often. There were signs of the 'normalisation' of drug use in that the cohort used a wider range of drugs, at a younger age, than would have been the case 20 years ago. Moreover, this diverse drug use did not indicate a progression or funnelling towards heroin or cocaine use. Instead, heavier users tended to use alcohol and cannabis frequently and other drugs occasionally. Despite high prevalence of use, few of the cohort reported dependence and only 15% were rated as at high risk of substance abuse problems. However, this rate is about ten times the prevalence of high-risk youth found in a large school survey. Forty per cent or more of the cohort felt there was some relationship between their substance use and their offending.

While these findings tell us that young offenders are far more likely to have used a drug, they say nothing about use by young offenders while in detention.

Drugs in the workplace

There has been a surge of interest in monitoring drug use in the workplace. The Institute of Personnel and Development (IPD) reported in the autumn of 1998 that 18% of 1,800 firms surveyed for them by the Reward Group reported illegal drug-taking by staff (IPD 1998a). This was an increase of 3% on the corresponding figure two years previously. Although 81% of firms encouraged individuals to seek counselling and help, time off for rehabilitation was only allowed by 38% of companies. Dismissals were used by firms in 31% of cases. Individuals' job performance deteriorated as a result of drug-taking, according to 64% of respondents. There was seen to be a worsening in working relationships with colleagues as a result of drug abuse in 57% of firms, and in relationships with clients according to 27% of companies. Nearly half (47%) of firms surveyed did not have a drugs policy and only 15% had an illegal drugs awareness policy. The two main ways in which personnel or management sections became aware of drug misuse were deterioration in work performance (75%) or notification by other members of staff (72%). In one-third of instances, there was a voluntary admission by the individual concerned. Accidents in the workplace accounted for 14% of notifications and random drug testing only 4% (IPD 1998b).

Armed Forces

Random testing for drugs was introduced for the Army on 2 May 1995, the Royal Navy on 1 April 1997 and for the Royal Air Force on 1 November 1998 (Hansard 2000). During the first two years, the proportion of positive tests for the Army fell from 1.4% in 1995 to 0.7% in 1996 (Hansard 2007b). For the Armed Forces overall, positive results have fluctuated over the years within the range 0.49% to 0.71%; the Royal Air Force consistently having the lowest rates, followed by the Royal Navy and then the Army (Hansard 2007a). Average rates of positive tests increased from 0.53% in 2000 to 0.65% in 2006 (Table 3.10).

Positive findings for Class A drugs have risen for the Armed Forces as a whole, and for each branch of the Services, from 42.5% of positive results in 2000 to 56.9% in 2006 (Table 3.10). The most common drugs identified in 2006 were: cocaine (45.4%); cannabis (28.0%); and ecstasy (10.0%). Stimulants, whether alone or in combination with each other, were by far and away the most common drugs detected; heroin accounted for only 0.24% of all positive findings (Table 3.11).

Table 3.10 Drug testing (%) in the Armed Forces, 2000 to 2006

Branch of Services	2000	2001	2002	2003	2004	2005	2006
Royal Navy							
Positive rates among those tested	0.35	0.39	0.33	0.41	0.39	0.37	0.46
Proportion of positives that were Class A	55.30	44.00	30.20	62.50	55.30	76.60	79.00
Army							
Positive rates among those tested	0.59	0.65	0.58	0.56	0.69	0.83	0.74
Proportion of positives that were Class A	41.20	49.50	46.50	47.00	37.20	61.20	55.00
Royal Air Force							
Positive rates among those tested	0.12	0.13	0.09	0.15	0.21	0.15	0.14

Branch of Services	2000	2001	2002	2003	2004	2005	2006
Proportion of positives that were Class A	35.70	39.00	30.00	20.00	45.80	57.10	66.70
Armed Forces overall							
Positive rates among those tested	0.53	0.57	0.50	0.49	0.61	0.71	0.65
Proportion of positives that were Class A	42.50	48.80	45.00	47.50	38.70	62.00	56.90

Source: Hansard 2007b

Table 3.11 Drug testing in the Armed Forces, 2006

	Royal Navy	Army	Royal Air Force	Armed Forces overall
Number of random tests performed on military personnel	12,505	104,499	12,884	129,888
Number of personnel testing positive (% of tests conducted)	57 (0.46%)	769 (0.74%)	18 (0.14%)	844 (0.65%)
Drug or combination of drugs involved				**(% of positive tests)**
Heroin	1	1		2 (0.24)

	Royal Navy	Army	Royal Air Force	Armed Forces overall
Cocaine	35	340	8	383 (45.4)
Cocaine/ecstasy		34	2	36 (4.3)
Cocaine/ecstasy/ amphetamine		3		3 (0.36)
Cocaine/ecstasy/ cannabis		6		6 (0.71)
Cocaine/amphetamine		6		6 (0.71)
Cocaine/ amphetamine/ cannabis		1		1 (0.12)
Cocaine/cannabis		33		33 (3.9)
Ecstasy	9	73	2	84 (10.0)
Ecstasy/amphetamine		9		9 (1.1)
Ecstasy/ amphetamine/ cannabis		3		3 (0.36)
Ecstasy/cannabis		10		10 (1.2)
Cannabis	11	221	4	236 (28.0)
Amphetamine		15		15 (1.8)
Amphetamine/ cannabis		4		4 (0.47)
Benzodiazepine	1	10	2	13 (1.57)

Source: Hansard 2007a

Drinking patterns within the Armed Forces were examined by researchers in March 2003 (Fear et al 2007). A random representative sample of regular members of the forces (7,937 males, 749 females) had their alcohol consumption assessed using the Alcohol Use Disorders Identification Test (AUDIT) – a widely used and validated instrument. Two-thirds (67%) of males and half (49%) of females had an AUDIT score of 8 or more – denoting hazardous drinking; this compares to 38% of males and 16% of females in the general population. Binge drinking was associated with being younger, being in the Army, being single, being a smoker and being white. Heavy drinking (AUDIT score of 16 or more) among male service personnel was associated with: holding a lower rank, being younger, being single, being in the Naval Services or Army, being deployed to Iraq, not having children, being a smoker, having a combat role, and having a parent with a drink or drug problem.

How many people are hurt by drug use?

Prevalence figures indicate the number of people using drugs but say little about the effects drugs have on individuals, families and society. The effect which generates most interest, particularly among academics, health professionals and politicians – ie those who usually carry out and commission research – is harm. Traditionally, 'harm' has been generally categorised into four areas: addiction, health (morbidity), drug-related deaths (mortality) and accidents – in other words, the consequences of drug consumption for individuals. However, harm has also been viewed in criminological terms, focusing on the effects of drug use on society. Particular emphasis has been given to issues such as: violence, the fear of crime, antisocial behaviour and acquisitive crime.

This broader perspective has led to an interest in developing instruments to estimate the full extent of the effects of drugs, and thus the costs – financial and others – to society. This development has come about as politicians, civil society, law enforcement agencies and health professionals – to name but a few stakeholders – have advocated a range of approaches on how to tackle the problems associated with drugs. There is no longer a straight dichotomy between law and order and health perspectives. Approaches now considered appropriate to explore include: demand and supply reduction, harm reduction, harm minimisation, education and prevention, etc; some are championed by previously unlikely supporters, such as harm reduction by the police. One of the key problems here is to come up with a holistic, comprehensive and balanced approach, based on evidence, and with limited resources. Thus, there has been more effort put into evaluation and monitoring, as well as cost-benefit analyses.

The Home Office commissioned research on the development of a Drug Harm Index (DHI). The DHI captures the harms generated by the problematic use of any illegal drug by combining robust national indicators into a single-figure time-series index. The harms include drug-related crime, community perceptions of drug problems, drug nuisance and the various health consequences that arise from drug abuse (eg HIV, overdoses, deaths, etc). The relative importance of each of the harm indicators in the DHI is captured by the economic and social costs that they generate. This follows from work to estimate the economic and social costs of Class A drug use (Godfrey et al 2002).

The DHI does not capture all the harms that illegal drugs might possibly generate, but rather a subset of harms for which robust data are available. Thus, this measure is an index indicating change over time, rather than an estimate of the absolute level of harm at any one time. Interpreting changes in the DHI requires care, as it is a single measure that summarises much detail. Different categories of harm may evolve differently over time and no single index can fully capture this diversity. The authors recommended that the DHI should be considered alongside a 'basket' of individual indicators in order to determine which particular types of harm are becoming dominant, or are being moderated (MacDonald et al 2005).

The value of the Index, using 1998 as the base year (value = 100) to coincide with the launch of the Drug Strategy in that year, rose to 112 in 1999, fell slightly to 110.3 in 2000, before rising to 117.0 in 2001, followed by a slight decline to 115.8 in 2002. Between 2003 and 2004 the DHI fell in value from 104.8 to 87.9, a drop of 16.9 points (or 16.1%); this compares to a 9% drop between 2002 and 2003. The previously reported fall in the DHI between 2002 and 2003 was primarily driven by reductions in the number of drug deaths, hepatitis C episodes, commercial and domestic burglaries, BCS perceptions of drug nuisance and thefts of (domestic) vehicles. Taken together, these accounted for 75% of the change in DHI value between 2002 and 2003. The change in the DHI value between 2003 and 2004 was mostly due to substantial falls in a number of drug-related crime types (eg burglary, shoplifting, robbery and vehicle theft) (MacDonald et al 2006). The only significant health-related driver is drug-related deaths, but between 2003 and 2004 these increased in England and Wales from 1,255 to 1,427 (according to figures published at that time).

Where detailed studies of estimating costs and harms have been undertaken, their authors have highlighted methodological problems (for example, in placing a value on the intangible costs of drug abuse, such as pain and suffering) and the lack of data on key drug-related harms in even the most advanced drug policy research institutions. In the UK context, this means having more timely data, eg drug seizure and offender data. The Beckley Foundation argues that if these forms of analysis are to be used to routinely inform policy decisions, policy-makers must be aware of the scale and nature of the costs of different patterns of drug use to their citizens, the costs (and collateral costs) of the policies and programmes designed to reduce drug problems, and the impact and effectiveness of these policies and programmes (Roberts et al 2006).

Addiction

Addiction, dependence or problematic use is a difficult concept to survey. Those with drug-related problems tend to be difficult to find, and addiction is difficult to measure. Experts consistently fail to agree on what constitutes an addict, dependence, problematic use or a problematic user (see Ghodse 2002 pp 2–5). What to one person is a manageable activity can be seen by others as problematic. While the debate goes on, estimates as to how many people are experiencing drug problems have to be pooled from a number of sources, using a range of criteria – none of which measure addiction directly or comprehensively.

Treatment

Traditionally, the only source of information on the number of problematic drug users in the UK was the Home Office Addicts Index. The epidemiological function of the Index, which closed in April 1997, was superseded by the Regional Drug Misuse Databases (RDMDs) (Hickman et al 2004). In essence, the RDMDs logged the number of people seeking new help for their drug use. The databases, therefore, counted not the number of people addicted to a drug, but those who were using drugs and seeking help. These figures revealed only the number of individuals with problem drug use presenting to RDMD-participating services for the first time within a six-month period. The data were not submitted by all agencies and so were not comprehensive. They gave only the number of new, not ongoing, treatments.

The RDMDs in England were replaced on 1 April 2001 by the National Drug Treatment Monitoring System (NDTMS), which itself is undergoing change and

Table 3.12 Number and percentage of clients starting treatment episodes, by country and primary drug of use, in 2004/05

Drug	England		Scotland		Wales		Northern Ireland		United Kingdom	
	No.	%	No.	%	No.	%	No.	%	No.	%
Amphetamines	3,045	3	269	2	398	13	19	1	3,731	3
Benzodiazepines	1,395	1	791	6	135	4	182	10	2,503	2
Cannabis	12,021	12	1,593	11	377	12	810	46	14,801	13
Cocaine	4,637	5	278	2	52	2	126	7	5,093	4
Crack	5,715	6	48	0	76	2	3	0	5,842	5
Opiates	60,030	61	8,162	57	1,627	53	360	21	70,179	60
Other/Not known	11,641	12	3,143	22	402	13	246	14	15,632	13
Total	98,684		14,284		3,067		1,746		117,781	

Source: Treatment Demand Indicator data supplied to UK Focal Point for Annual Report 2006, Eaton et al 2006

development. There are also national Drug Misuse Databases (DMDs) in Wales, Scotland and Northern Ireland (which still retains an Addicts Index).

The number of people in contact with specialist drug treatment in England during 2006/07 was 195,454 (177,055 in 2005/06); this is an increase of 130% since 1998 (85,000). Just over half (53% or 104,000) of these individuals either entered structured drug treatment for the first time or re-entered services in 2006/07 (National Treatment Agency 2007).

Counting the figures for the NDTMS and the national DMDs it is possible to derive an estimate of the total number of clients starting treatment episodes. The number of treatment demands of individuals presenting for treatment has risen from 74,546 in 2002/03 to 99,482 in 2004/05 in England and Wales. However, this does not necessarily reflect an increase in the number of problematic drug users but is more likely to be a response to the increased number of places made available by treatment services. These figures, it should be noted, still exclude those receiving treatment in prisons and provided by other service providers.

While Table 3.12 provides an estimate of the number of individuals in treatment, it fails to cover those experiencing problems but not receiving treatment. However, Hay et al (2006b) have estimated that 32.2% of opiate users and about 25.4% of opiate and/or problem cocaine users were in treatment in 2004 in Northern Ireland. Furthermore, the often hidden nature of problem drug use means that population-based surveys are of limited use for estimating the full extent of problematic drug use. Although it is almost impossible to count the number of people experiencing problems at any one time, there are methods for deriving estimates.

Capture–recapture

A number of local studies have used what is called the capture–recapture method. Originally used to estimate the number of fish in a pool, this method simply calculates the number of recaptured or missed fish every time the net is cast, and applies this ratio to the whole population. In essence, two consecutive samples of the same population are taken. The first sample tags and releases all that are captured. The second then reveals the number of fish recaptured and those that are not (by way of the tags). This ratio can then be applied to the rest of the population. Therefore, if, on the second sampling, five out of 100 fish are tagged, then we can estimate that every time we cast the net, we catch only 5% of the total fish population. From this we can estimate that in that pool, there are roughly 500 fish.

Using this method, several studies have estimated the number of problematic drug users in their area. For example, estimates of prevalence of crack cocaine in 12 London boroughs for 2000–01 was approximately 15.4 per 1,000 population (20,972) in 12 boroughs and approximately 13 per 1,000 (47,000) in London as a whole (Hope et al 2005).

The multivariate (or multiple) indicator method has been employed also by UK researchers to provide such estimates. This approach combines local prevalence estimates (typically based on capture–recapture techniques) with routinely available regional/national indicator data, eg seizures, treatments, arrests and deaths.

Table 3.13 UK national prevalence estimates for problem drug use

Country	Year	Age range	Estimate		Rate per 1,000 population	
			Number	95% Confidence Interval	Rate	95% Confidence Interval
England	2004/05	15–64	327,466	325,945– 343,424	9.93	9.88 – 10.41
Wales*	2004/05	15–64	18,402	18,316– 19,299	9.93	9.88 – 10.41
Scotland	2003	15–54	51,582	51,456– 56,379	1.84	1.84 – 2.01
Northern Ireland	2004	15–64	3,303	3,093– 4,307	3.03	2.84 – 3.95
United Kingdom	2003–05	15– 54/64	400,753	398,810– 423,409	–	–

* Not yet undertaken, same rates as England assumed

Sources: Hay et al 2005, 2006a, 2006b

There are currently differences between the countries of the UK as to what constitutes 'problematic' use and in the age groups covered; therefore it is difficult to get a single comprehensive estimate for the UK. Table 3.13 presents the most recent estimates that are in the public domain. At the local level, estimates of problematic drug use can vary enormously. For example, in Scotland the estimates range from 1.6 in the Orkneys to 33.1 per 1,000 population in Glasgow (Hay et al 2005). UK prevalence estimates for injecting drug use concentrate on current injecting status. These are given in Table 3.14.

Table 3.14 UK national prevalence estimates for injecting drug use

Country	Year	Age range	Estimate		Rate per 1,000 population	
			Number	95% Confidence Interval	Rate	95% Confidence Interval
England	2004/05	15–64	137,141	133,118–149,144	4.16	4.04–4.52
Wales*	2004/05	15–64	7,707	7,480–8,381	4.16	4.04–4.52
Scotland	2003	15–54	18,737	17,731–20,289	0.67	0.63–0.71
Northern Ireland†	2004	15–64	451	551–800	0.41	0.51–0.73
United Kingdom	2003–05	15–54/64	164,036	158,880–178,614	–	–

* Not yet undertaken, same rates as England assumed

† Same rates as England and Scotland assumed

Sources: Hay et al 2005, 2006a, 2006b

Morbidity – drug-related illness

There are a number of medical conditions which are related to the use or misuse of drugs. The following sections deal with the most common diseases and conditions associated with drug use: blood-borne viruses and infections (eg HIV/AIDS, hepatitis) and psychiatric co-morbidity (dual diagnosis). Other physical conditions can include septicaemia, gangrene, myocardial infarction, seizures, poisoning, etc.

HIV/AIDS

Information on infectious disease is based on *Shooting up: infections among injecting drug users in the United Kingdom 2006* (Health Protection Agency et al 2007). Data on the prevalence of HIV/AIDS, hepatitis and other diseases among drug injectors is provided by a number of agencies:

- Health Protection Agency Centre for Infections
- Health Protection Scotland
- National Public Health Service for Wales
- Communicable Disease Surveillance Centre Northern Ireland
- Centre for Research on Drugs and Health Behaviour, London School of Hygiene and Tropical Medicine.

The information on HIV/AIDS in England, Wales and Northern Ireland is collated by the Health Protection Agency (HPA) through its unlinked anonymous HIV prevalence monitoring programme. The programme gets its data from screening the saliva of injecting drug users attending specialist treatment and support agencies or genitourinary medicine clinics. The sampling is neither random nor comprehensive, and fails to screen those not attending participating clinics, failing to do a saliva test or failing to declare their injecting. Scottish data are provided by the Scottish Centre for Infection and Environmental Health (SCIEH – Health Protection Scotland), and are for all persons coming forward for a named test and who are tested in an NHS laboratory. Cases are referred for testing from a wide range of settings – GPs, GUM clinics, counselling clinics, prisons, drug clinics, hospital inpatients/outpatients, etc. Coverage is national (not sampled), as all positive tests are confirmed by one of the main reference labs in Edinburgh or Glasgow.

The HPA reports that by the end of 2006 there had been a cumulative total of 4,662 HIV diagnoses reported in the UK where infection was believed to have been acquired through injecting drug use. This figure represents 5.4% of all HIV diagnoses in the UK: 4.2% in England; 26% in Scotland; 3.8% in Wales; and 2.1% in Northern Ireland. There was an average of 140 reports of HIV among injecting drug users (IDUs) during the period 1998–2006. A survey of current and former IDUs in England, Wales and Northern Ireland carried out by the Unlinked Anonymous Prevalence Monitoring Programme (UAPMP) indicates an overall HIV prevalence of 1.3% in 2006. In London, the prevalence was 4%; elsewhere in England it was 0.65%. Combined data for 2005 and 2006 show the prevalence of HIV infection among IDUs in Northern Ireland was 1.9% and in Wales was 1.1%. The prevalence among recent initiates has remained higher than it was prior to 2003, with the prevalence being 0.77% in 2006 (0.25% in 2002). In Scotland, the prevalence of HIV among IDUs in 2006 was 0.79%, compared to 1.4% to 3.2% in the early to mid-1990s and 0.5% to 0.9% during the period 1998 to 2005. HIV prevalence among IDUs continues to be much lower than in other western European countries of comparable size.

Hepatitis C

Hepatitis C is currently the most common infectious disease affecting those who inject drugs. Very high prevalence has been reported among IDUs in many countries. Up to 80% of those acquiring hepatitis C develop chronic infection and are at risk of developing cirrhosis and liver cancer.

Figures for hepatitis C are gathered by the UAPMP and reported to the HPA Centre for Infections (CfI). Up to the end of 2006, laboratories in England had reported a total of 62,424 diagnoses of hepatitis C infections to the CfI since reporting began in 1992. The majority of these infections will most probably have been acquired through injecting drug use, as over 90% of those diagnoses with risk factor information gave this as the route of infection. Welsh laboratories have reported a total of 4,198 diagnoses of hepatitis C infection, including 428 diagnoses in 2006. Over 90% of infections in individuals with a known risk factor were associated with injecting drug use. In Northern Ireland, laboratories have reported a total of 1,049 cases, including 140 new ones in 2006 – the highest yearly total to date – and all associated with injecting drug use. The prevalence of hepatitis C infection among IDUs remains high overall. Of the (current and former) IDUs in 2006, 41% had antibodies to hepatitis C, similar to that seen in recent years (42% in 2005). The overall hepatitis C prevalence in England was 43%, but with very marked regional variations: from 22% in the North-East to 57% in London and 60% in the North-West (2005 and 2006 data combined). The prevalence rates in Wales and Northern

Ireland were lower than in most of the English regions: Wales 18%; and Northern Ireland 29%. Among current IDUs, hepatitis C prevalence has increased from 33% in 2000 to 42% in 2006: 44% in England in 2006; in Wales (combined 2005 and 2006 data) 17%; in Northern Ireland 25%. There were higher prevalence rates among several sub-groups. Those reporting injecting crack cocaine in the past four weeks were more likely (59%) to have hepatitis C than those who had not (34%); those who had injected into their groins in the past four weeks (54%) than those who had not (37%); and those who injected into their legs (49%) than those who had not (41%). In 2006, throughout England, Wales and Northern Ireland the prevalence was 21%, similar to 2001–05. However, the prevalence among this group remains higher than it was in 2000 (11%) and earlier years.

During 2005, it was estimated that about 50,000 people were infected with hepatitis C in Scotland (1% of the population). Of these, it was estimated that 37,500 (75%) were chronically infected (including 33,800 individuals who had ever injected drugs) and that 35–40% had had their infection diagnosed. By the end of 2006, a total of 22,073 people had been diagnosed hepatitis C positive in Scotland. In 2006, 1,520 new diagnoses were reported, compared with an annual average of 1,682 reports during 2001–05; 89% were known to have ever injected drugs.

The prevalence of hepatitis C among IDUs in Glasgow reduced substantially between 1990 (all IDUs: 89%; IDUs aged under 25 years: 91%) and 1999/2000 (62% and 41% respectively), suggesting that there had been a decrease in hepatitis C incidence during the 1990s. Since then, the prevalence of hepatitis C among IDUs in Glasgow has remained broadly unchanged (rising only slightly in 2002/03: all IDUs, 64%; IDUs aged under 25 years, 43%). A review of epidemiological studies showed that the incidence of hepatitis C among IDUs in many parts of Scotland remains high (in the range 12 to 29 per 100 person-years).

Hepatitis B

In the UK, hepatitis B infection is usually acquired in adulthood, with sexual activity or injecting drug use being the most commonly reported routes of infection. In England and Wales there was a substantial deterioration in the quality of hepatitis B reporting in 2004, and data for 2004 to 2006 are not available. In 2003, however, injecting drug use was the main risk associated with hepatitis B infection, accounting for 34% of individuals with a known risk factor in England, and 27% in Wales.

The proportion of case reports indicating injecting drug use as the main risk declined in Scotland from 30% in 1999 – the year in which an outbreak occurred among the IDU population in Aberdeen – to 3% in 2006. In Northern Ireland, the total number of reports prior to 2002 had fluctuated at about 30 per year. Numbers have since risen: 67 in 2002, 61 in 2003, 60 in 2004, 72 in 2005, and 78 in 2006. Some of these infections will have been related to injecting drug use. Overall, about one in five IDUs have had hepatitis B infection. In 2006, 21% of current and former IDUs in England, Wales and Northern Ireland had antibodies to hepatitis B core antigen (anti-HBc, a marker of previous or current hepatitis B infection, similar to the level seen since 1995). Prevalence varied by country (combining 2005 and 2006 data). In Wales the prevalence was 11%, and was 8% in Northern Ireland. The prevalence of anti-HBc among recent initiates increased from 3.4% in 1997 to 9.1% in 2003, 6.7% in 2004, 7.1% in 2005 and 10% in 2006.

Other infections

IDUs are vulnerable to a range of bacterial infections, such as wound botulism, 'gas gangrene', and bacteraemia, as a result of non-sterile injecting or injecting contaminated drugs. In recent years these acute infections have caused growing public health problems. Cases of severe infection related to both meticillin resistant *Staphylococcus aureus* (MRSA) and Group A streptococci continue to occur among IDUs.

Clostridia are a group of spore-forming bacteria that are widely found in the environment. The spores produced by these bacteria may end up in drugs, such as heroin, through environmental contamination. They may cause wound infections among IDUs, particularly if they enter an intramuscular or subcutaneous injection site, and can then produce toxins, causing illnesses such as tetanus or 'gas gangrene' with potentially severe or fatal outcomes.

Cases of wound botulism continue to occur among IDUs in the UK. Prior to 2000, no cases of wound botulism had been reported; by the end of 2006 a total of 134 suspected cases had been reported. In 2006, 22 suspected cases were reported (28 in 2005, 40 in 2004). In 2006 one of the three cases of tetanus reported to the HPA in England was known to have been an IDU; there were no cases elsewhere.

In 2005, four of the six cases of tetanus reported in the UK were in IDUs. During 2000 there was an outbreak of serious illness and death among IDUs, due to *Clostridium novyii*. Laboratory work has shown that *C.novyii* spores can easily survive the 'cooking-up' process prior to heroin injection.

Psychiatric co-morbidity

Provisional data on psychiatric discharges in Scotland shows that, in 2004/05, 6% had a diagnosis of drug misuse (68% of these had only a main diagnosis). Where a main diagnosis of drug misuse was recorded with a supplementary diagnosis, the most commonly mentioned ones were: mood (affective) disorders (16% of those cases which recorded a supplementary diagnosis) and personality disorders (15%). Where drug misuse was a supplementary diagnosis, the most common main diagnosis was schizophrenia (32%) followed by mood (affective) disorders (19%) (ISD 2006).

A cross-sectional prevalence survey of 1,808 patients in a semi-rural area of south-east England was conducted with detailed assessments from a representative sample of 373 patients identified as having a combination of severe mental illness and substance misuse (Trathen et al 2007). One-tenth of patients attending Community Mental Health Teams (CMHTs) reported problematic use of illicit drugs and 17% reported alcohol problems in the past year. One-fifth (22%) of Community Drug and Alcohol Service (CDAS) clients reported a severe mental illness and 46% reported some other form of psychiatric disorder. Of patients with a combined diagnosis of mental illness and substance misuse, cannabis use was four times more common among patients attending the CMHT than CDAS (33% versus 8%) while use of amphetamines was five times higher in the CMHT group (10% versus 2%). Patients with concurrent psychiatric and substance misuse problems represent a similar proportion of the aggregate caseload of both treatment services, with observed prevalence among CDAS and CMHT patients with a diagnosis of anxiety disorder (18% versus 26%), minor depression (42% versus 32%), personality disorders (32% versus 36%), histories of self-harm (52% versus 46%) and violence (33% versus 30%) respectively.

Current and lifetime substance use were recorded for 123 consecutive referrals to a specialist early intervention service in Cambridge and South Cambridgeshire of people experiencing a first psychotic episode (Barnett et al 2007). Substance use among people with first-episode psychosis was twice that of the general population (estimated from BCS figures) and was more common in men than women. Cannabis abuse was reported in 51% of patients (n=62) and alcohol abuse in 43% (n=53). More than half (n=68, 55%) had used Class A drugs, and 38% (n=43) reported poly-substance abuse. Age at first use of cannabis, cocaine, ecstasy and amphetamine was significantly associated with age at first psychotic symptom.

Mortality

There are two main types of source in the UK for information on 'acute' deaths:

- three General Mortality Registers (GMRs) – the General Register Offices for England & Wales, Scotland and Northern Ireland (although the data from the latter is analysed by the Northern Ireland Statistics and Research Agency – NISRA)
- one Special Mortality Register (SMR) – the National Programme on Substance Abuse Deaths (np-SAD) based at St George's, University of London. The Scottish Crime and Drug Enforcement Agency (SCDEA) also collates information on drug-related deaths (chiefly accidental overdoses) reported to police forces.

ICD10 Underlying cause code (from 2001)	ICD9 Underlying cause code (up to 2000)	Description
F11–F16, F18–F19	292, 304, 305.2–305.9	Mental and behavioural disorders due to drug use (excluding alcohol and tobacco)
X40–X44	E850–E858	Accidental poisoning by drugs, medicaments and biological substances
X60–X64	E950.0–E950.5	Intentional self-poisoning by drugs, medicaments and biological substances

ICD10 Underlying cause code (from 2001)	ICD9 Underlying cause code (up to 2000)	Description
Y10–Y14	E980.0–E980.5	Poisoning by drugs, medicaments and biological substances, undetermined intent
X85	E962.0	Assault by drugs, medicaments and biological substances

The essential data recorded by GMRs are derived from medical death certificates. In England & Wales and Scotland some supplementary information is provided. The details of substances recorded by the GMRs are those recorded on the death certificate. No detailed information is passed to them on toxicology, eg levels of drugs and/or alcohol found in body tissues, blood or urine, neither are post-mortem reports. The Office for National Statistics (ONS) database of drug-related deaths records all deaths in England and Wales from 1993 where the underlying cause of death was assigned one of the following codes according to the International Classification of Diseases (ICD).

This data has been entered in such a way that deaths can be sorted, counted and analysed according to any substances which are mentioned on the death certificate. For each record the database also contains information collected at death registration – eg age, sex marital status, place of death, occupation and place of usual residence (to postcode level). Deaths involving more than one drug or alcohol can also be identified.

There are various problems associated with quantifying deaths from specific drugs. The coroner can note any drugs implicated in a death in the 'cause of death' section of the coroner's certificate of death. However, coroners do not always know or record this information, often recording only a general description such as 'drug overdose'. Many deaths involve a mixture of drugs, often taken in combination with alcohol, and there is usually no recorded indication of the relative quantities or which substance was likely to have caused death. It is, therefore, not possible to obtain precise figures on deaths caused by specific substances using data collected at death registration. ONS estimates of the number of deaths due to specific drugs are therefore based on the number of deaths where the *underlying* cause of death was drug-related (ie, assigned one of the ICD codes above) and where the drug is mentioned on the coroner's certificate, regardless of whether it was the *primary* cause of death. The figures presented in Table 3.15 overleaf should therefore be regarded as an estimate of the number of deaths associated with particular substances rather than the exact number directly due to these substances.

Using the ONS definition, from 1993 to 2005 more than one drug was mentioned on the death certificate in 27.1% (9,663 out of 35,616) of cases, and alcohol in 23.4% (8,340 out of 35,616) of drug poisoning deaths in England and Wales (ONS 2007). Most deaths are associated with opiates (chiefly heroin/morphine and methadone), often in combination with other drugs and/or alcohol. Large numbers of deaths also involve benzodiazepines such as Temazepam and diazepam. However, the non-opioid types of drug most often mentioned are antidepressants and paracetamol (either on its own or in compound preparations such as co-proxamol).

The number of deaths where heroin/morphine was mentioned was six times higher in 2001 (at 981) than in 1993 (155), but fell to 696 in 2003, before rising to 842 in 2005. The number of cases in which methadone was implicated rose steadily from 206 in 1993, to peak at 437 in 1997, falling to 199 in 2002, before rising to 220 in 2005. Mentions of cocaine, although still comparatively few compared to heroin/morphine, rose more than 16-fold over the period 1993–2005 as a whole (from 11 to 176). Deaths involving ecstasy accounted for only 1.1% of drug-related deaths; they rose from 12 in 1993 to 56 in 2002, fell to 43 in 2004 before rising again to 58 in 2005. GHB was mentioned in 24 deaths recorded by the ONS between 1996 and 2005.

The number of deaths in Scotland using the ONS 'Standard' definition rose by 23% between 1996 and 2002, from 460 to 566, but fell 13% to 493 in 2003. This figure then rose again by 11% in 2004 to 546, but fell again in 480 in 2005 (GROS 2006). Heroin/morphine was involved in 40% of deaths in 2005, diazepam in 19% and methadone in 15%. The involvement of heroin/morphine trebled between 1996 and 2002, fell by 27% in 2003, rose by 29% in 2004 and then fell by 14% in 2005. Diazepam mentions rose by 2.5 times between 1996 and 2002, but had returned to their 1997 level by 2005. The number of methadone-related deaths fell between 1996 and 2000, rose in 2001 and 2002, fell in 2003,

Table 3.15 Number of deaths where selected substances were mentioned on the death certificate, including with other drugs and alcohol, England and Wales, 1993–2005

Substance	1993	1994	1995	1996	1997	1998	1999	2000	2001	2002	2003	2004	2005
All mentions	2,178	2,350	2,540	2,618	2,817	2,976	3,110	2,932	3,093	2,830	2,623	2,787	2,762
Heroin/ morphine	155	270	331	440	444	609	755	851	981	865	696	751	842
Methadone	206	262	304	322	437	398	336	269	244	199	201	219	220
Cocaine	11	14	22	13	27	65	88	83	97	128	129	154	176
All amphetamines	51	37	49	46	56	63	82	61	79	94	81	80	103
Ecstasy	12	20	17	16	15	17	21	28	55	56	50	43	58
Cannabis	13	19	16	9	14	10	8	9	16	13	11	19	19
GHB	0	0	0	1	0	0	3	3	1	5	6	1	4
Temazepam	165	159	159	102	97	111	95	70	77	70	70	78	45
Diazepam	52	62	89	84	111	117	120	87	123	131	121	94	101
Zopiclone/ Zolpidem	0	0	6	10	12	14	20	41	37	47	40	57	48

Substance	1993	1994	1995	1996	1997	1998	1999	2000	2001	2002	2003	2004	2005
Barbiturates	42	45	40	41	21	27	30	21	26	22	20	16	14
Tricyclic antidepressants	412	448	488	480	488	490	474	374	361	293	310	313	272
Dothiepin	181	262	244	273	254	260	242	186	190	170	158	134	107
Amitriptyline	171	138	154	146	175	184	184	148	134	92	125	148	127
Paracetamol	236	215	202	215	254	233	195	177	192	168	153	174	153
Co-proxamol	304	306	369	328	385	383	388	375	353	312	264	287	202
Dihydrocodeine	58	55	50	55	48	45	29	25	25	27	19	27	19
Tramadol	0	0	0	1	5	7	23	24	28	36	36	43	53

Notes: (1) Some deaths may be counted more than once in the table above. For example, if heroin and cannabis are recorded on the death certificate, the death will be recorded once under heroin and once under cannabis.

(2) As heroin breaks down in the body into morphine, the latter may be detected at post-mortem and recorded on the death certificate. Therefore, where heroin and/or morphine were mentioned on the death certificate, a combined figure is included.

Source: ONS 2007

rose again in 2004 before falling in 2005. Cocaine deaths increased up to 2002, remained little changed in 2003 but rose to a new peak in 2004. Ecstasy mentions stabilised in 2002, fell in 2003 but rose slightly in 2004 and then fell back to their 2000 levels. Drug-related deaths in Northern Ireland have varied in number from year to year; there are no clear patterns emerging. Deaths involve mostly opiates and related narcotics, as well as anti-depressants and benzodiazepines.

One of the objectives of the UK Drug Strategy (Department of Health 2003) was to reduce drug-related deaths (DRDs) by 20% by 2004, using 1999 as the base year. Following the recalculation by ONS of their figures for DRDs it is necessary to revise what has previously been reported on this aspect. Using the Drug Strategy definition (which is much narrower than the ONS definition), the UK target was a reduction of 388 DRDs by 2004. This is against the background of a 34% increase across the UK in the five-year period 1996–2000, followed by a rise of 12.5% in 2001, falls of 6.2% in 2002 and 12.8% in 2003. An increase of 6% in 2004 means that at the UK level the reduction between 1999 (1,941) and 2004 (1,884) was of 57 deaths or 2.9% – clearly in the right direction but totally insufficient to achieve the set target. However, at a national level the picture is more complex. There was a reduction between 1999 and 2004 in England & Wales of 8.2% (from 1,628 to 1,493) but an increase of 22.3% (from 291 to 356) in Scotland, and an increase of 50% in Northern Ireland (from 22 to 33). In England, the Department of Health has lead responsibility for the government's action plan (Department of Health 2007) to reduce drug-related harms. The action plan will support improvements in reducing blood-borne viruses and drug-related deaths through a range of activities within three areas:

- surveillance
- improving delivery
- campaigns.

Since publication of the action plan, work has been undertaken by the Department of Health, in association with the National Treatment Agency, on its implementation over the next three years.

Data from the SMR (np-SAD) database are broadly consistent with those from the ONS. However, the database records not only the presence of particular substances found at post-mortem, but the involvement of particular substances in a death. The np-SAD annual report for 2007 (Ghodse et al 2007) shows that in 2006:

- There was a decrease of about 1% over the number of recorded deaths by the same sources for 2005 (from 1,382 to 1,366)
- The demographic profile remains consistent with previous reports. The majority of cases were males (76%), under the age of 45 years (71%) and white (96%).
- Throughout the period 1997–2006 about two-thirds of cases had a history of drug abuse or dependence, and on average death was 14 years earlier than for those without such a history.
- In 2006, 70% of cases died in a defined residential address, 23% in hospital and 7% elsewhere (eg a public place).
- In 2006, 48% of those who died were unemployed. Forty-three per cent lived with others, compared to 42% who lived alone, while 4% were of no fixed abode.
- Opiates/opioids (ie heroin/morphine, methadone other opiates/opioid analgesics), alone or in combination with other drugs, accounted for the majority (68%) of fatalities. Heroin/morphine alone or in combination with other drugs, accounted for the highest proportion (46%) of fatalities.
- Deaths involving methadone were more likely to be the result of possibly illicit (62% or more) rather than prescribed drugs.
- The number of cases involving methadone rose from 198 to 217.
- The proportion of cases involving methadone increased from 12% to 17%.
- The proportion of cases involving alcohol-in-combination increased from 26% to 32%.
- The proportion of cases involving heroin/morphine decreased from 46% to 44%.

HIV/AIDS deaths

Deaths of IDU (including sex between men and IDU) AIDS victims accounted for 8.4% (1,333 out of 15,914) of the total number of AIDS deaths in England and Wales up to the end of March 2007. In Northern Ireland, the figure was 5.1% (4/79), but in Scotland it was 51% (718 out of 1,408). The figure for the Channel Islands was 1/11. The decline in the number of deaths of IDU AIDS victims seen in recent years has levelled off. The UK figure of 69 for 2005 (63 in 2004) is about 33% of the peak level in 1995 (212). By the end of March 2007, 46 deaths had been reported for 2006; the number is likely to increase (personal communication from Health Protection Agency, 8 May 2007).

Volatile substance abuse deaths

Data on deaths since 1971 associated with volatile substance abuse (VSA) has been collected since 1973 by a special national register based at St George's Hospital Medical School. There were 45 deaths associated with VSA in 2005, compared to 47 in the previous year (Field-Smith et al 2007). This is the lowest figure since 1983 and compares with the all-time peak of 152 in 1990 (see Table 3.16, p 104). Concern about these high rates led to an advertising campaign by the Department of Health in 1992 throughout Great Britain. There was a sharp fall in deaths among children which has persisted, and a small fall among adults. It is estimated that these decreases represent falls of 60% and 19% respectively for those under 18 or 18 or over compared to the previous trends.

In 2005, VSA deaths among 10–14-year-olds accounted for 0.8% of all deaths in this age group; for 15–19-year-olds this proportion rose to 0.4%. Children aged less than 18 accounted for 49% of all VSA deaths in the period 1971–2005. Compared to previous years, there was a shift in 2005 towards higher ages at death. Although VSA rates are similar for both genders, over the last ten years males have accounted for 80% of VSA deaths. Nearly three-fifths (56%) of deaths in 2005 occurred in the home of the deceased, reflecting the fact that 73% of the abuse took place in this location-type. Over the last decade, there was no gender differences in the location where deaths occur. Children are more likely to die in a public place, and adults at home or a friend's home. Standard Mortality Ratios for the last ten years were highest in the Northern Ireland (163), North-East (159), East Midlands (134), and Scotland (132), compared to the UK average (100). The South-East (76), South-West (75) and London (69) had lower rates than would be expected.

In most cases, only one substance was implicated in death. In 5% of instances were two or more substances involved in a death. In the decade ending 2005, the frequency of glue-related deaths decreased. The movement away from using chlorofluorocarbons (CFCs) as propellants in aerosols has led to a reduction in such deaths. There has been a statistically significant fall in gas fuel-related deaths. Consequently, butane now accounts for a much greater proportion of deaths. In 2005 in the under-18 age group, for the first time, more deaths were associated with aerosols than with gas fuels. The principal method of abusing fuel gases (mainly butane lighter refills) is by discharging them directly into the mouth. Most glues are abused by inhalation of the fumes/vapours from plastic bags, and aerosols by spraying through a cloth.

Drug-related road accidents

In 1997 the Department for the Environment, Transport and the Regions (DETR) began a three-year study (the first for ten years) into the incidence of drugs in road accidents. Research by the Transport Research Laboratory (TRL) covering the period October 1996 to June 2000 shows that there has been a significant increase in the number of road traffic accident fatalities who had consumed drugs (Tunbridge et al 2001). Between 1985 and 1987, 7.4% of the sample population of a similar study were found to have used medicinal or illicit drugs, and 35% alcohol (Everest et al 1989). A decade later, the proportion taking drugs has risen to 24.1% but that for alcohol has fallen slightly to 31.5%. In total, 1,184 fatalities were examined, of whom 17.7% tested positive for a single drug and 6.3% for multiple drugs – ie a quarter of cases where drugs were detected had multiple drugs implicated. This contrasts with only 5.3% in the earlier study. Two or more drugs were found in the majority (89%) of multiple drug users. Apart from cannabis, which was found in 11.9% of all cases examined, opiates (5.6%), benzodiazepines (4.8%) and amphetamines (4.5%) were the drugs most commonly detected. The majority of the combinations found would normally be regarded as illicit. Most of all illicit drug consumption (75.3%) was in those aged under 40, while most (78.3%) medicinal use was in those aged 40 and over.

The TRL has also investigated the effects of cannabis and alcohol on driving (Sexton et al 2002). Male drivers who were experienced cannabis and alcohol users were required to carry out laboratory-based tasks and to drive in the TRL driving simulator under two cannabis conditions: (a) placebo; and (b) low dose cannabis. The low dose was herbal cannabis containing about 10mg active ingredient (Δ9-THC). There were also two alcohol conditions: placebo and a dose to give a blood alcohol concentration (BAC) of 50mg of alcohol per 100ml of blood. Experimental procedures included the formal sobriety testing of participants, conducted by two experienced police surgeons/forensic medical examiners. Participants also completed a mood questionnaire at different times during their visit. The results confirmed and extended those from previous studies. There was a reduction of average driving speed and an increase in the minimum time headway on simulated motorway driving when participants had had the active dose of cannabis, regardless of the alcohol dose. Participants' responses on the mood questionnaire showed that they were aware of their impairment. The results suggest that they attempted to compensate for their impairment by driving more cautiously. The results of simulator tracking tasks, which required subjects to stay within their lane on a

Table 3.16 VSA deaths by country, United Kingdom, 1971–2005

Year	England	Wales	Scotland	Northern Ireland	Channel Islands	Isle of Man	United Kingdom
1971–89	748	39	147	30	2	0	966
1990	129	7	12	4	0	0	152
1991	89	1	21	10	1	0	122
1992	70	6	7	2	0	0	85
1993	57	7	9	6	0	0	79
1994	55	1	9	2	0	0	67
1995	62	3	9	1	2	0	77
1996	57	3	13	3	1	1	78
1997	68	1	5	3	0	1	78
1998	64	3	10	3	0	0	80
1999	54	7	8	6	0	0	75
2000	52	1	9	2	1	1	66
2001	49	1	9	4	0	0	63

Year	England	Wales	Scotland	Northern Ireland	Channel Islands	Isle of Man	United Kingdom
2002	51	5	8	1	0	0	65
2003	42	1	6	5	0	0	54
2004	41	4	1	1	0	0	47
2005	35	1	4	5	0	0	45
Total	1,723	91	287	88	7	3	2,199

Source: Derived from Table 4, Field-Smith et al 2007

bend, showed that participants tended to drive less accurately when they had been given the active cannabis dose. This again confirms previous observations that cannabis adversely affects drivers' tracking ability. Measurements of an adaptive tracking task (a laboratory task which measures ability to track a moving object on a computer screen) also produced statistically significant results.

A study of 1,008 17–39-year-old drivers in Scotland found that 9% had ever driven under the influence of any drugs and 5% had done so in the previous year (Ingram et al 2001). These figures represent 26% and 36% respectively of those who had used drugs ever or in the last 12 months. Males were 2.6 times more likely than females to have ever driven under the influence of drugs and 2.7 times more likely in the last year. Thirteen percent of people aged 20–24 had driven under the influence of drugs in the last 12 months, compared to only 3% of those aged 30–34, reflecting the pattern in general drug use. It appears that such driving decreases as age increases. Looking at the last occasion upon which they had driven under the influence of drugs in the last year, 39 out of 57 said they had only consumed cannabis, and only 4 out of 57 ecstasy. The remaining three reported taking a combination of drugs. Thirty of these 57 respondents felt the drugs had not affected their driving. They were usually just going to or from a friend or relative's house, typically at the weekend, and on a journey of five miles or less.

A qualitative study of clubbers and drivers found similar patterns (Neale et al 2001). Drug-driving is associated with a particular lifestyle, ie clubbing. It is not uniformly distributed throughout society. However, most drug-driving episodes involve cannabis and are not associated with travelling to or from clubs and dance venues. Driving under the influence of cannabis was considered by respondents to be less dangerous than driving under the influence of stimulants or hallucinogens. Driving under the influence of LSD or alcohol was considered to be even more dangerous.

How much does it cost?

Exploratory work to estimate the size of the market for illicit drugs in the UK was undertaken by National Economic Research associates for the Home Office at the end of the last decade. The method finally chosen followed a 'bottom-up' approach, identifying the prevalence of different types of users (eg regular and occasional users) and their consumption characteristics to derive estimates of the value and size of the market.

Data from the NEW-ADAM programme provided the basis for estimating the number of regular users – defined as individuals using a particular drug at least once a week. The estimates derived from NEW-ADAM indicated that in the UK there are around 270,000 regular heroin users. The data suggested that regular use of crack is more prevalent than regular use of cocaine.

NEW-ADAM was also used to identify drug expenditures by regular users. The results suggested that a regular heroin user spends around £16,500 a year (on all their drugs) and a regular crack user spends almost £21,000 a year (on all drugs). These expenditures are in line with estimates derived from other research. Occasional use of drugs is a relatively minor part of the overall market for heroin, cocaine and crack. Heavy (and poly) drug users dominate these markets. The prices paid by regular, occasional and prison users were then converted to quantities using street and prison prices. Finally, these were converted back to financial values. The results of this work are given in Table 3.17.

Table 3.17 Estimates of the size of the UK market for illicit drugs, 1998

Drug	Value of market	Street price	'Street quantity' (= value of market/ street price, converted to kg)
Amphetamines	£257.7m	£10 per gram	25,722
Cannabis	£1,577.9m	£92 per oz (28 grams)	486,224
Cocaine	£352.8m	£77 per gram	4,582
Crack	£1,817.0m	£20 per dose (0.2 gram)	18,174
Ecstasy	£294.6m	£11 per dose	26,786,000 (tablets)
Heroin	£2,313.0m	£74 per gram	31,257

Source: Bramley-Harker 2001 p 29

This work formed the foundation for developing the model further to estimate the economic and social costs of Class A drug use (Godfrey et al 2002). Class A drug users were first identified by type of user: young recreational, older regular and problematic; and then prevalence estimates were derived for each type of drug user using established methods. Consequences by type of drug user were derived from available treatment data. Unit costs are then applied to the consequences where reliable data are available – mainly healthcare services, the criminal justice system and state benefits. Total economic costs, defined as government reactive expenditure, were estimated by adding all the various cost consequences identified for each drug user type. Adding victim costs of crime and value for premature deaths to other resource costs results in total economic and social costs. Other potential social costs were identified but not included in the final estimates.

Problem drug users accounted for the majority of total economic and social costs. Further developments of the model were proposed in terms of the definition of user groups and consequences. The proposed typology of consequences comprised five domains (health, work, driving, crime and other social impacts) and six different groups who may bear the costs (users, families/carers, other individuals directly affected, wider community effects, industry, and the public sector). There is uncertainty with all methods for estimating the number of Class A drug users, especially problematic drug users. Three methods were therefore used to derive a range of estimates for problem drug users: multivariate indicator method, treatment coverage method, and treatment demographic method (which produced the lowest estimate but was closer to previously reported estimates in the literature). The total number of Class A drug users was derived by summing the numbers of problem drug users, young recreational users and older regular users. This process yielded the following range of estimates: 1,771,000 (low); 1,827,000 (medium); and 3,486,000 (high).

Data for estimating the economic and social costs of drug misuse are very scarce. However, data for consequences were available from the National Treatment Outcomes Research Study (NTORS) and comprised healthcare services, the criminal justice system and employment. Cost consequences are identified for each type of drug user: recreational, older regular and problematic. Consequences identified include healthcare services: GP, accident and emergency, hospital days, mental health services; state benefits; and the criminal justice system: police arrests/ acquisitive crime, police custody, court appearances and prison. In addition, a number of other healthcare costs were identified, such as those associated with injecting, but not included in the final estimates.

A total of £6 million a year health service and criminal justice costs were associated with young recreational users, or a cost of £7.50 to £15 per user. Total social costs for this group were estimated at £28.8 million a year, a cost per user between £36 and £72. Older regular users were estimated to cost around £6.2 million each year, a cost per user between £3 and £6. Estimates for young recreational and older regular users excluded any allowance for productivity effects and effects from driving and drug taking. For problem drug users, total economic costs ranged from £2.9bn to £5.3bn (the medium estimate is £3.5bn – ie £10,402 per user per annum). Total economic and social costs for this group increase the range of figures to between £10.1bn and £17.4bn – ie £35,455 per user per annum. Problem drug users account for almost all economic and social costs (99%), and drug-related crime accounts for around 88% of total economic and social costs.

References

Barnett J H, Werners U, Secher S M, Hill K E, Brazil R, Masson K, Pernet D E, Kirkbride J B, Murray G K, Bullmore E T and Jones P B (2007) 'Substance use in a population-based clinic sample of people with first-episode psychosis', *British Journal of Psychiatry*, Jun, 190, pp 515–20

Bennett T (1998) *Drugs and Crime: the results of research on drug testing and interviewing arrestees*, Home Office Research Study No. 183, London: Home Office Research and Statistics Directorate

Bennett T (2000) *Drugs and crime: the results of the second developmental stage of the NEW-ADAM programme*, Home Office Research Study No. 205, London: Home Office Research and Statistics Directorate

Bennett T, Holloway K and Williams T (2001) *Drug use and offending: summary results from the first year of the NEW-ADAM research programme*, Home Office Research Findings No. 148, London: Home Office Research and Statistics Directorate

Boreham R and Shaw A (ed.) (2001) *Smoking, drinking and drug use among young people in Scotland in 2000*, London: The Stationery Office

Bramley-Harker E (2001) *Sizing the UK market for illicit drugs*, RDS Occasional Paper No 74, London: Home Office Research Development and Statistics Directorate. Available at: http://www.homeoffice.gov.uk/rds/pdfs/occ74-drugs.pdf

Branigan P, Kuper H and Wellings K (1997) *The Evaluation of the London Dance Safety Campaign*, London: London School of Hygiene and Tropical Medicine

Brown M and Bolling K (2007) *Drugs misuse in Scotland: findings from the 2006 Scottish Crime and Victimisation Survey*, Edinburgh: Scottish Government Social Research. Available at: http://www.scotland.gov.uk/Resource/Doc/198856/0053157.pdf

Budd T, Sharp C, Weir G, Wilson D and Owen N (2005) *Young people and crime: findings from the 2004 Offending, Crime and Justice Survey*, Home Office Statistical Bulletin 20/05, London: Home Office Research Development and Statistics Directorate, November 2005. Available at: http://www.homeoffice.gov.uk/rds/pdfs05/hosb2005.pdf

CACI (1993) *ACORN User Guide*, London: CACI

Carlen P (1996) *Jigsaw: a political criminology of youth homelessness*, Buckingham: Open University Press

Craske V, Stevenson N, Halfin M and French P (2000) 'The *Mixmag* drugs survey 2000', *Mixmag*, February 2001, 117, pp 54–65

Deehan A and Saville E (2003) *Recreational drug use among clubbers in the south east of England, Findings 208*, London: Home Office Research Development and Statistics Directorate. Available at: http://www.homeoffice.gov.uk/rds/pdfs2/r208.pdf

Department of Health (2003) *Government action plan to prevent drug related deaths*, London: Department of Health, 13 December 2003. Available at: http://www.dh.gov.uk/en/Publicationsandstatistics/Publications/PublicationsPolicyAndGuidance/DH_4006533

Department of Health (2007) *Reducing drug-related harm: an action plan*, London: Department of Health, 23 May 2007. Available at: http://www.dh.gov.uk/en/Publicationsandstatistics/Publications/PublicationsPolicyAndGuidance/DH_074850

Eaton G, Lodwick A, Bellis M A and McVeigh J (2006) *United Kingdom drug situation: annual report to the European Monitoring Centre for Drugs and Drug Addiction (EMCDDA) 2006*, London: United Kingdom Focal Point at the Department of Health & Liverpool: North West Public Health Observatory, The Centre for Public Health, Liverpool John Moores University, Submitted to the EMCDDA on 31 October 2006. Available at: http://www.ukfocalpoint.org.uk/documentbank/2006_AR_Full_version.pdf

ESRC (2007) Question bank. Available at: http://qb.soc.surrey.ac.uk/surveys/bcs/crimeintro.htm

Everest J T, Tunbridge R J and Widdop B (1989) *The incidence of drugs in road traffic fatalities*, Research Report RR202, Crowthorne: TRL Ltd

Farrell M, Howes S, Taylor C, Lewis G, Jenkins R, Bebbington P, Jarvis M, Brugha T, Gill B and Meltzer H (2003) 'Substance misuse and psychiatric comorbidity: an overview of the OPCS National Psychiatric Morbidity Survey', *International Review of Psychiatry*, Feb-May, 15(1–2) pp 43–9

Fear N T, Iversen A et al (2007) 'Patterns of drinking in the UK Armed Forces', *Addiction*, November, 102(11) pp 1749–59

Field-Smith M E, Butland B K, Ramsey J D and Anderson H R (2007) *Trends in deaths associated with volatile substance abuse, 1971 to 2005*, Report 20, Division of Community Health Sciences, London: St George's, University of London, 25 July 2007. Available at: http://www.sgul.ac.uk/dms/16669E93D4AAEF9E9F1E7FBAD1BDE330.pdf

Fountain J and Howes S (2002) *Home and dry? Homelessness and substance misuse*, London: Crisis. Available at: http://www.crisis.org.uk/downloads.php/141/HomeDry.pdf

Fraser F (2002) *Drug misuse in Scotland: Findings from the 2000 Crime Survey*, Edinburgh: Scottish Executive Central Research Unit. Available at: http://www.scotland.gov.uk/cru/kd01/green/dmis.pdf

French P (2003) 'The Mixmag drug survey 2003', *Mixmag*, March 2003, 142, pp 74–80

Fuller E (ed.) (2006) *Drug use, smoking, and drinking among young people in England in 2005*, London: The Information Centre, 30 August 2006. Available at:

http://www.ic.nhs.uk/cmsincludes/_process_document.asp?sPublicationID=11749
87644774&sDocID=1755

Fuller E (ed.) (2007) *Smoking, drinking and drug use among young people in England in 2006*, London: The Information Centre, 31 August 2007. Available at: http://www.ic.nhs.uk/pubs/icpublication.2006-01-04.0315032678

Ghodse H (2002) *Drugs and addictive behaviour: a guide to treatment*, 3rd edition, Cambridge: Cambridge University Press

Ghodse H, Corkery J, Oyefeso A, Schifano F and Tonia T (2007) *Drug-related deaths in the UK: annual report 2007*, Drug-related deaths reported by coroners in England, Wales, Northern Ireland, Guernsey, Jersey and the Isle of Man; police forces in Scotland; and the Northern Ireland Statistics and Research Agency – *Annual Report January-December 2006* and *19th Surveillance Report July-December 2006*, London: International Centre for Drug Policy, St George's University of London, July 2007

Gill B, Meltzer H and Hinds K (2003) 'The prevalence of psychiatric morbidity among homeless adults', *International Review of Psychiatry*, Feb-May, 15(1–2) pp 134–40

Godfrey C, Eaton G, McDougall C and Culyer A (2002) *The economic and social costs of Class A drug use in England and Wales, 2000*, Home Office Research Study 249, London: Home Office Research Development and Statistics Directorate, July 2005. Available at: http://www.homeoffice.gov.uk/rds/pdfs2/hors249.pdf

Goulden C and Sondhi A (2001) *At the margins: drug use by vulnerable young people in the 1998/99 Youth Lifestyle Survey*, Home Office Research Study 228, London: Home Office Research, Development and Statistics Directorate. Available at: http://www.homeoffice.gov.uk/rds/pdfs/hors228.pdf

GROS (2006) *Drug-related deaths in Scotland in 2005*, Edinburgh: General Register Office (Scotland), 30 August 2006. Available at: http://www.gro-scotland.gov.uk/statistics/library/drug-related-deaths/05drug-related-deaths.html

Hammersley R, Marsland L and Reid M (2003) *Substance use by young offenders: the impact of the normalisation of drug use in the early years of the 21st century*, Home Office Research Study 261, London: Home Office Research Development and Statistics Directorate February 2003. Available at: http://www.homeoffice.gov.uk/rds/pdfs2/hors261.pdf

Hammersley R and Pearl S (1997) 'Show me the way to go home: young homeless and drugs', *Druglink*, Jan-Feb 12(1) pp 11–13

Hansard (2000) HC, 11 April 2000, *Random drug tests*, vol. 348, col. 93, WA. Available at: www.publications.parliament.uk/pa/cm199900/cmhansrd/v0000411/text/00411w04.htm

Hansard (2007a) HL, 17 April 2007, *Armed Forces: Drug tests*, vol. 691, cols. 35–8, WA. Available at: http://www.publications.parliament.uk/pa/ld200607/ldhansrd/text/70417w0001.htm

Hansard (2007b) HL, 18 April 2007, *Armed Forces: Drug tests*, vol. 691, col. 56, WA. Available at: http://www.publications.parliament.uk/pa/ld200607/ldhansrd/text/70418w0001.htm#070418105000073

Hay G, Gannon M, MacDougall J, Millar T, Eastwood C and McKeganey N (2006a) 'Local and national estimates of the prevalence of opiate use and/or crack cocaine use (2004/05)', pp 3–40 in Singleton N, Murray R and Tinsley L (eds) *Measuring different aspects of problem drug use: methodological developments*, Home Office Online Report 16/06, London: Home Office research Development and Statistics Directorate. Available at: http://www.homeoffice.gov.uk/rds/pdfs06/rdsolr1606.pdf

Hay G, Gannon M, McKeganey N, Hutchinson S and Goldberg D (2005) *Estimating the national and local prevalence of problem drug misuse in Scotland – Executive Report*, Glasgow: Centre for Drug Misuse Research, University of Glasgow and Scottish Centre for Infection and Environmental Health. Available at: http://www.drugmisuse.isdscotland.org/publications/local/prevreport2004.pdf

Hay G, Higgins K, Gannon M and Carroll C (2006b) *Estimating the prevalence of problem opiate and problem cocaine use in Northern Ireland*, Belfast: Drug and Alcohol Information and Research Unit, Department of Health, Social Services and Public Safety Northern Ireland. Available at: http://www.dhsspsni.gov.uk/opiate_cocaine.pdf

Hickman M, Griffin M, Mott J, Corkery J, Madden P, Sondhi A and Stimson G (2004) 'Continuing the epidemiological function of the Addicts Index – evidence from matching the Home Office Addicts Index with the National Drug Treatment Monitoring System', *Drugs: education, prevention and policy*, April, 11(2) pp 91–100

HMPS (2001) *HMPS Annual Report and Accounts 2000–2001*, London: The Stationery Office, HC 29, 19 July 2001. Available at: http://www.hmprisonservice.gov.uk/resourcecentre/publicationsdocuments/index.asp?cat=38

HMPS (2002) *HMPS Annual Report and Accounts 2001–2002*, London: The Stationery Office, HC 957, 18 July 2002. Available at: http://www.hmprisonservice.gov.uk/assets/documents/10000149AnnualReport2002part1.pdf

HMPS (2003) *HMPS Annual Report and Accounts 2002–2003*, London: The Stationery Office, HC 885, 15 July 2003. Available at: http://www.hmprisonservice.gov.uk/assets/documents/100001B42003Part_1.pdf

HMPS (2005) *HMPS Annual Report and Accounts 2004–2005 – Appendices*. London: The Stationery Office, HC 193, 19 July 2005. Available at: http://www.hmprisonservice.gov.uk/assets/documents/10000DFDappendices1–5.pdf

HMPS (2006) *HMPS Annual Report and Accounts 2005–2006 – Appendices*, London: The Stationery Office, HC 1291, 17 July 2006. Available at: http://www.hmprisonservice.gov.uk/assets/documents/10001E58annual_rep_0506_appendices.pdf

HMPS (2007) *HMPS Annual Report and Accounts 2006–2007 – Appendices*, London: The Stationery Office, HC 717, 17 July 2007. Available at: http://www.hmprisonservice.gov.uk/assets/documents/10002CC8annual_rep_0607_appendices.pdf

Home Office (2001) *Prison Statistics England and Wales 2000*, Cm 5250, London: The Stationery Office

Home Office (2003) *Prison Statistics England and Wales 2001*, Cm 5743, London: The Stationery Office

Hope V D, Hickman M and Tilling K (2005) 'Capturing crack-cocaine use: estimating the prevalence of crack cocaine use in London using capture-recapture with covariates', *Addiction*, November, 100(11), pp 1701–08

Ingram D, Lancaster B and Hope B (2001) *Recreational drugs and driving: prevalence survey*, Edinburgh: Scottish Executive Central Research Unit

Health Protection Agency, Health Protection Scotland, National Public Health Service for Wales, CDSC Northern Ireland and the CRDHB (2007) *Shooting up: infections among injecting drug users in the United Kingdom 2006 – an update,*

London: Health Protection Agency, October 2007. Available at: http://www.hpa.org.uk/infections/topics_az/injectingdrugusers/shooting_up_2006_data.pdf

IPD (1998a) Press release 16 November 1998, London: Institute of Personnel and Development

IPD (1998b) Press release 22 December 1998, London: Institute of Personnel and Development

ISD (2002) *Drug Misuse Statistics Scotland 2001*, Edinburgh: ISD Scotland. Available at: http://www.drugmisuse.isdscotland.org/publications/abstracts/drugstats2001b.htm

ISD (2003) *Drug Misuse Statistics Scotland 2002*, Edinburgh: ISD Scotland. Available at: http://www.drugmisuse.isdscotland.org/publications/02bull/02bullb.htm

ISD (2005) *Drug Misuse Statistics Scotland 2005*, Edinburgh: ISD Scotland. Available at: http://www.drugmisuse.isdscotland.org/publications/05dmss/05dmss-000.htm

ISD (2006) *Drug Misuse Statistics Scotland 2006*, Edinburgh: ISD Scotland. Available at: http://www.drugmisuse.isdscotland.org/publications/06dmss/06dmssb.htm

Kershaw A, Singleton N and Meltzer H (2003) 'Survey of the health and well-being of homeless in Glasgow', *International Review of Psychiatry*, Feb–May, 15(1–2) pp 141–3

Klee H and Reid P (1998) 'Drugs and youth homelessness: Reducing the risk', *Drugs: education, prevention and policy*, November, 5(3) pp 269–80

MacDonald Z, Collingwood J and Gordon L (2006) *Measuring the harm from illegal drugs using the Drug Harm Index – an update*, Home Office Online Report 08/06, London: Home Office Research Development and Statistics Directorate. Available at: http://www.homeoffice.gov.uk/rds/pdfs06/rdsolr0806.pdf

MacDonald Z, Tinsley L, Collingwood J, Jamieson P and Pudney S (2005) *Measuring the harm from illegal drugs using the Drug Harm Index*, Home Office Online Report 24/05, London: Home Office Research Development and Statistics Directorate. Available at: http://www.homeoffice.gov.uk/rds/pdfs05/rdsolr2405.pdf

Maxwell C, Kinver A and Phelps A (2007) *Scottish Schools Adolescent Lifestyle and Substance Use Survey (SALSUS) National Report – Smoking, drinking and drug use among 13 and 15 year olds in Scotland in 2006,* Edinburgh: Undertaken by the BMRB Social Research, commissioned by the ISD Scotland on behalf of the Scottish Executive, 29 May 2007. Available at: http://www.drugmisuse.isdscotland.org/publications/local/SALSUS_2006.pdf

McCambridge J, Mitcheson L, Winstock A, Hunt N (2005) 'Five-year trends in patterns of drug use among people who use stimulants in dance contexts in the United Kingdom', *Addiction,* Aug, 100(8), pp 1140–9

McCambridge J, Winstock A, Hunt N and Mitcheson L (2007) '5-year trends in use of hallucinogens and other adjunct drugs among UK dance drug users', *European Addiction Research, 13,* p 57–64 (DOI: 10.1159/000095816)

McKeganey N, Connelly C, Knepil J, Norrie J and Reid L (2000) *Interviewing and drug testing of arrestees in Scotland: a pilot of the Arrestee Drug Abuse Monitoring Methodology (ADAM),* Crime and Criminal Justice Research Findings No 48, Edinburgh: Scottish Executive Central Research Unit

McMullan S and Ruddy D (2006) *Experience of drug misuse: findings from the 2005 Northern Ireland Crime Survey,* Research and Statistical Bulletin 8/2006, Belfast: Statistics and Research Branch of the Northern Ireland Office. Available at: http://www.nio.gov.uk/bulletin_8_2006_-_experience_of_drug_misuse__findings_from_the_2005_northern_ireland_crime_survey.pdf

McVie S, Campbell S and Lebov K (2004) *Scottish Crime Survey 2003,* Edinburgh: Scottish Executive Social Research. Available at: http://www.scotland.gov.uk/Resource/Doc/30859/0024985.pdf

Miller R and Dowds L (2002) *Drug and alcohol use among young people in Northern Ireland: a secondary analysis of Drug and Alcohol Use Surveys – Final Report,* Belfast: ARK Northern Ireland & Queen's University, Belfast and the University of Ulster. Available at: http://www.dhsspsni.gov.uk/drug_alcohol_use_among_young_people.pdf

Murphy R and Roe S (2007) *Drug misuse declared: findings from the 2006/07 British Crime Survey – England and Wales,* Home Office Statistical Bulletin 18/07, London: Home Office Research Development and Statistics Directorate, October 2007. Available at: http://www.homeoffice.gov.uk/rds/pdfs07/hosb1807.pdf

Murray L and Harkins J (2006) *Drugs misuse in Scotland: findings from the 2004 Scottish Crime and Victimisation Survey*, Edinburgh: Scottish Executive Social Research. Available at: http://www.scotland.gov.uk/Publications/2006/07/19095705/0

National Treatment Agency (2007) 'New national statistics reveal more drug users in treatment', press release, 18 October 2007. Available at: http://www.nta.nhs.uk/media/media_releases/2007_media_releases/new_national_statistics_reveal_more_drug_users_in_treatment_media_release_181007.aspx

Neale J, McKeganey N, Hay G and Oliver J (2001) *Recreational drug use and driving: a qualitative study*, Edinburgh: Scottish Executive Central Research Unit

NIO (1998) *Patterns of drug use in Northern Ireland – some recent survey findings: 1996–1997*, Research Findings 2/98, Belfast: Northern Ireland Office, November 1998. Available at: http://www.nio.gov.uk/patterns_of_drug_use_in_northern_ireland_1996–1997.pdf

Office for National Statistics (2007) 'Deaths related to drug poisoning: England and Wales, 1993–2005', *Health Statistics Quarterly*, Spring, 33, pp 82–8. Available at: http://www.statistics.gov.uk/downloads/theme_health/HSQ33.pdf

O'Shea J, Jones A and Sondhi A (2003) *Statistics from the Arrest Referral Monitoring Programme from October 2000 to September 2002*, Arrest Referral Statistical Update, London: Research Development and Statistics Directorate

Owen K (2002) *The hard evidence: rough sleeping in Edinburgh: an update*, Edinburgh: Streetwork

Owen K and Henry T (2001) *Rough sleeping in Edinburgh: the hard evidence. A pilot study by Edinburgh Street Work Project*, Edinburgh: Shelter Scotland

Parker H, Bury C and Egginton R (1998) *New heroin outbreaks amongst young people in England and Wales*, Crime Detection and Prevention Series Paper 92, London: Home Office Police Research Group

Ramsay M and Partridge S (1999) *Drug Misuse Declared in 1998: results from the British Crime Survey*, Home Office Research Study 197, London: Home Office Research Development and Statistics Directorate. Available at: http://www.homeoffice.gov.uk/rds/pdfs/hors197.pdf

Ramsay M and Percy A (1996) *Drug misuse declared: results of the 1994 British Crime Survey*, Home Office Research Study 151, London: Home Office Research and Statistics Directorate. Available at: http://uk.sitestat.com/homeoffice/homeoffice/s?rds.hors151pdf&ns_type=pdf&ns_url=[http://www.homeoffice.gov.uk/rds/pdfs2/hors151.pdf]

Ramsay M and Percy A (1997) 'A national household survey of drug misuse in Britain: a decade of development', *Addiction*, 92(8), pp 931–7

Release (1997) *Release dance and drugs survey: an insight into the culture*, London: Release

Roberts M, Bewley-Taylor D and Trace M (2006) *Monitoring drug policy outcomes: the measurement of drug-related harm*, Report Nine: The Beckley Foundation Drug Policy Programme, July 2006. Available at: http://www.internationaldrugpolicy.net/reports/BeckleyFoundation_Report_09.pdf

Roe S and Man L (2006) *Drug misuse declared: findings from the 2005/06 British Crime Survey – England and Wales*, Home Office Statistical Bulletin 15/06, London: Home Office Research Development and Statistics Directorate, October 2006. Available at: http://www.homeoffice.gov.uk/rds/pdfs06/hosb1506.pdf

Scottish Prison Service (2001) *Fourth prison survey: the prisoners results.* Research Bulletin Issue 6, Edinburgh: Research and Evaluation Services, Scottish Prison Services

SEU (2001) *Preventing social exclusion*, London: Social Exclusion Unit, Office of the Deputy Prime Minister

Sexton B F, Tunbridge R J, Board A, Jackson P G, Wright K, Stark M M and Englehart K (2002) *The influence of cannabis and alcohol on driving – Prepared for Road Safety Division, Department for Transport*, TRL Report TRL543, Wokingham, Berks: Transport Research Laboratory. Available at: http://www.trl.co.uk/store/report_detail.asp?srid=2694&pid=211

SHEU (2005) *Trends – illegal drugs 1987–2004*, Exeter: Schools Health Education Unit. Available at: http://www.sheu.org.uk/publications/trendsdrugs.htm

SHEU (2006) *Young people into 2006*, Exeter: Schools Health Education Unit. Available at: http://www.sheu.org.uk/publications/yp06.htm

Singleton N, Pendry E, Simpson T, Goddard E, Farrell M, Marsden J and Taylor C (2005) *The impact of mandatory drug testing in prisons*, Home Office Online Report 03/05. Available at: http://www.homeoffice.gov.uk/rds/pdfs05/rdsolr0305.pdf

Sondhi A, O'Shea J and Williams T (2002) *Statistics from the Arrest Referral Monitoring Programme for October 2000 to September 2001*, Arrest Referral Update, London: Research Development and Statistics Directorate

Trathen B, O'Gara C, Sarkhel A, Sessay M, Rao H and Luty J (2007) 'Co-morbidity and cannabis use in a mental health trust in South East England', *Addictive Behaviours*, Oct, 32(10), pp 2164–77, Epub 2007 Mar 7

Tunbridge R J, Keigan M and James F J (2001) *The incidence of drugs and alcohol in road traffic fatalities*, TRL Report 495, Crowthorne: TRL Ltd

Wincup E, Buckland G and Bayliss R (2003) *Youth homelessness and substance use: report to the Drugs and Alcohol Research Unit*, Home Office Research Study No. 258, London: Home Office Research

Wozniak E, Dyson G and Carnie J (1998) *The third prison survey*, Scottish Prison Service Occasional Paper No 3, 1998, Edinburgh: Research and Evaluation Services, Scottish Prison Service

Wright N (2002) *Homelessness: a primary care response*, London: Royal College of General Practitioners

Yanetta A, Third H and Anderson I (1999) *National monitoring and interim evaluation of the rough sleepers initiative in Scotland*, Edinburgh: Scottish Executive

4 How do drugs affect children and the family?

Harry Shapiro and Martin Barnes

Harry Shapiro, Director of Communications & Information, DrugScope,
harrys@drugscope.org.uk
Martin Barnes, Chief Executive, DrugScope, martinb@drugscope.org.uk

Female drug users

According to the British Crime Survey (the main household survey of drug use in the general population for England and Wales) around twice as many males report they have used an illegal drug as women. In Scotland, the figure is closer to 1.5. In terms of drug treatment, figures for England and Wales suggest that for every three male drug users presenting to services, there is one female user. In Scotland, the balance between males and females in treatment seems more evenly split. However, for women, it is assumed that the figures underestimate the true picture because:

- treatment services are less appropriate to women's needs
- social norms make it difficult for women to present (Hunter and Judd 1998).

A number of studies have found that women feel more stigmatised for their drug use than men (eg Barnard 1993). Female drug use conflicts with the traditional view of women as carers, mothers and wives. A common concern of women drug users presenting to services is that their children may be taken from them, and many services have tried to reduce this fear with positive policy statements (Thom 1986).

Pregnant drug users

Similarly, it is accepted that pregnancies involving women who use drugs under-estimate the true incidence. Hospital records for England in 2003/04 indicate that just under 500 foetuses and newborns were affected by maternal drug use, with just over 3,000 newborn babies showing some kind of withdrawal symptoms.

What are the effects of drugs on the foetus?

The answer to a question such as 'I took some x before I found out I was pregnant. Is it likely to hurt the baby?' is almost certainly 'no'. There are many factors affecting the level of damage a drug can do to the foetus. The main ones are:

- the amount of drug taken

Benzodiazepines (tranquillisers, Valium, Librium, etc)

Studies have shown a link between benzodiazepine use in the first trimester of pregnancy and a mouth deformity known as cleft palate – all of the various benzodiazepines should be treated as having the potential to cause malformations. Breastfeeding can be a problem with cleft palate babies, who may have trouble sucking.

Caffeine

There is some limited evidence to suggest an association between caffeine consumption in excess of 300mg a day (approximately five cups of instant coffee or tea) and a small decrease in birthweight. Irregular foetal heart rate has been associated with very large daily amounts of caffeine intake late in pregnancy, but this returns to normal after caffeine intake is stopped.

Cannabis

A study in Canada (Fried 1986) which compared cannabis users to non-users found there were no significant differences in rates of miscarriage, type of presentation at birth, frequency of obstetric complications, birthweight or physical birth defects, among even the heaviest users. There was some evidence of slightly shorter (about a week) gestation periods among the heavier smokers. Other studies that have shown adverse effects (eg prematurity, low birthweight) for the babies of heavy cannabis users have involved women whose drug-taking, diet and general lifestyle have been more potentially detrimental than the effects found in the Canadian study.

The most recent review of cannabis by the World Health Organization (1997) failed to demonstrate any distinct problems for infants or children linked to parental use of cannabis during pregnancy.

Cocaine and crack

Possibly more than any other drug, heavy cocaine or crack use in pregnancy has been associated with harmful effects on the foetus, most seriously premature rupture of the membrane. Foetal growth is also retarded, due, it is thought, to the strong stimulatory effect on the circulation – ie it restricts the supply of blood and oxygen to the foetus. However, as with most of the research on the adverse effects of drug use on the foetus, the studies suggesting such associations have been conducted with women from very poor socio-economic backgrounds where more general problems for babies are more likely to occur in any case. Also, many of the women in these studies had little or no antenatal care.

A study of social cocaine users (ie not dependent) who stopped when they realised they were pregnant, concluded that no adverse effects were experienced (Graham et al 1989).

Ecstasy

There are no published case reports implicating use of ecstasy in foetal damage.

Heroin and other opiates

The main direct effect of opiate use in pregnancy appears to be low birthweight babies. There is also evidence of growth retardation with heroin use (Thornton et al 1990). Other effects such as prematurity are at least in part associated with factors such as poor diet and ill health. Irregular use of heroin in pregnancy can cause foetal distress in labour and significant respiratory problems after delivery.

LSD

In the 1960s LSD was the subject of much press scaremongering. There is no evidence of foetal damage caused by LSD.

Solvents

Inhaled solvents reduce oxygen levels in body tissue and easily cross the placenta, so sniffing during pregnancy theoretically might reduce oxygen supply to the foetal brain, although there appear to be no cases on record. However, there is a study by Goodwin (1988) which suggests an association between chronic daily paint sniffing (toluene) for several months and renal problems in the newborn.

What effect does withdrawal have on the mother and child?

Many drug-using women who find they are pregnant will want to come off drugs, seeing the pregnancy as an opportunity for a change of lifestyle. Withdrawal from drugs can cause problems, mainly as a consequence of the physical trauma, and success depends on the mother's ability to stay stable and healthy. The main effects and complications are briefly discussed below.

Stimulants

Substitute withdrawal or maintenance (see Chapter 9 for definitions) is not appropriate for stimulant drugs (amphetamine or cocaine) and is potentially harmful to the foetus.

Benzodiazepines

When benzodiazepines have been taken in ordinary therapeutic doses they should be withdrawn on an outpatient basis. The whole point of the withdrawal regime is to prevent fits. A one-week detoxification period is adequate on medical grounds, but on social grounds a longer period may be required if a woman cannot cope.

Heroin and other opiates

Traditionally, detoxification during pregnancy has been viewed as dangerous as it carries an unacceptable risk of spontaneous abortion or pre-term labour. However, detoxification mid-trimester is generally considered safe if a strict regime of reduction is followed. Therefore, methadone substitution or maintenance therapy tends to be advocated. A pregnant woman can choose in- or outpatient detoxification. Where the pregnant user does not have an overly unstable lifestyle and has support at home, outpatient detox can prove a more successful option, although it is less widely available. The advantages of outpatient detox are:

- methadone doses can be adjusted to prevent either intoxication of withdrawal symptoms
- the foetus can be monitored
- the availability and use of other drugs can be restricted
- other services such as counselling and exercise is more readily at hand
- stability can be restored to a normally chaotic life in some circumstances.

Breastfeeding

Most drugs do not pass into the breastmilk in quantities which are sufficient to have any major effect on the newborn. With opiates, for example, the quantities ingested are so small that they will not prevent the onset of the neonatal opiate withdrawal syndrome. Breastfeeding is encouraged in mothers who are using drugs as long as the user is stable and the breastfeeding is not suddenly stopped. There is some variation among the benzodiazepines. Diazepam passes into the milk, and can cause sedation in the child. Chlordiazepine and nitrazepam also go into the breastmilk, but in quantities too small to have an effect.

Women who are HIV positive, or whose HIV status is unknown, are advised not to breastfeed. Studies show that if an HIV-positive mother breastfeeds her baby, there is twice the risk of passing on the infection, especially if the mother has only recently been infected.

HIV/AIDS and hepatitis

Various studies show the risk of mother-to-baby transmission of HIV ranges from 14 to 39%. All infants born to HIV-positive mothers will have maternal HIV antibodies; however, this does not mean they will be necessarily infected.

Hepatitis B is common among injecting drug users. The transmission routes are the same for HIV, but the disease is even more infectious. Hepatitis B may be transmitted from mother to child, although prompt immunisation of babies born to known carriers has proved effective. Infection, if it occurs, will happen in the first three months of life.

Hepatitis C is also common among injecting drug users but is far more dangerous than hepatitis B. Up to 50% of all carriers develop serious liver disease (Carey 1995). Immunisation for hepatitis C is not possible and the only reliable test is a non-standard (and therefore expensive) PCR (polymerase chain reaction) test.

How do drugs affect the family?

For some time there has been growing evidence of the emotional, behavioural and learning problems experienced by many children of problem substance users. The issue was highlighted in 2003 by a major report called *Hidden Harm* published by the Advisory Council on the Misuse of Drugs (which advises the UK government on drug legislation and policy). The Council estimated that between 250,000 and 350,000 children in the UK had a parent who was a problem drug user, representing 2–3% of children under 16 in England and Wales and about 4–6% of all children under 16 in Scotland.

Although the report emphasised that many problem drug users work hard to do the best for their children, drug use can harm a child's development from conception onwards. Problems associated with parental drug use include poverty, physical and emotional abuse or neglect, inadequate supervision, harmful substances in the home and social isolation. The impact on children can vary enormously and may be difficult to detect, but the adverse effects can be 'multiple and cumulative', ranging from a failure to thrive and doing badly at school to emotional and behavioural problems. Parental substance misuse is often a factor in child protection cases and many children do not live with their drug-using parents.

The UK government accepted most (but not all) of the ACMD report's 48 recommendations, which included the collection of information about the children of people in drug treatment, better links and coordination between drug misuse services and children's and social care services, and improved training on parental substance misuse for professionals in child and adolescent mental health services. In an updated version of *Hidden Harms*, published in 2007, the ACMD acknowledged progress in protecting and supporting the children of problem drug users – for example, in the provision of dedicated services for children affected and their families – but was critical of responses in England compared, in particular, with the approaches of the devolved administrations Scotland and Wales. In Scotland, for example, all areas are required to develop protocols setting out how different agencies and staff work together and respond to parental substance misuse.

Drug use among young people

There are many reasons for taking drugs and a number of 'risk' and 'protective factors' have been identified (see below). However, despite sometimes alarmist media reports about levels of drug use and concern about the potential harms, the majority of young people do not use illegal drugs and many overestimate levels of use among their peer group. More young people report being offered drugs than use them.

Information about illegal drug use among young people aged 11–15 years in England is collected in an annual school-based survey (Department of Health 2007) and similar information for 16–24 year olds is available from the annual British Crime Survey (Home Office 2007b), which is a household study. The prevalence of illegal drug use by young people aged 11–15 has overall fallen slightly after considerable increases in the early 1990s and following a period of relative stability since 1999. Drug use rises sharply with age and is highest among

16–24-year-olds. Volatile substance use (eg glues and aerosols) among 11–15-year-olds is a particular concern and more young people in this age group die from volatile substances than from illegal drugs.

An authoritative study on the use of tobacco, alcohol and other drugs by young people in the UK was published by the ACMD in 2006. The *Pathways to Problems* report examined patterns and trends in substance use, the availability of alcohol and other drugs and the characteristics of young people who are most at risk of harm (ACMD 2006). It found that many young people who use drugs from an early age have a troubled background in terms of family, schooling or antisocial behaviour.

Risk and protective factors

A number of factors increase the risk that young people will develop problems with drug use. No single factor is predictive of drug use or problem use and nor should it be assumed that the existence of risk factors are a direct *cause* of drug use – but the greater the risk factors the more likely it is that problems will occur. Protective factors, where it may be less likely that a young person uses drugs or develops problems, have also been identified.

Risk factors	Protective factors
Chaotic home environment	Strong social bonds
Parents who misuse drugs or suffer from mental illness	Experiences of strong parental monitoring with clear family rules
Behavioural problems	Family involvement in the lives of children
Lack of parental nurturing	Successful school experiences
Inappropriate and/or aggressive classroom behaviour	Strong bonds with the local community
School failure	A supportive relationship with at least one adult
Low commitment to school	

Risk factors	Protective factors
School exclusion and truancy	
Early age of first drug use	
Low socio-economic status	

Source: DrugScope (2006) *Guidance for the Youth Service*

Responses to drug use and support for families and children

Every Child Matters

Measures designed to tackle drug use among young people should be seen in the context of *Every Child Matters: Change for Children*, the UK government's overarching approach to the well-being of children and young people (www. everychildmatters.org.uk). Although encapsulating a broad range of strategic and multi-layered issues – everything from how local authorities organise children and young people's services to the provision of childcare – *Every Child Matters* seeks five outcomes: be healthy, stay safe, enjoy and achieve, make a positive contribution and achieve economic well-being.

The UK government will publish a new drug strategy in 2008, with the Department for Children, Families and Schools (DCSF) leading on children and young people's substance misuse issues. The main components of strategies to tackle drug use among young people are drug education, prevention and treatment.

Drug education

Drug education can take place in formal and non-formal settings and, in England, is an entitlement for every young person in school. Many schools deliver drug education as part of wider Personal Social Health and Citizenship Education (PSHCE) to address children and young people's health and well-being. There is no statutory provision for drug education for students at Further Education (FE) or sixth form colleges.

The *Pathways to Problems* report (ACMD 2006) concluded that there was little evidence that classroom-based education is effective in reducing rates of drug use and called for a reassessment of the role of schools in drug *prevention* (see below). However, the aims of drug education are broad and should include increasing knowledge and understanding and clarifying misconceptions about the effects and risks involved in drug use, laws relating to drugs, and the prevalence and acceptability of drug use among peers. The aims also include developing young people's personal and social skills to make informed decisions and keep themselves healthy and safe.

Further research on 'what works' in drug education is needed and, to this end, the UK government commissioned a major research programme called Blueprint to determine its effectiveness in schools. A report on the outcomes and impact of the programme is expected to be published in 2008, but the need for high-quality and intensive training for those delivering drug education has been highlighted (Home Office 2007a).

Prevention

Drug 'prevention' describes policies and interventions aimed at minimising the number of young people who use drugs, although outcomes may also include delaying the onset of first use and reducing the harms that drugs cause. The terms 'drug education' and 'drug prevention' are often used interchangeably but, as noted above, the aims of drug education should be broader than just stopping young people using drugs; drug education can be seen as a component of drug prevention.

A broad range of interventions aim to 'prevent' drug use, from the provision of leisure and sports-based activities (eg 'diversion' activities) to measures designed to support families and vulnerable young people, including housing, access to higher education, training and employment activities. A common theme is to address (directly and indirectly) the underlying 'risk factors' that increase the likelihood of problem drug use.

The role of family support services and family-based programmes (as preventive measures as well as supporting treatment, see below) has been highlighted time and again – for example, the provision of parenting skills training, the important role of health visitors and ensuring closer working between children and adult services. Recommendations by the National Institute for Health and Clinical Excellence (NICE), in a report on interventions to reduce young people's substance misuse, include, for example, offering family-based programmes of structured support involving parents and carers (NICE 2007).

Treatment and support

Although the majority of young people who use illegal drugs do not come to harm, it has been estimated that around 20,000 young people a year become adult 'problem drug users' (Department for Education and Skills 2005).

To enable front line professionals and agencies to better identify the needs of young people (and to facilitate processes of referral and inter-agency working) there is a shared assessment tool called the Common Assessment Framework (CAF) for young people. Substance use is not specifically mentioned in the standard tool (although a trigger question has been introduced in some areas) but is intended to help practitioners assess a range of needs which may, for example, include a specialist assessment for substance misuse (National Treatment Agency 2007). Following assessment a young person may be referred to a specialist service for treatment and support with drug problems.

Even if a young person is not physically or psychologically dependent on drugs there may be a number of risks associated with their drug use – for example, overdose or deliberate self-harm; association with offending behaviour or sexual exploitation; using drugs in dangerous physical environments (eg while driving); injecting drugs; and physical and mental health problems.

Every young person receiving treatment for drug problems should have a care plan which sets out goals and interventions. Depending on the needs of the young person, interventions can include individual and group work sessions ('psychosocial interventions'), information and advice on harm reduction and the use of prescribed drugs (eg during detoxification or opiate substitute prescribing). All services providing support should be involved in the care planning process coordinated by a lead professional.

Treatment interventions need to operate in the wider context of legal requirements to safeguard young people from harm. These include the duty under the Children Act 2004 on all agencies to safeguard and promote the welfare of children and, where necessary, to refer to social services where a young person may be 'in need' (section 17 of the Children Act 1989) or 'suffering or at risk of suffering significant harm' (section 47 of the Children Act 1989). Parental drug misuse may be a factor in such proceedings.

Notes

Advisory Council on the Misuse of Drugs (2003) *Hidden Harm – Responding to the needs of children of problem drug users*

Advisory Council on the Misuse of Drugs (2007) *Hidden Harm three years on: realities, challenges and opportunities*

Advisory Council on the Misuse of Drugs (2006) *Pathways to Problems – hazardous use of tobacco, alcohol and other drugs by young people in the UK and its implications for policy*

Barnard M A (1993) 'Needles sharing in context: patterns of sharing among men and women injectors and HIV risks', *Addiction*, 88, pp 805–12

Carey P (1005) 'HIV, pregnancy and the drug user', in Siney C, *The pregnant drug addict*, London: Midwives Press

Department for Education and Skills (2005) *Every child matters: change for children: young people and drugs*. Available at: http://www.everychildmatters.gov. uk/_files/9660D91BB1755A6E288998AAE145297F.pdf

Department of Health (2007) *Smoking, drinking and drug use among young people in England in 2006*

Fried P (1986) 'Marijuana and human pregnancy', in Chasnoff I J (ed.) *Drug use in pregnancy: mother and child*, Norwell, MA: MTP Press

Goodwin T M (1988) 'Toluene abuse and renal tubular acidosis in pregnancy', *Journal of Obstetrics and Gynaecology* 71 (5) pp 715–18

Graham K et al (1989) 'Pregnancy outcome following first trimester exposure to cocaine in social users in Toronto', *Veterinary and Human Toxicology*, 2, pp 143–48

Home Office (2007a) *Blueprint Drug Education Research Programme – summary of delivery report and practitioner report findings*. Available at: http://drugs. homeoffice.gov.uk/publication-search/blueprint/dpreports/

Home Office (2007b) *Drug misuse declared: findings from the 2006/07 British Crime Survey*

Hunter G and Judd A (1998) 'Women injecting drug users in London: the extent and nature of their contact with drug and health services', *Drug and Alcohol Review*, 17, pp 267–76

Koren G et al (1989) 'Bias against the null hypothesis: the reproductive hazards of cocaine', *Lancet*, 2 (8677) pp 1140–42

National Institute for Clinical Excellence (NICE) (2007) *Community-based interventions to reduce substance misuse among vulnerable and disadvantaged children and young people*

National Treatment Agency for Substance Misuse (2007) *Assessing young people for substance misuse*, London: NTA

Thom B (1986) 'Sex differences in help-seeking for alcohol problems: the barriers to help-seeking', *British Journal of Addiction*, 81 pp 777–88

Thornton L et al (1990) 'Narcotic addiction: the expectant mother and her baby', *Irish Medical Journal*, 83(4), pp 139–42

World Health Organization (1997) *Cannabis: a health perspective and research agenda*, Report by Programme in Substance Abuse, Geneva: WHO

5 Drug use and criminal behaviour

Trevor Bennett

Professor of Criminology, Director, Centre for Criminology, University of Glamorgan,
thbennet@glam.ac.uk
Based on original text from *Understanding drugs, alcohol and crime*, T H Bennett and K R
Holloway, Buckingham: McGraw-Hill/Open University Press, 2005

The drugs–crime connection

It is widely believed that drug use and crime are in some way associated. One of the
stated aims of the current UK drugs strategy is to reduce crime by reducing drug
misuse. However, it is not at all clear whether there is a connection between drugs
and crime. There have been few reviews of empirical research on the drugs–crime
connection, and those that have been done have produced mixed results.

Gandossy et al (1980), for example, conducted one of the first thorough reviews
of the literature on the connection between drug use and crime covering studies
from the US, Australia, Canada and Europe. The review looked mainly at the links
between heroin and crime and concluded that '...it was difficult to avoid concluding
that addicts engage in substantial amounts of income-generating crimes. This is
true when analyzing the charges against drug-using arrestees, convictions of addicts
in prisons, arrest records of treatment populations, or the observations of street
addicts' (p 52).

Hough (1996) also found some support for a relationship between drug use and
crime in his review of British research on the drugs–crime connection. He noted that
it is clear drug misuse makes a significant contribution to the overall total number
of crimes committed in England and Wales. However, he was concerned about the
quality of research available and concluded, 'current knowledge about the volume
and cost of drug-related crime is so patchy that all we can say with certainty is that
problem drug misuse is responsible for a significant minority of crime in England
and Wales' (p 19).

Chaiken and Chaiken (1990) were more sceptical of the existence of a general
association between drug use and crime. In their review of the literature on the
relationship between drug use and predatory crime, they found no evidence of a
simple or unified association. They concluded that when behaviours of large groups
of people are studied in aggregate no coherent general pattern exists associating

drug misuse with predatory crime. They also noted that even in relation to heroin and cocaine there was no clear evidence of a relationship between consumption and offending.

Explaining the connection

The connection between drug use and crime has been discussed in the literature mainly in terms of the statistical association and the causal connection. A statistical association concerns the extent to which drug use and crime are found together. In other words, when you find one do you tend to find the other? This does not mean that the two are in any way causally connected. A causal connection between drug use and crime means that one of them is the cause of the other. In order for two variables to be causally connected they must meet fairly well established criteria. The three most commonly cited essential conditions are: (1) there must be an association between the variables; (2) the connection must show that the cause occurs before the effect; and (3), the connection must not disappear when the influence of other variables is taken into account.

There are a number of ways in which drugs and crime might be causally connected. Some of the most common causal models are: the 'drug use causes crime' model, the 'crime causes drug use' model, the 'reciprocal' model, the 'common-cause' model and the 'coincidence' model. The first two models ('drug use causes crime' and 'crime causes drug use') are the most straightforward. The first indicates that drug use in some way causes criminal behaviour and the second argues that criminal behaviour in some way causes drug misuse. The third model (the 'reciprocal' model) is a more complex model, based on the idea that drug use sometimes causes crime and crime sometimes causes drug use. This model presumes that the relationship between drug use and crime is bi-directional. Menard et al (2001) argued that drug use and crime might be causally linked and mutually reinforcing. Illegal behaviour might lead to the initiation of drug use and serious drug use might lead to the continuity of illegal behaviour. The fourth model (the 'common-cause' model) proposes that drug use does not cause crime, nor does crime cause drug use. Instead, they are both caused by a third or common variable. The fifth model (the 'coincidence' model) is sometimes described as a spuriousness model. This model purports that drug use and crime are not causally connected at all. Instead, they exist within a nexus of correlated variables and problematic behaviours.

Evidence for a statistical association

Research on the statistical association tends to be based on estimating the proportion of drug users who commit crimes or the proportion of criminals who use drugs.

Are drug users more likely than non-drug users to commit crimes?

Studies based on drug users typically find that they are more likely than comparable samples of non-drug users to commit crimes. Hunt et al (1984) conducted interviews in the USA with 368 users on methadone maintenance and 142 narcotics users not in treatment. The results showed that heroin users were more likely than non-users to report having recently committed property crimes and drug dealing. In a study of adolescent drug users, Hawke et al (2000) found that amphetamine users were significantly more likely than non-users to have committed property crimes and drug supply offences at some point in their lives. Studies based on users in the community also show that drug users are more likely than non-users to commit crimes. Nurco et al (1993) compared changes in the severity of criminal behaviour among narcotics addicts and various control groups. In total, 74 per cent of the narcotics addicts, compared with 31 per cent of the non-addict controls, reported involvement in crime.

Are criminals more likely than non-criminals to use drugs?

The relationship between involvement in drug use and crime can also be determined by looking at samples of arrested or convicted offenders. Goulden and Sondhi (2001) conducted research on young people in the general population as part of the second wave (1998/99) of the Youth Lifestyles Survey. The study showed that significantly more offenders than non-offenders in the general population had used drugs. Approximately half of the offenders reported using an illicit drug in the last year compared with one in seven non-offenders. Potterat et al (1998) looked at the prevalence of illegal drug use among prostitutes and a comparison group of non-prostitutes. Drug use was more commonly reported by the prostitutes than the comparison group (86% versus 23%). A similar study by Yacoubian et al (2001) compared 182 female arrestees charged with prostitution offences with over 3,000 female arrestees charged with other non-prostitution offences. Seventy-eight per cent of prostitutes tested positive for at least one drug, compared with 51% of non-prostitutes.

Are certain types of drugs associated with certain types of crime?

The results so far have focused mainly on the prevalence of offending and drug use in general. It might be the case that only some drug types are related to crime or only some crimes are related to drug use. There are a number of reasons mentioned in the literature why the relationship between drug misuse and crime might vary by types of drug and types of crime. Drugs vary substantially in terms of their pharmacological properties, their addictive qualities and their costs (Farabee et al 2001). Hence, it is unlikely that their impact on criminal behaviour would be the same. Similarly, criminal behaviour varies substantially in terms of its nature and motivation. Some forms of criminal behaviour have clear theoretical links with drug misuse (such as certain kinds of acquisitive crime), while others have fewer plausible connections (such as expressive crime).

There are a number of studies that have used disaggregated measures to investigate the connection between types of drug and types of crime. Makkai et al (2000) analysed data collected as part of the Drug Use Monitoring in Australia (DUMA) programme to investigate the relationship between drug misuse and the prevalence of offending. The results showed some variations in the relationship between offence types and drug types. Property offenders were more likely to test positive for opiates (55%) than those charged with drug offences (38%) or violent offences (32%). Arrestees charged with drug offences were more likely to test positive for cannabis (76%) than property offenders (52%) or violent offenders (46%).

The results of the NEW-ADAM (New England and Wales Arrestee Drug Abuse Monitoring) programme showed that the relationship between drug misuse and offending was much stronger when certain kinds of drugs and certain kinds of crime were looked at together (Bennett and Holloway 2005). Cannabis and diazepam use were significantly associated with eight of the ten offence types investigated. In other words, these drug types were associated with crime generally. Other drugs were associated with specific offences only. Amphetamine use was associated with the commission of five crime types, and ecstasy was associated with three types. Heroin use was also associated with just three offence types (shoplifting, 'burglary non-dwelling' and 'theft person'). In particular, heroin use was strongly associated with the offence of shoplifting. Heroin users were five times more likely than non-heroin users to have committed shoplifting offences in the last 12 months.

Overall, the research tends to show that drug users are more likely than non-drug users to be criminals and that criminals are more likely than non-criminals to be drug users. However, it also shows that the drugs–crime connection is characterised by some very specific connections between particular drugs and particular offences. The drugs most strongly implicated in the connection are heroin and crack, and the crimes most strongly implicated are shoplifting, commercial burglary and theft.

Evidence for a causal connection

Drug use and crime are often found together. Drug users (especially those who consumed heroin or crack) are likely to have committed crimes, and offenders (especially those who committed shoplifting and general theft) are likely to have consumed drugs. However, this does not mean that drug use causes crime or crime causes drug use. They might be found together because they are both caused by other factors or co-exist within a nexus of problematic behaviours.

The causal connection between drug use and crime has been investigated in the research literature in four main ways: 'age of onset' studies that investigate whether drug use preceded crime or crime preceded drug use in time; 'changes over time' studies that investigate the relationship between changes in involvement in drug use on crime and changes in involvement in crime on drug use; qualitative interview studies that investigate the causal connection by asking drug users and offenders their views on whether the two are connected; and quantitative interview studies that estimate the proportion of respondents who report pre-coded models of the connection.

'Age of onset' studies

'Age of onset' studies address the issue of causality, specifically whether drug use causes the onset of a career in crime or crime the onset of a career in drug use. The results of these studies vary considerably, depending on whether drug use concerns first drug use (usually a recreational drug) or first 'hard' drug use (usually heroin, crack or cocaine).

The results of studies on the connection between *first* drug use (usually a recreational drug) and crime tend to show that *drug use precedes crime*. Byqvist (1999), for example, found in a study of drug users receiving treatment in Sweden, that first drug use occurred at an average age of 15 years, while first recorded crime occurred at 18.4 years of age. McCoy et al (1995) found from interviews with crack users in residential treatment in Miami, Florida that the average age of first crime was several years older than the average age of first drug use. Inciardi and Surratt (2001) interviewed 708 cocaine-dependent women in Miami and found that the average age of first cannabis use was 15 years and the age of first crime was 18. Another study that looked specifically at age of first solvent use and age of first crime found that the average age of first solvent-inhalant use was 13.9 years, while the average age of first crime was 15.7 years (Inciardi and Pottieger 1986).

However, not all studies show that first drug use preceded first crime. Pudney (2002) used data from the Youth Lifestyles Survey to investigate sequences of initiation into drugs and crime in the UK. A total of 3,901 young people were questioned about their current and past behaviour. The results show that *the onset of criminal behaviour occurred prior to the use of all illicit drug types*, with the exception of solvents (14.5 years at onset of criminal behaviour compared to 14.1 years at use of solvents). The author concluded that there is '...a tendency towards a chain of events beginning with petty crime and truancy, and only later developing into drug use'. He goes on to suggest that if 'we were prepared to assume that this tendency has causal significance, then we might conclude that a policy addressing truancy and other problems at school might be more effective than a policy attacking drug use directly' (Pudney 2002, p 187).

The results of studies on the connection between first *'hard'* drug use and crime show quite different findings. Most of the studies find that the onset of crime precedes the onset of hard drug use. Inciardi and Pottieger (1986), for example, in their study of female narcotics users in Miami found that the average age of first heroin use was 17.5 years, whereas the age of first crime was 15.7 years. Datesman (1987) found among a sample of 153 female heroin users that the average age of first cocaine use was 19 years and the average age of first crime was 15. Some studies have explored the age of onset of crack use and crime. All of the studies found that the average age of onset of crime preceded the average age of onset of crack use by a number of years. The average age of first crack use ranged from 20 to 24 years and the average age of first crime ranged from 14 to 19 (depending on the crime type).

The finding that age of first drug tends to precede crime and age of first 'hard' drug use usually follows first crime might at first seem hard to explain. At first sight, these two findings appear to be in opposition. However, the mechanism by which the two might be connected could be different. Recreational drug use might lead to minor crimes, perhaps as a result of judgement impairment or by providing the courage to commit minor crimes. At a slightly older age, crime (perhaps slightly more serious crime) might lead to hard drug use as a result of involvement in wider criminal subcultures and access to drug dealers. It is also possible that neither connection is causal. Instead, they both might be the products of natural age variations in the onset of various kinds of problematic behaviours.

'Changes over time' studies

'Changes over time' studies are able to provide greater insight than 'age of onset' studies into the continuing relationship between drug use and crime following the onset of drug use and crime. Like 'age of onset' studies, 'changes over time' studies have the advantage of being able to address the issue of whether drug use preceded crime or crime preceded drug use. They also have the additional advantage that they can identify changes in the rates of drug use and crime over time. In other words, they can determine whether, for example, crime increased following an increase in drug use or decreased when drug use decreased. In this sense, these studies offer some of the best quantitative evidence on the causal connection between drug use and crime.

Most of these studies focused on the effects on crime of changes in use of hard drugs such as heroin or crack cocaine. Hanlon et al (1990), for example, interviewed a sample of 132 narcotics addicts in the USA about various periods of addiction and non-addiction during their drug-using careers. They found that the mean number of days per year spent offending in the last period of addiction was more than double the number of offences committed in the last period of non-addiction. Anglin and Speckart (1986) looked at groups of male subjects undergoing methadone maintenance treatment in the USA. They found that in the 12-month period prior to addiction, subjects reported a mean of 2.3 crime days per month, whereas in the 12-month period after addiction, subjects reported a mean of nine crime days per month.

It is possible that changes in drug use are associated with changes only in certain kinds of crime. One study provided breakdowns of the findings in terms of type of offences committed. Hanlon et al (1990) presented data on the mean rates of different crime types during periods of addiction and non-addiction. The greatest increase in offending over the last period of addiction occurred in relation to 'theft offences', 'con games/forgery', and 'drug distribution'. There was little change in the rate of 'violent offences' or 'other offences'.

Studies based on offenders also showed a connection between changes in drug use and changes in crime. Ball et al (1981) examined changes in drug use and crime among a sample of 243 opiate addicts drawn from police files in the USA. The results showed that there were substantially more crime days during periods of addiction than during periods of abstinence (248 days per year compared with 40.8 days per year). The authors concluded that 'criminality decreased markedly during the months or years that these addicts were not dependent on heroin and other opiates' (Ball et al 1981, p 60). Nurco et al (1984) found in a similar study that the mean number of crime days per year was significantly lower during periods of addiction than periods of non-addiction (62 during the last period of non-addiction and 280 in the last period of addiction).

There have been very few 'changes over time' studies based on the general population. One such study conducted by Mason and Windle (2002) investigated the relationship between self-reported substance use and delinquency through a multiple follow-up data survey of more than 1,000 high school students in the USA. The authors found that both sets of measures were closely correlated. They noted that 'changes in delinquency were positively associated with subsequent changes in substance use...' (p 72). The authors concluded that these findings provide some support for the view that adolescent drug use and delinquency are reciprocally related and potentially reinforcing.

Overall, this small group of studies provides evidence that drug use and crime could be causally connected. In general, these studies find that increases in drug use are associated with increases in crime and (to a more limited extent) that increases in crime are associated with increases in drug use. However, this general conclusion is based on some very specific findings that relate primarily to periods of addiction and non-addiction to heroin. Few of these studies disaggregate the findings to show the effects of different drugs on different crimes or to show the effect of different user characteristics.

Qualitative interview studies

There is a small body of research that investigates the drugs–crime connection by obtaining the views of drug users or offenders. These sometimes include statements from the subjects about their perceptions of the way in which drug use and crime are connected.

The most common explanation given by respondents is that crimes are committed to raise money for drugs. Many of these studies are based on drugs and crime among samples of prostitutes. Erickson et al (2000) explored the impact of crack addiction on women in Toronto, Canada who were involved in the sex trade. The study involved in-depth interviews with a sample of 30 women who were recruited by a local street worker and who were heavy crack users over several years. The study identified a clear link between drug use and prostitution. One subject explained:

> 'I've been doing it [prostitution] since I was 16 years old, that's like what I know best. I started prostitution to support my habit for alcohol and marijuana.' (Erickson et al 2000, p 775)

The authors explain, '...it is clear that they work in the sex trade to get money and/ or crack to support their own usage when few other sources of income are available to them' (p 784). Graham and Wish (1994) identified a relationship between drug use and prostitution in a study of female arrestees in the USA. They quote one arrestee who explained that:

> 'For the past year I have been hustling to support my habit. I started out hustling the men I met while hitchhiking into the city to cop (purchase drugs) and I am now working the streets. All my proceeds go towards drugs.' (Graham and Wish 1994, p 326)

Similarly, in a study of female crack users in the USA, Sterk et al (2000) found some evidence of a causal relationship between crack use and prostitution. One subject is reported to have said:

> 'I wouldn't be out there doing what I'm doing if it wasn't because of getting high.' (Sterk et al 2000, p 359)

Other studies have been based on samples of drug users or offenders. Brain et al (1998) interviewed crack cocaine users in the north of England about the relationship between their drug use and criminal behaviour. One male subject reported on the links between shoplifting and his own drug use:

'Now I wake up and I go out shoplifting and I don't come back in until I've got enough for at least a stone and a bag and then I'll be out again once or twice more.' (Brain et al 1998, p 43)

Another group of explanations concerned the pharmacological effects of certain kinds of drugs on the motivation for crime. Carpenter et al (1988) conducted structured open-ended interviews with a sample of 100 youths in the USA. They found that the young people in their study had a 'rich repertoire of common-sense theories about the association between drugs and crime' (p 27). The authors report that the subjects emphasised the irrationality that results from drug use and the 'criminogenic aspects of drug addiction' (p 37). Some of these youths believed drug and alcohol use resulted in impulsive behaviour, which included a wide range of crime including theft and vandalism.

Some explanations given were based on the idea that crime caused drug use. The most common 'crime causes drug use' explanation is that the proceeds of crime are used to finance pleasure-seeking activities. Wright and Decker (1997) in their study of street robbers in St Louis, Missouri used the concept of 'life as a party' to explain why offenders took drugs and the role of drugs in 'keeping the party going'. One of the robbers explained that money from crime might be used to buy drugs or alcohol:

'I'm walking around, sometimes if I have any money in my pocket I go get high, buy a bag of [marijuana], a forty-ounce (malt liquor) or something. Get high and then I ain't got no more money and then the highness makes you start thinking until you go out and do [a robbery].' (Wright and Decker 1997, p 36)

Brain et al (1998) provide an example of a male subject who claimed that he would commit crime (burglaries) and only afterwards would think about using drugs:

'It's just that I've chosen to spend the proceeds on drugs.' (Brain et al 1998, p 43)

In summary, qualitative studies provide evidence of a number of potential connections between drug use and crime. The greatest number of quotations fell under the heading of 'drug use causes crime' explanations.

Quantitative interview studies

Some studies have attempted to enumerate the proportion of respondents who give different explanations of the drugs–crime connection in their own case. Liriano and Ramsay (2003) found that the vast majority of subjects who thought there was a connection gave explanations that fell into the 'drug use causes crime' category. A similar conclusion was drawn by Holloway and Bennett (2004), who found that the majority of subjects who thought that there was a connection gave 'economic necessity' explanations. Among those arrestees who reported any drug use in the last 12 months, the majority (70%) of those who saw a connection between drug use and acquisitive crime said it was because they needed money to buy drugs. The remainder said they thought that drugs affected their judgement, which thereby caused them to commit crime (30% of those who saw a connection), and/or that they used the money from crime to buy drugs (12%). Users of both heroin and cocaine/crack were more likely than other arrestees to perceive a connection between their drug use and offending behaviour (78% compared with 40% overall).

Conclusion

In summary, studies of drug users, offenders and members of the general population have identified a strong statistical connection between drug use and crime. However, the strength of the relationship depends on the type of drugs used and the type of crimes committed. The drugs most strongly connected to crime are heroin and crack, and the crimes most strongly connected to drug use are shoplifting and theft.

The main research question is whether the association between drug use and crime is causal or simply spurious (eg a product of the clustering of problem behaviours in particular individuals). There is little evidence on this topic. However, the evidence that does exist suggests that changes in drug use are associated with changes in crime (when one goes up the other goes up) and that drug users and criminals tend to believe that, in some instances at least, their drug use and their criminal behaviour are causally connected. The most common explanation given is that crime is committed to fund drug misuse. Other connections mentioned include the pharmacological effect of the drug on their decision-making.

Overall, the research evidence leads to the conclusion that there is no general connection between drug use and crime in the sense that all drugs are associated with all crimes. However, there does appear to be some highly specific connections between particular drug types and particular crimes. In these cases, there is some evidence that the connection between the two might be causal. The challenge now is to find out precisely which connections are causal and the way in which they are causal. In particular, it would be useful to know the role of moderating and mediating factors and the extent to which the connection varies between individuals and different groups of individuals.

Notes

Anglin M D and Speckart G (1986) 'Narcotics use, property crime, and dealing: structural dynamics across the addiction career', *Journal of Quantitative Criminology* 2(4), pp 355–75

Ball J C, Rosen L, Fluceck J A and Nurco D N (1981) 'The criminality of heroin addicts when addicted and when off opiates', in Inciardi J A (ed.) *The drugs–crime connection*, Beverly Hills, CA: Sage, pp 39–65

Bennett T and Holloway K (2005) 'Disaggregating the relationship between drug misuse and crime', *The Australian and New Zealand Journal of Criminology*

Brain K, Howard P and Bottomley T (1998) *Evolving crack cocaine careers: new users, quitters and long-term combination drug users in N.W. England*, Manchester: University of Manchester

Byqvist S (1999) 'Criminality among female drug abusers', *Journal of Psychoactive Drugs*, 31(4), pp 353–62

Carpenter C, Glassner B, Johnson B D and Loughlin J (1988) *Kids, drugs, and crime*, Toronto: Lexington

Chaiken J M and Chaiken M R (1990) 'Drugs and predatory crime', in Tonry M and Wilson J Q (eds) *Drugs and crime,* London: The University of Chicago Press, pp 203–39

Datesman S (1987) 'Women, crime, and drugs', in Inciardi J A (ed.) *The drugs–crime connection*, Beverly Hills, CA: Sage, pp 85–104

Erickson P G, Butters J, McGillicuddy P and Hallgren A (2000) 'Crack and prostitution: gender, myths and experiences', *Journal of Drug Issues* 30(4), pp 767–88

Farabee D, Joshi V and Anglin D M (2001) 'Addiction careers and criminal specialization', *Crime and Delinquency* 47(2), pp 196–220

Gandossy R P, Williams J R, Cohen J and Harwood H J (1980) *Drugs and crime: a survey and analysis of the literature*, Washington: US Department of Justice

Goulden C and Sondhi A (2001) *At the margins: drug use by vulnerable young people in the 1998/99 Youth Lifestyles Survey*, Home Office Research Study 228, London: Home Office

Graham N and Wish E D (1994) 'Drug use among female arrestees: onset, patterns, and relationships to prostitution', *Journal of Drug Issues* 24(2), pp 315–29

Hanlon T E, Nuren D N, Kinlock T M and Duszynski K R (1990) 'Trends in criminal activity and drug use over an addiction career', *American Journal of Drug and Alcohol Abuse* 16, pp 223–38

Hawke J M, Jainchill N and De Leon G J (2000) 'Adolescent amphetamine users in treatment, client profiles and treatment outcomes', *Journal of Psychoactive Drugs* 32(1), pp 95–105

Holloway K and Bennett T (2004) *The results of the first two years of the NEW-ADAM programme*, Home Office Online Report 19/04, London: Home Office, available at <www.homeoffice.gov.uk/rds/pdfs04/rdsolr1904.pdf>

Hough M (1996) *Drug misuse and the criminal justice system: a review of the literature*, London: Home Office

Hunt D E, Lipton D S and Spunt B (1984) 'Patterns of criminal activity among methadone clients and current narcotics users not in treatment', *Journal of Drug Issues* 14(4), pp 687–702

Inciardi J A and Pottieger A E (1986) 'Drug use and crime among two cohorts of women narcotics users: an empirical assessment', *Journal of Drug Issues* 16(1), pp 91–106

Inciardi J A and Surratt M A (2001) 'Drug use, street crime and sex-trading among cocaine-dependent women: implications for public health and criminal justice policy', *Journal of Psychoactive Drugs* 33(4), pp 379–89

Liriano S and Ramsay M (2003) 'Prisoners' drug use before prison and the links with crime', in Ramsay M (ed.) *Prisoners' drug use and treatment: seven research studies*, Home Office Research Study 267, London: Home Office

Makkai T, Fitzgerald J and Doak P (2000) 'Drug use among police detainees', *Crime and Justice* 49 (March), Sydney: NSW Bureau of Crime Statistics and Research

Mason W A and Windle M (2002) 'Reciprocal relations between adolescent substance use and delinquency: a longitudinal latent variable analysis', *Journal of Abnormal Psychology* 111(1), pp 63–76

McCoy V, Inciardi J A, Metsch L R, Pottieger A E and Saum C A (1995) 'Women, crack, and crime: gender comparisons of criminal activity among crack cocaine users', *Contemporary Drug Problems* 22, pp 435–51

Menard S, Mihalic S and Huizinga D (2001) 'Drugs and crime revisited', *Justice Quarterly* 18(2), pp 269–99

Nurco D N, Shaffer J W, Ball J C and Kinlock T W (1984) 'Trends in the commission of crime among narcotic addicts over successive periods of addiction and non-addiction', *American Journal of Drug and Alcohol Abuse* 10, pp 481–89

Nurco D N, Kinloch T and Balter M B (1993) 'The severity of pre-addiction criminal behaviour among urban, male narcotic addicts and two non-addicted control groups', *Journal of Research in Crime and Delinquency* 30(3), pp 293–316

Potterat J J, Rothenberg R B, Muth S Q, Darrow W W and Phillips-Plummer L (1998) 'Pathways to prostitution: the chronology of sexual and drug abuse milestones', *The Journal of Sex Research* 35(4), pp 333–40

Pudney S (2002) *The road to ruin? Sequences of initiation into drug use and offending by young people in Britain*, Home Office Research Study 253, London: Home Office

Sterk C E, Elifson K W and German D (2000) 'Female crack users and their sexual relationships: the role of sex-for-crack exchanges', *The Journal of Sex Research* 37(4), pp 354–60

Wright R and Decker S (1997) *Armed robbers in action: stickups and street culture*, Boston: Northeastern University Press

Yacoubian G S, Urbach B J, Larsen K L, Johnson R J and Peters R J (2001) 'A comparison of drug use between prostitutes and other female arrestees', *Journal of Alcohol and Drug Education* 46(2), pp 12–25

6 The economic impact of illegal drugs

From: *Drugs – facing facts. The report of the RSA Commission on Illegal Drugs, Communities and Public Policy*, RSA, 2007

How big is the 'drugs industry'?

It is necessary to start with a caveat: 'The organisation of this field of activity is outside the law, and therefore outside any system of controlled information... The time has come today to face up to the fact that we are in an exceptional area of an "informational circus" ' (Geffray et al 2002). In more circumspect language, the most recent World Drugs Report from the UN Office on Drugs and Crime (UNODC) agreed: 'The obscurity of the global illicit drug market makes the exercise of estimating its size extremely difficult... because the most basic inputs which are needed for such an estimation – data on production, prices, quantities exported, imported and consumed – are themselves often estimates and are frequently based on less than complete data.'

The accuracy of these estimates is further compromised by the politicisation of statistics in this area. Critics point out that it is in the interests of bodies like UNODC and the other agencies responsible for enforcing drug prohibition policies to maximise the threat of drugs in order to justify ever-increasing budgets. They produce very large figures, which then become established as part of the discourse (Thoumi 2005): 'Both supporters and adversaries of the current drug control regime [in the USA] use the mythical number of US$400 or $500 billion for the global illicit trade as evidence either to reinforce or do away with current drug policies, although nobody really knows if the figures are right – and many question them.'[1]

However, it is generally agreed that the trade in illegal drugs is a multi-billion dollar global business, with more than 50 million regular users of heroin, cocaine and synthetic drugs worldwide, and 200 million if cannabis is included.

Millions more people, 'from the cocaleros of Bolivia to the bouncers of London' (*The Observer*, 21.4.02), are involved in supplying these users at the various different stages in the drugs trade:
- cultivation of crops
- wholesaling of raw materials

---

1 TNI Crime and Globalisation seminar – 'The economic impact of the illicit drug industry' – Dec 2003

- processing and manufacturing
- transport and distribution
- retail
- money laundering and investment of proceeds.

Besides the farmers/producers, the marketers, traffickers and lower-level dealers, there is a large financial infrastructure of accountants, lawyers, and bankers operating in a 'grey economy' between the 'black' and legitimate economies.

The UNODC's best estimate of the value of the market in 2003 (the latest year for which figures are available) was US$13 billion at the production level, $94 billion at the wholesale level (taking seizures into account), and US$322 billion at the retail level (based on retail prices and taking seizures and other losses into account). According to the same UNODC calculations (UNODC 2004), the value measured at retail prices is higher than the GDP of 88 per cent of the countries in the world and equivalent to about three-quarters of Sub-Saharan Africa's total GDP. The sale of drugs measured at wholesale prices was equivalent to 12 per cent of the global export of chemicals (US$794 billion) and 14 per cent of global agricultural exports (US$674 billion) and it exceeded global exports of ores and other minerals (US$79 billion) in 2003.

The largest market is for cannabis herb (with a retail market size of $113 billion),[2] followed by cocaine (US$71 billion), the opiates (US$65 billion) and cannabis resin (US$29 billion). The ATS [amphetamine type stimulants] markets together (methamphetamine, amphetamine and ecstasy) amount to US$44 billion.

As for trends in the world market, the UNODC concludes that the overall market is growing, though in different degrees for different drugs. The market for opiates is up slightly (mostly due to increased demand in Asia); production levels and prices will depend very largely on Afghanistan, where it is unclear whether 2005 will equal the bumper crop produced in 2004. The overall market for cocaine is up, production is increasing, and the market is diversifying with a particularly noticeable rise in demand in Europe. There is no sign of any slowing in the

---

2 The document continues, 'While UNODC is reasonably confident with its estimations on opiates, cocaine and the ATS [amphetamine type stimulants], the degree of certainty is far lower for cannabis, notably for cannabis herb, as information for production and consumption of this substance is highly contradictory. If better information becomes available, a major revision cannot be ruled out.'

consistent increase of the market for cannabis; perhaps more significantly, the numbers of people in treatment for cannabis is growing worldwide. The market for amphetamines and ecstasy has declined slightly, largely due to a reduced demand for amphetamine in south-east Asia and for ecstasy in the US.

In terms of money spent, cocaine is the world's number one drug, thanks to the combination of high demand and a relatively high price, as compared with heroin (high price but relatively low demand) and cannabis (high demand but relatively low price).

What are the profits and who makes them?

It is certainly not the original producers of illegal drugs who receive most of the profits from them. Value is largely embedded in the distribution network, with high premiums paid for the taking of risk, with the producers of some drugs receiving no more than 1 per cent of the eventual retail price.

Prices, and therefore profits, vary from time to time and from drug to drug, but the overall mark-up between production price and retail price is invariably steep. To take the heroin trade as an example:

- An *Observer* report in 2002 (21.4.02) stated, 'Afghan-originated heroin, transported in bulk, costs as little as £600 per kilo. The so-called "Turkish route" importers will trade "tens of kilos" for around £7,000 per kilo. Middle-level brokers will purchase a single kilo for about £22,000. "At this level, it will often be bulked out with cutting agents before being sold for up to £1,000 an ounce (£35,000 a kilo)," says Customs latest analysis. That's a mark-up of 60 times the original price.'
- The Prime Minister's Strategy Unit the following year claimed that the annual turnover for a major Afghan opium trafficker would be £11–37 million in annual profits, allowing for seizures. The profit margin per kilo would be between 26 per cent and 58 per cent. For comparison the Unit cited private sector profit margins for such companies as LVMH/Moet Hennessy Louis Vuitton – 48 per cent, Exxon – 8 per cent and Procter and Gamble – 7 per cent (Strategy Unit 2003).

This large gap between production and retail costs is also to be found for legal commodities such as chocolate and coffee – but illegal drugs have a much shorter distribution chain than do similar agricultural commodities. ' "It is a surprise how few links in the supply chain there are; for heroin there are as few as four," says HM

Customs and Excise,' (*The Observer*, 21.4.02), which means bigger profits for fewer people.

These inflated profits appear to be largely concentrated near the top end of the chain, in the hands of major traffickers. Detailed evidence is lacking on profits further down the chain – for example, for middle market distributors – but they almost certainly do not reach the lower levels of street dealers. In a chapter of their book *Freakonomics* focussing on low-level crack dealers in Boston, Stephen Levitt and Stephen Dubner ask, 'Why do drug dealers still live with their moms?', and broader academic research suggests that at the lowest level dealers are poorly paid (Reuter 2000). (They may make relatively more profit per gram than players at other levels, but deal in much smaller quantities.) This is broadly consistent with the assumption that the markets are competitive; and competition may mean that middle-market margins are also tight.

The salient points are that:
- at every level people can make more from drugs than from anything else open to them (although at the lowest level this may be because, besides being street dealers they are also users, quite possibly with criminal records, and little else actually is open to them)
- profits are sufficiently substantial for the industry as a whole to be able to absorb any losses caused by interdiction. At a higher level these losses may be written off, at a lower level they can be balanced by decreases in purity of the drug sold rather than increases in its price.

What form does the 'drugs industry' take?

Generally speaking, the drugs industry is characterised by competition rather than cartelisation, and there is little evidence of central price fixing. This leads to larger production, lower prices and faster growth in response to world demand (Byrd and Ward 2004). One American source reported in 2000, 'Despite finding that some dealers within the US have enormous incomes and traffic in large quantities, no researcher has found evidence, except on the most local basis (eg a few blocks) that a dealer organization has the ability to exclude others or to set prices, the hallmarks of market power... Even at the trafficker level, market power seems elusive. Notwithstanding references to the Medellin and Cali "cartels" [trafficking cocaine in Colombia], these seem to be only loose syndicates of independent entrepreneurs who sometimes collaborate but who also have to compete with other, smaller Colombian smuggling enterprises. ... The continuing decline of prices over an almost twenty-year period at all levels of the market suggests that, if market power ever existed, it has now been dissipated' (Reuter 2000).

It is no longer believed that there is a single integrated structure, or even a limited number of vertically integrated structures, to the drugs industry, nor any one 'Mr Big' at its head. For years the trend has been towards growing decentralization. The trade is certainly closely intertwined with organised crime networks, as one of their many 'earners', but these criminal organisations themselves take many forms and do not necessarily have uniform structures, stable hierarchies or long-established leaders.

In some cases, drugs networks may be vertically integrated to a greater or lesser degree, with the same network controlling several stages in the process, from production to retail. This may be the case, for example, where the trade is in the hands of immigrant communities. 'Immigrant groups may have strong links with producing countries; they speak languages the police rarely understand; they have close ties of loyalty to each other ' (*The Economist* 2001) – all of which makes them more likely to form 'communal businesses', to quote Michael Hough and M Natarajan (2000). Hough and Natarajan also identify 'corporations' in the drugs trade – large, formal hierarchies with well-defined divisions of labour, which are also more likely to be vertically integrated. But they stress that there are other types of organisation – 'freelancers', for example, small, non-hierarchical entrepreneurial groups which tend only to operate at one or two levels, or 'family businesses', cohesive groups with a clear structure and authority derived from family ties but not organised on the same scale as 'corporations'. It is not always clear how lower-level retail markets, where the freelancers and family businesses may be operating, are linked to the upper-level distribution systems.

In general, the various different business functions involved in the drugs trade are often accomplished by a range of loosely aligned associations of independent producers, shippers, distributors, processors, marketers, financiers and wholesalers. It is this looseness, flexibility and readiness to adapt which makes the drugs trade so difficult to disrupt. The Strategy Unit report observes: 'The capacity of the drugs industry to source and supply heroin and cocaine is enhanced by the wide diversity of routings, methods and types/scales of organisations involved', the constant variation in transport types, size of consignments, degree of central organisation, numbers of players involved and degree of integration in the supply chain.

This is an industry of considerable technological sophistication, with an apparently inexhaustible supply of new recruits and, in some areas, growing levels of managerial expertise. *The Economist* comments, 'Mexican distributors operate with great professionalism, sometimes employing top managers with degrees in business studies, and relying heavily on honour, credit and collateral. "The recruitment process is very like that for IBM or Xerox".' '"We dealt with a team a while ago that had a director of operations and a director of finance, and they actually called them that," says Bill Hughes, the appointed director-general of SOCA [Serious Organised Crime Agency]' (The Economist 2001, 2004).

The drugs industry in Britain

Commentators point out that there is a need in this area too for more reliable statistics. According to the Strategy Unit report, 'Less is known about the UK drugs market than about drug production and trafficking overseas. Data across the UK drug supply chain has not been consistently collected, analysed and interpreted. UK drug suppliers are numerous, operate in a fluid fashion and adapt effectively to surveillance efforts. As a result, there are still significant gaps in government knowledge about the UK market in drugs:

- the typical number of links in the domestic supply chain is estimated at between four and seven, but there is insufficient evidence to be certain
- the buy and sell rates at the various points in the chain (other than wholesale and retail) are largely unknown; revenues and profits along the chain can only be estimated
- though the numbers of individuals involved in the chain can be estimated, there is little hard evidence or intelligence available.'

The Strategy Unit report offers rough estimates of the numbers of people involved in the heroin and cocaine trades in Britain – eg 80–120 major importers of cocaine selling to 'hundreds' of major distributors and 'thousands' of wholesalers, and 30–50 major importers of heroin selling to 120–160 major distributors and more than 1,500 wholesalers.

Five years ago the Office for National Statistics estimated the size of the drugs market in the UK as between £3.9 and £8.5 billion a year. A Home Office Research Study in 2001 made a more precise estimate of £6.6 billion, but suggested that this figure might be inflated (Bramley-Harker 2001). In 2003, however, the Strategy Unit valued the heroin and cocaine market alone as worth more than £4 billion.

There is some production of drugs within the UK. About 50 per cent of cannabis consumed in Britain is now cultivated here, with an increasing amount home-grown (Hough et al 2003). One report in 1999 (*The Independent* 20.6.99) suggested that a quarter of all ecstasy tablets seized in Britain (about one million in total) had been manufactured here, and that the UK was actually exporting ecstasy to the US. The report also claimed an increase in the manufacture of amphetamines: 'Last year, police raided a drugs factory on a farm in Norfolk which had the capacity to produce £15m of amphetamine a week – £780m over a year. Les Fiander, a member of the drugs unit at the NCIS [National Criminal Intelligence Service], which is instrumental in helping police to raid drug factories in the UK at the rate of one a month, said: "We are picking up intelligence that there is a lot more interest from criminal gangs to manufacture drugs over here. They are bringing in chemicals from Eastern Europe where there is a lot of corruption in the chemical and pharmaceutical industries".'

However, most British involvement in the international drugs trade takes the form of import, distribution, retail and money laundering. While import and distribution at the middle-market level are largely dominated by a relatively small number of criminal groups, these groups are again more usefully understood as networks or partnerships of independent traders or brokers than as tightly organised units. This is particularly evident in the case of the cocaine trade, according to a recent *Economist* report. 'The drugs trade used to be dominated by stable, vertically integrated outfits resembling mini-Mafia families. That was a response to the risks of doing business. Drug buyers may be undercover police officers; promises to pay may be broken (these are criminals, after all); trusted contacts may be jailed and rivals get shopped. Stable partnerships reduced these risks, as did recruitment from a shallow ethnic pool. But market forces have gradually pushed these cumbersome organisations out of business. Competition in the cocaine trade has cut margins to minuscule levels, considering the risks involved. Powder cocaine from Central America is sold in multiple-kilogram loads for £15,000–30,000 ($28,000–56,000). But the price for a single kilogram, £18,000–32,000, is barely higher, and the retail price not much more than that. Last year, the National Criminal Intelligence Service estimated that cocaine was selling for £56 per gram (equivalent to £56,000 per kilo) but the current London price is said to be around £40 per gram... The reason why the cocaine price has fallen so much is that the market is opening up... The London-based Colombian importers who traditionally controlled the import and wholesale trades now contract freely with British entrepreneurs. A recent trend is for Britons living in Spain to deal directly with Central American suppliers before selling on to Colombians in London or directly to an army of middlemen.'

'By contrast,' the report continues, 'the heroin trade is more closed and less innovative... partly because demand for heroin is more inflexible than demand for other drugs. Reliability of supply is more important than price, which means there is less shopping around at any stage of the supply chain. Another barrier to greater competition is linguistic. To move cocaine from producer to market, English and Spanish are essential; to move ecstasy, it helps to speak Dutch. But as many as 120 languages, from Italian to Pashto, are spoken by those involved in the heroin trade. That makes it tricky to seek out new sources or new routes.' In consequence, margins are fatter in the heroin trade. 'Importers, many of them London-based Turks, sell multi-kilo loads to white British middlemen at £16,000–22,000 per kilo. The middlemen, who rarely deal in any other product, sell on to retailers at prices up to £33,000 for a single kilo, enhancing profits further by adulterating the drug. Heroin is then cut again before being sold on the street for the equivalent of £60,000 per kilo.

Heroin traffickers do not constitute a cartel, though. They behave more like members of an oligopoly, with a mixture of competition and co-operation at the highest levels of the trade. Paul Evans, chief investigation officer at Customs and Excise, says that this can extend to emergency relief: "If your shipment hasn't arrived, someone else will loan you stuff to tide you over." Such cosy arrangements are likely to break down as new players enter. Turkish importers have already lost business to Kurds and Albanians – both groups now scattered across Europe, thanks to instability at home and higher immigration into rich countries. British-based Colombians squeezed out of the cocaine trade are dabbling in the more profitable opiates. The dissolving of ethnic and family bonds is likely to mean still freer trade' (*The Economist* 2004).

What is the impact of the drugs trade on economies?

The impact of the drugs trade is less significant in more developed consumer economies, more significant in less developed economies.[3] It is most significant, obviously, in less-developed producing countries.

---

3 TNI Crime and Globalisation seminar

In these countries the trade undeniably produces short-term profits, bringing relatively large amounts of money into the local economies and improving the trade balance, while providing thousands of jobs for farmers, itinerant labourers, laboratory workers, wholesale distributors and their employees (INCB 2002). 'The example of Colombia... shows how large a part this sector can play in the national economy of a large country, affecting not only employment, incomes, investments... commerce, economic property, financial flows and the external balance of payments, but also the rules, standards, regulations and laws which govern the functioning of that economy. In situations where there is little supervision by government institutions, the presence, withdrawal or re-routing of this trade can enable whole medium-sized towns to develop or cause them to falter. In such places the redistribution of the profits involved may also sustain large sections of a region's economy or firms belonging to the officially recognised economy. Together with the proceeds of other criminal activities, they swell the funds in these regions' financial and banking systems in an utterly disproportionate way... In the great metropolitan conurbations, drug money can make a considerable difference to neighbourhoods, indeed to whole city districts' (UNESCO 2002). (It is worth noting that this can hold true even in developed economies. 'In a lot of poor communities, drug dealers are the only equal-opportunity employer,' says Deborah Small, director of public policy at the Lindesmith Centre, a drug-campaigning organisation in the United States.)

But these short-term gains are counteracted, according to the UN, by more severe long-term damage. The International Narcotics Control Board points to a negative correlation between illicit drug production and economic development, citing the recent examples of Bolivia and Peru where increases in drug cultivation have not been accompanied by corresponding increases in economic growth (INCB 2002). According to the UNODC (1997), money from the illegal drugs trade will ultimately have the effect of destabilising the economy in producer countries, through:

- inflating the domestic currency: 'Unexplained currency surpluses can occur when there is a high degree of underground activity in the economy.'
- damaging licit export businesses: 'The so-called "Dutch disease" refers to a market distortion resulting from a boom in an isolated sector of the economy which causes stagnation in the other core sectors... The disproportionately high foreign exchange earnings of illicit drug production can result in a stagnation of exports in non drug-related sectors.' In consequence, an economy may become dangerously dependent on a single trade. In addition, 'licit business

can be crowded out through intimidation or corruption, while criminal entrepreneurs with liquid cash have no need to borrow and can undercut the prices of legitimate competitors.'

● disrupting monetary policy: 'Large-scale movements of illicit sector capital... can disable a government's ability to plan and control monetary policy. For example one of the traditional tools of macroeconomic stabilization is a Central Bank's capacity to make credit (and therefore consumption and investment) more or less expensive by increasing or decreasing the money supply. However, when the underground economy is large in relation to the legitimate one, these conditions no longer apply... Decreased financial control undercuts financial credibility and as a result, the benefits to a given country of drug-related capital can be more than offset by reduced access to legitimate sources of finance.'

In addition, 'the actual multiplier effect of the income generated from illicit drug trade will be less than those arising from comparable lawful activity' (INCB 2002). This is because it will more often go into conspicuous consumption, very often on imported goods, contributing nothing to local economic development, or into non-productive sectors like real estate and gambling, rather than being saved or productively reinvested. 'One of the reasons why "black" money behaves differently from licit sector capital is because the investment decision often prioritizes disguising the capital over the maximization of profits.'

In the worst case, drugs profits will be used to destabilise political regimes in less developed countries (van der Veen 2000) – through the financing of electoral campaigns, straightforward corruption, or the subsidy of insurgency and terrorism. This can damage the business climate and lead to decreasing investment. 'Even though the drug problem does not, itself, rank high as a risk factor for foreign investment, it has a significant impact on other risk factors rated high by investors, such as insurgency, terrorism, land disputes, social violence and corruption.'[4]

It has been suggested by UNESCO researchers that money laundering for the drugs trade has contributed to financial crises in poorer countries – for example, in Mexico in 1994–5 and Thailand in 1997.[5] In richer consumer countries, where most drugs profits are made and reinvested, even though the sums involved are

---

4 UNDCP Technical Report 6
5 UNESCO, 'The social and economic impact of drug trafficking" http://portal.unesco.org/en/ ev.php-URL_ID=6906&URL_DO=DO_TOPIC&URL_SECTION=201.html

much larger they will not have the same destabilising effect because of the relative size of the economies. Logically, the most significant impact is likely to stem from money laundering, but it is not at all clear what form this impact takes. A recent seminar on the economic impact of the illicit drug industry asked what happens to the 'dirty money' from illegal drugs. Does it become 'gentrified' – for instance, in the establishment of new companies, mixed with other funds? Is it hoarded to be handed on as an inheritance? How is it transferred into real estate or valuables which can be traded? What happens to it after it is moved to tax havens? Does it flow into the capital market? Delegates concluded that 'there is a near total vacuum of knowledge... with regard to criminal money flows and money laundering'.[6]

One other crucial datum is unknown and appears not to have been estimated: the added monetary value of illegality. There has only been a limited amount of research on what the economic impact of the world drugs trade would be if it were legalised. Harvard professor Jeffrey Miron has recently calculated that legalizing marijuana would save the United States $7.7 billion in government expenditure on enforcement of prohibition; and legalization would yield tax revenue of $2.4 billion annually if marijuana were taxed like all other goods, $6.2 billion if it were taxed at rates comparable to those on alcohol and tobacco (Miron 2005). Similar calculations were performed for the whole British drugs market by the Independent Drug Monitoring Unit in 2004, projecting savings of between £3.5 billion and £6 billion per year. 'The financial effects of legalisation and regulation of the drugs trade would have benefits – in excise duty, VAT, general economic growth and expenditure savings, with modest additional expenditure required to establish a regulatory authority and give the regulator effective "teeth" to tackle abuses of the system' (Atha 2005). Figures as diverse as Milton Friedman and Mo Mowlam have advocated legalizing and taxing drugs as a means of increasing funding for drugs strategies. The recommendation is also incorporated in the recent report from Transform Drug Reform Foundation, *After the war on drugs: options for control*, but the report stops short of projecting the revenue that might accrue from this move. A mainstream study would greatly enrich the debate on possible drugs policy options.

---

6 TransNational Institute, Amsterdam, December 2003

How does the drugs industry adapt to changing market conditions and changes in the law?

There is not enough research on this subject to draw more than the most general conclusions. 'Markets seem to adapt to changing preferences', according to the recent Foresight study on 'Brain science, drugs and addiction' (Cave and Godfrey 2005). These preferences may have a variety of sources – changing fashions in youth culture, for example – which will almost certainly include price. It is now generally accepted that the drugs industry is not set apart by the nature of its products but will behave much like other industries. It used to be thought that demand for many drugs was inelastic and would remain steady, because of the addictive nature of the commodities, regardless of price. But it is now acknowledged that the position is more complex. High prices for heroin, for instance, may be tolerated for a while without any change in behaviour; equally, they might force non-offending users into crime to finance their habit. Alternatively, they might force addicts into treatment and off the market, or push them sideways into using a different drug in a different market for a while. In other words, 'in a departure from conventional wisdom, both economic theory and empirical evidence suggest that drug prices influence demand' (Cave and Godfrey 2005).

The most obvious recent example of a change in the law relating to illegal drugs was the reclassification of cannabis from Class B to Class C in January 2004. A year later some sources were claiming that this relaxation in the law had prompted a sales drive from the industry. ' "One of the biggest growth areas is the shifting of organised crime towards cannabis importation," said a senior officer connected to the Met's organised crime unit. "The supply side has reacted to the liberalisation because they think law enforcement has taken its eye off the ball. We are now recovering tons of the drug at one time and that is something we were never doing before"' (*The Observer* 20.2.05). In contrast, the decriminalisation of cannabis in South Australia, Portugal, the Netherlands and a number of individual American states would not appear to have increased its prevalence in the long term (McCoun and Reuter 2001).

Mapping responses to market conditions is complicated by the fact that many if not most drug users use more than one substance at the same time or on different occasions. Very many use alcohol as a drug as well as illegal drugs, and drugs in a growing range of combinations. Suppliers both respond to this and encourage it – for example, by selling combination packs of heroin and crack for simultaneous injection as 'speedballs'. 'There has been a growth of poly-drug use among consumers and some evidence of suppliers becoming more concentrated on this demand' (Cave and Godfrey 2005). It is not clear what happens if one substance is made more difficult or expensive to obtain. Some maintain that the natural response is to switch to another. 'Most illicit drug use is controlled and involves sales in small amounts. Purchases are often opportunistic and if a specific drug is in short supply, there is a range of licit and illicit alternatives' (Hough and Natarajan 2000). Others argue, on the contrary, that tightening policy on one drug may reduce consumption of another. 'In general, drugs are complementary, so relaxing policies on any one drug may increase the consumption of all substances,' whereas tightening them may reduce overall consumption (Cave and Godfrey 2005). In particular, increasing the price of alcohol will often reduce both drinking and marijuana consumption. There are similar overlaps between smoking and marijuana use, and drinking and the use of both heroin and cocaine.

It is hard to predict how the drugs market may adapt to accommodate new technological possibilities. The 2005 Foresight study raises the prospect that 'minimally refined agricultural products (eg the 'big three' of heroin, cocaine and cannabis) may be threatened by 'high-tech' synthetic alternatives. This could well present problems for countries – like Britain – with advanced biotechnology sectors.

What are the costs to the community of drug misuse ?

Cost statistics are the figures most commonly used to justify policy choices and budget allocations. Costs are usually calculated taking a variety of factors into account:
- harms to individuals from drug use – ill health, loss of earnings and other opportunities, premature death
- harms to society – impaired productivity, lost output and lower GDP, environmental damage, drug-related crime
- the costs of the various strategies for combating these harms – education, treatment and criminal justice.

Two points are worth making:
- Critics argue that these calculations should not be used as if they were significant in themselves; they would become significant only if they were set against similar calculations for alternative policy options – eg

decriminalisation, legalisation, zero-tolerance, etc (see for example Miron 2005).

●   The most expensive item in the list is 'drug-related crime', but the precise definition of this term and the methodology used to calculate its costs is strongly challenged by those who argue that the relationship between drugs and crime is far more complex and reciprocal than such calculations often assume.

The Strategy Unit report in 2003 put the estimated total costs of drug misuse in the UK at £24 billion per year. The Foresight Brain Science, Addiction and Drugs report in 2005 projects that this total may have risen to £35 billion by 2025. The most thorough analysis of the economic and social costs of Class A drug use in England and Wales (Godfrey et al 2002) breaks down the factors that should be included in calculating such costs as follows:

Personal costs
●   Mortality – premature death
●   Morbidity – drug-related illness
●   Loss of earnings – through criminality and imprisonment, sickness, temporary or permanent unemployment. (The lost earnings of carers also have to be taken into account.)
●   Educational attainment – eg some argue that the impact of marijuana on educational achievement translates into reduced future earnings.

External/social costs
●   Lost output, lower GDP – from sickness absence, theft in the workplace, the cost of security and testing, etc. The cost to industry of the use of illegal substances has recently been estimated at £800 million per year
●   Damage to communities – environmental damage, drug litter, lowered house prices, etc
●   The costs of caring for the children and other dependants of drug users – estimated by Godfrey at £63 million in England and Wales in 2000
●   The other costs of social care and social security benefits
●   The costs of the drugs education programme and other preventive strategies
●   The costs of drugs treatment services
●   The costs of healthcare for drug users – including GP care, Accident and Emergency, ambulance services, hospital days, mental health services, death

costs, plus specialist services such as the care of babies born to drug-using parents (Godfrey estimates £4.3 million spent on neonates in 2000) or treatment for HIV and hepatitis. (Godfrey produces a figure of £888,753 for each new case of HIV presenting in 2002, incorporating figures for the predicted loss of 20 years' life, valued at a total of £714,229, plus 15 years of treatment at £15,000 per year.)

- The costs of healthcare for people affected by the drug misuse of others – Godfrey estimates the average yearly loss of health for people in Britain as a result of fear of crime at £19.50 per head
- The costs of drug-related crime itself

'Drug-related crime' is used loosely in much policy literature, including the national drugs strategy, to cover:

- criminal offences in breach of drug legislation – trafficking, dealing, etc
- offences committed as part of the operation of drug markets and the supply of illegal drugs – bribery, turf war fights, etc. (The Home Affairs Committee's report in 2003 related an upsurge in shooting incidents in London and other major cities to drugs, principally crack cocaine – a lucrative market well worth fighting to protect.)
- crimes committed under the influence of drugs
- crimes committed by users to support their habit.

It is not always clear which of these are included in calculations of the crime-related costs of drug misuse.

The Strategy Unit report refers to 'drug-motivated crime' and focuses under this heading on acquisitive crime committed to fund drug use, as well as drug driving (which caused more than 200 deaths in 2002), mugging (around 238,000 per year) and murder (130 per year). The report asserts that drug-motivated crime has risen over the last seven years while other types of crime have remained stable or fallen, and it attributes 85 per cent of shoplifting, 80 per cent of domestic burglary, 71 per cent of non-domestic burglary, 55 per cent of theft from cars and 54 per cent of robbery to drug misuse. The Godfrey report stated that in 2000 Class A drug-related crime accounted for more than £10 billion worth of crime, 88 per cent of the total. The 2003 Strategy Unit report estimated that drug-motivated offences account for around 56 per cent of the total number of criminal acts and a third of the total cost of crime – £19 billion – with £16 billion of this attributable to heroin and crack users. (This compares with £12 billion as the cost of alcohol-related crime

– but it should be noted that drug-motivated crime is far more likely to take the form of property theft than violence, while the reverse is almost certainly true of alcohol.)

The Strategy Unit report adds that the 280,000 users of heroin and/or crack are responsible for the vast bulk (87 per cent) of the cost of drug-motivated crime and that the 30,000 highest offending heroin/crack users commit more than 50 per cent of it. 'The highest offending heroin and/or crack users could be responsible for crime costing over £360,000 per user per year.' This contrasts with the much more conservative statistics on the DrugScope website to the effect that 'between one and 21 per cent of the total cost of acquisitive crime is associated with people who were dependent on heroin'. The divergence can most plausibly be explained by DrugScope's more nuanced view of the relationship between drugs and crime and its greater reluctance to see this relationship as linear and uni-directional (see below).

Criminologists Trevor Bennett and Katy Holloway (2005) observe that drugs and crime are unquestionably connected. Drug users are more likely than non-users to be criminals and the vast majority of offenders have consumed at least one drug recently. But not all drug types are associated with all crime types and some drug types are not associated with crime at all: for instance, there is little evidence of a link between crime and the recreational use of cannabis or ecstasy. The association between drugs and crime is multi-faceted and traffic between the two may be moving in both directions, with the additional possibility that the association is not causal at all.

Some alternative theories suggest:
- The pharmacological effects of drugs might cause crime – though this is more likely in the case of violent crime than the property crime that makes up the bulk of drug-related offences. (It can also be argued that the effects of using some drugs 'might sometimes be so inhibiting that they reduce the risk of offending'.)
- It has also been suggested that drugs may be used as a means of celebrating a crime – ie after the event, not before it.
- The most popular 'drugs cause crime' explanation is the 'enslavement' argument that users offend to raise money for their habits. However, it has also been argued that surplus funds from crime can be used to finance drug

use – ie crime causes drug use. 'Drug use is part and parcel of the criminal lifestyle that revolves around criminal behaviour and having a good time.'
● The link between drug use and crime could be forged by a third variable, or cluster of variables (deprivation, social exclusion, childhood abuse, etc) that explains both drug use and crime.
● Research indicates that much offending tends to begin *after* the use of recreational drugs (which are not generally associated with eg acquisitive crime) but *before* the use of 'hard' drugs – ie that there is no clear-cut temporal progression from drug use to offending, as it seems that 'most people who are likely to be involved in crime are already offending by the time they begin serious drug misuse'.
● 'It is possible that drug use and criminal behaviour merely co-exist in perhaps rather chaotic lifestyles of some individuals: neither drug use can be seen as causing crime, nor can crime be seen as causing drug use.'

Bennett and Holloway point out that current government strategy relies heavily on the assumption that the relationship between drugs and crime is causal and that reducing the prevalence of drug use will automatically reduce crime. If the relationship is not causal – or not to the degree that they suppose – then the strategy is unlikely to be successful – or not as successful as they suppose.

What are the costs of the present regime(s) for dealing with drug misuse?

The government Spending Review for 2000 carried out a cross-departmental review of public spending plans on illegal drugs. The plans for 2003/04 were as follows:

	£million
Drug treatment	401
Protecting young people (education)	120
Safeguarding communities	95
Reducing availability (criminal justice)	380
TOTAL	**996**

These figures have since been substantially increased in the Spending Reviews for 2002 and 2004, following the updating of the drug strategy in 2002. The government's projected direct annual expenditure on the drug strategy for 2004/05 and 2005/06 is as follows:

2004/05

Drug treatment	512
Protecting young people	155
Safeguarding communities	297
Reducing supply	380
TOTAL	**1,344**

2005/06

Drug treatment	573
Protecting young people	163
Safeguarding communities	367
Reducing supply	380
TOTAL	**1,483**

Expenditure for 2005/06 will probably increase following the settlement of the 2004 Spending Review. Funding for 2006/07 and 2007/08 was also agreed and expenditure information for these years will be published later in 2005/06.

How do existing public policies and the implementation of those policies affect the economics of the drugs industry?

The Strategy Unit report seeks to demonstrate that the current focus on supply reduction is not cost-effective in that it seems to have little impact on the economics of the drugs industry. The logic of the current policy is that a reduction in the supply of drugs reaching users in Britain will force up prices to the point where it discourages demand and, in reducing the consumption of drugs, will reduce the amount of drug-related crime. Even if it were possible to assume that the relationship between drug use and crime was a causal one, the Strategy Unit report argues that:

● It would be necessary to seize some two-thirds of drugs being imported into Britain in order to affect prices. (A UN study suggests a figure nearer to 75 per cent (Commission on Narcotic Drugs 1996).) The current seizure rate is much lower than that (the Strategy Unit report estimated 20 per cent), and prices seem to be little affected.

● Even if prices went up, consumption would not necessarily go down. The nature of drug use might change, but not its overall quantity.

- If prices did rise, the effect might well be a corresponding rise in crime to fund the increasing cost of drug use. It is also suggested that higher prices might push people towards stronger drugs, in search of a better return on their money – in other words, a reduction in consumption would not automatically mean a reduction in drug-related harm.

The report concludes:

'Interventions to reduce production are complex, time-consuming and expensive to achieve. They often result in displacement of production elsewhere. Traffickers have adapted effectively to government interventions. They run highly profitable businesses and can withstand shocks to their profitability. Interventions have been short-lived or have had a negligible impact on the retail market. Cash is of critical importance for traffickers, but the money laundering business has become increasingly sophisticated and difficult to disrupt. The UK drugs business is highly fluid; dealers manipulate purity and alter the weights sold to maintain revenue. Even if supply interventions did successfully increase price, the evidence is not sufficiently strong to prove that this would reduce harm.'

From the point of view of economics, many would argue that treatment and demand reduction are far more cost-effective than supply reduction. One commonly quoted statistic suggests that £1 spent on treatment saves £3 on criminal justice. An old but much-quoted American study (Rydell and Everingham 1994) reckoned the various returns on a dollar invested in combating cocaine as follows:

Coca plant eradication in South America	17c
Cocaine interdiction between South and North America	32c
Domestic law enforcement (customs and police)	52c
Treatment for dependence	$7.48

A recent National Treatment Outcome Research Study suggested that money spent on drug treatment has saved nine to 15 times as much again in social costs (Godfrey et al 2004). Again, a simulation model has suggested that getting 10,000 more problem users a year into community-based methadone treatment over the next five years would reduce the social costs of drug misuse by £3–4 billion (Godfrey et al 2005). (However, the authors note that it is hard to estimate how much it would cost to attract more users into treatment and add that in the short-term health costs would probably rise as a result of bringing to light health problems that had simply been neglected while these drug users were not in treatment.)

Key points for consideration

- There is still no comprehensive cost-benefit analysis of current drugs policy which evaluates the overall effectiveness of current UK policy and sets this calculation against the estimated future costs of alternative policies.
- The strongest influence on the price of illegal drugs is compensation for risk. There seems to have been little research on what the price of legalised drugs would be with this premium removed.
- Current enforcement policies are being implemented without a foundation of accurate evidence about the drugs trade. The Transform Drug Policy Foundation is calling on the government 'to instigate an audit of the effectiveness of enforcing the drug laws in order to expose expenditure to comprehensive scrutiny and to help in the process of defining success and failure'.
- Some evidence suggests that, in the short term at least, decriminalisation of cannabis in Britain may possibly be producing different results from similar measures in other countries. Further research into this over a longer period would be important in the consideration of any possible reclassification of cannabis.
- The relationship of the drugs trade with the alcohol trade needs more study.
- Given that current policy in the UK hinges on reducing 'drug-related crime', a deeper and subtler understanding at every level of the relationship between drugs and crime is important.

References

Atha M (2004) *Taxing the UK drugs market*, Independent Drug Monitoring Unit

Bennett T and Holloway K (2005) *Understanding drugs, alcohol and crime*, Open University Press

Bramley-Harker E (2001) 'Sizing the UK market for illicit drugs', Home Office RDS No. 74, 2001. Available at: www.homeoffice.gov.uk/rds/pdfs/occ74-drugs.pdf

Byrd W and C Ward (2004) 'Afghanistan's drug economy: a preliminary overview and analysis', Draft Technical Annex 2, Washington: World Bank. Available at:

http://www.af/resources/mof/recosting/chapter1/Recosting per cent 20Chapter per cent 201 per cent 20Annex per cent 202.pdf

Cave J and Godfrey C (2005) 'The economics of addiction and drugs', Foresight BSAD, 2005

The Economist (2001) 'Stumbling in the dark', 26 July

The Economist (2004) http://cocaine.org/cokecrime/prices.html

Geffray C et al (2002) 'Research on drug trafficking, economic crime and social consequences: contributions to formulate recommendations for national and international public control policies', UNESCO

Godfrey C, Eaton G, McDougall C and Culyer A (2002) *The economic and social costs of Class A drug use in England and Wales, 2000*, Home Office Research Study 249, London: Home Office Research Development and Statistics Directorate, July 2005. Available at: http://www.homeoffice.gov.uk/rds/pdfs2/hors249.pdf

Godfrey C, Stewart D and Gossop M (2004) 'Economic analysis of the costs and consequences of drug misuse and its treatment: two-year outcome data from the National Treatment Outcome Research Study (NTORS)', *Addiction* 99, pp 687–707

Godfrey C, Parrott S, Eaton G, Culyer A and McDougall C (2005) 'Can we model the impact of increased drug treatment expenditure on the UK drug market?', in Lindgren B (ed.) *The economics of substance use*, Elsevier

Hough M and Natarajan M (2000) 'Illegal drug markets, research and policy', in Hough M and Natarajan M (eds) *Illegal drug markets: from research to prevention policy*, Crime Prevention Studies, Volume 11, Monsey, New York: Criminal Justice Press

Hough M, Warburton H, Few B, May T, Man L-H, Witton J and Turnbull P J (2003) *A growing market: The domestic cultivation of cannabis*, York: Joseph Rowntree Foundation

INCB (2002) 'Illicit drugs and economic development', in *Report of International Narcotics Control Board for 2002*

McCoun R and Reuter P (2001) 'Evaluating alternative cannabis regimes', *British Journal of Psychiatry*, 178

Miron J (2005) 'The budgetary implications of marijuana prohibition', Marijuana Policy Project

Reuter P (2000) 'Epilogue: connecting drug policy and research on drug markets', in Hough M and Natarajan M (eds), *Illegal drug markets: from research to prevention policy*, Crime Prevention Studies, Volume 11

Rydell C and Everingham S (1994) *Controlling cocaine: supply versus demand*, RAND

Strategy Unit (2003) *Drugs Project Phase 1: Understanding the issues*, May

Thoumi F (2005) 'Numbers game: let's all guess the size of the illegal drug industry', *Journal of Drug Issues*, Winter

UNESCO (2002) 'The economic and social transformations connected with the international drug problem', in *Globalisation, Drugs and Criminalisation*

UNODC (1997) *World Drugs Report*

UNODC (2004) *World Drugs Report*

van der Veen H (2000) 'The international drug complex. When the visible hand of crime fractures the strong arm of the law. Understanding the intertwined dynamics of international crime, law enforcement and the flourishing drug economy', CEDRO

7 Drug legalisation: an overview of the arguments

Harry Shapiro

Director of Communications and Information, DrugScope, harrys@drugscope.org.uk

Introduction

Since the 1960s, there has been controversy over the prohibition of the non-medical use of cannabis, kept alive by a succession of campaigns aimed at reforming the law. Reforms proposed by successive pressure groups have been either the complete legalisation of cannabis smoking and the availability of a legal supply, or the decriminalisation of cannabis whereby possession would not be a criminal offence, but perhaps akin to being given a parking ticket.

Support for reform has come from many quarters, including from within government. In 1968 the UK Advisory Committee on Drug Dependence recommended a limit of two years' imprisonment for cannabis offences with no imprisonment simply for possession. These recommendations – contained in what became known as the Wootton Report – were rejected by the government of the day, with Home Secretary James Callaghan claiming that the committee had been unduly influenced by the 'pot lobby'. Renamed the Advisory Council on the Misuse of Drugs (ACMD), it made similar recommendations in both 1979 and 1982, which were similarly rejected.

During the 1990s, on the back of renewed interest about drugs among young people, the cannabis reform lobby sprang to life in various guises, ranging from the Green Party and the UK Cannabis Alliance making full use of the internet to promote their views, to supportive editorials in the broadsheets. More recently, a new organisation, Transform, has emerged as the leading pro-reform lobby group. Transform's primary aim is the creation of a legal, regulated market for all drugs currently controlled under the Misuse of Drugs Act.

As well as campaigning groups, some judges and serving senior policemen have expressed concerns about the viability of the existing laws. Also, the rapid growth of cautioning for simple possession of cannabis (and even other drugs) has been regarded as de facto admission that because of the large numbers of people who regularly flout the cannabis laws it is wasteful of resources to push them through the judicial system.

In 1998 the House of Lords decided to launch its own investigation into the medical evidence about cannabis. And, apparently frustrated by the government's refusal to enter into the debate in any meaningful way, the Police Foundation conducted a three-year study into the workings of the Misuse of Drugs Act published in 2000. Since then, the Home Affairs Select Committee in 2002, the Parliamentary Science and Technology Committee in 2006, the Royal Society of Arts Commission on Illegal Drugs and the UK Drug Policy Commission in 2007 have, while not recommending outright legalisation, all queried the rationale and effectiveness of the current structure of illegal drug control.

In response to all the public debate around drugs and on the recommendation of the ACMD, the government reclassified cannabis from Class B to Class C in 2004. However, this move proved highly controversial with claims from opposition politicians, sections of the media and campaigning groups that this sent 'the wrong message' about cannabis to young people. Renewed concerns about the link between cannabis and mental health problems and the increasing potency of cannabis (both often exaggerated by anti-drug campaigners and sections of the media) prompted the government to ask the ACMD to look again at the classification in 2006 and in 2007. Because of the political nature of the debate, it would appear at the time of writing, that cannabis will revert back to being a Class B drug.

Sticking to convention

International solidarity is often cited by government officials as one of the main reasons for maintaining the current legislation against drugs. The UK is one of the 109 major industrialised countries which signed the 1961 UN Single Convention on Narcotic Drugs and subsequent treaties in 1971 and 1988, all of which served to increase the obligations of signatory states. As a signatory, the UK is obliged to make possession and other drug-related activities involving a named set of drugs punishable offences. Because of this, it is often thought that in order for any relaxation of the current legislation to take place, the UK would have to opt out of the conventions.

As other countries such as the Netherlands have made clear, there is a large degree of flexibility in the interpretation of the law, particularly around possession. Some consider possession as relating only to the act of trafficking, and not for personal use – ie an individual found with a small amount of cannabis for personal use will not be considered as legally in possession of the drug. Other countries have deemed fines or censure as punishment enough for possession.

With this flexibility in interpretation, several countries have applied the convention in ways that best suit their approach to drug use. Only where there are 'serious offences' committed need a nation seek imprisonment. Countries that have relaxed their laws include Italy, Portugal and Spain.

What are the key points in the debate?

There are many discussion points around drug legislation. How far do we relax the laws? What is the impact of each level of relaxation? Should we restrict legal drugs even more? Who should pay for the health consequences if more drugs are used?

On a generic level, the legalisation arguments can be broken down into four elements:
- civil liberties versus the duty of the state
- the consequences of drugs being made legal and therefore more available
- whether harm is caused by enforcing prohibition
- how a legalised regime would be managed.

Civil liberties

Freedom to use

Civil liberties have always been an issue in the debate; that is, the degree to which the state is justified in interfering in the private life of the citizen, thereby restricting freedom of choice. The principle of personal choice is applied to a wide range of private activities so why not drug use?

Duty to protect

On the other hand, it is argued that if by using drugs an individual is causing significant harm to themselves or others, the state can rightfully seek to counteract that harm. In its duty to protect its citizens, the state has taken many steps in restricting what it sees as high-risk behaviour. For example, those travelling in cars are required by law to wear a seat belt, and those travelling on motorcycles must wear a motorcycle helmet. In legislating against drug use, the government is seen to be discouraging intoxication and therefore preventing potentially harmful behaviour which may not be of benefit to society as a whole.

Health impact

The issue about cannabis and health (as with other drugs) has probably been the central theme of the whole debate. A succession of national and international reports dating back to the last century have tried but failed to indict the moderate use of cannabis, although questions have remained about the long-term consequences of smoking a drug with mind-altering properties.

An international review of cannabis was conducted by the World Health Organization (WHO) and published in 1997. Controversially, the WHO took the decision not to publish details of a review which showed that in many respects, users of tobacco and alcohol were running the same, and in some cases more, risks to their health than smokers of cannabis. In March 2007, *The Lancet* published a 'league table of drug harm' by Professors David Nutt and Colin Blakemore which put alcohol and tobacco higher up the harm rating league table than cannabis and ecstasy to demonstrate that the legal status of a drug was often unrelated to health harms.

What happens elsewhere may not be applicable here in the UK. It is very difficult to predict what will happen in drug cultures from one country to another. For example, ecstasy has made a much bigger impact in the UK than in the USA, while PCP (Angel Dust) has been widespread in the States but virtually unknown here. Some argue that if we legalised and then had to re-impose a ban, more people would have been introduced to the drug during the period of licit supply, and would almost certainly carry on using it. Therefore, we would be worse off than before.

Others feel that by making cannabis illegal and talking about it in the same health terms as heroin and cocaine, we undermine the credibility of drug education in the eyes of young people. Education, it is argued, should focus more on the harmful aspects of drug use, instead of trying to convey a message that fails to address the most relevant issues.

On the other hand, many believe that any government legalising drugs would be sending out the message to society that intoxication is OK.

Whatever health harms might be caused by cannabis, the harms caused by the drug laws are regarded by some as worse. Those who believe this say we can only improve the situation by law reform. Evidence from the USA when some states decriminalised in the 1970s, and more recent evidence from Holland, shows that cannabis use does not rise dramatically with decriminalisation, leading many to conclude that such a move does not encourage more widespread use of other drugs.

The harm of current laws

While the purpose of drug laws is to prevent what the government sees as harmful behaviour, they are seen by some as harmful in themselves. They make users criminals, create strong and lucrative illegal markets and stigmatise those who need help the most – the addicts. Here are the main arguments for and against.

The arguments against prohibition

The worst aspect of prohibition is the way it hits the user. Many have been saddled with criminal records or even sent to prison just for possessing cannabis. Enforcement of drug laws causes tensions between police and otherwise law-abiding citizens. Users come into contact with criminal networks in order to buy drugs.

As well as potentially wrecking academic and career prospects, prohibition brings in its wake violence and corruption on a large scale, while making massive profits for organised crime. If the aim of prohibition is simply to reduce risks to health, it is a moot point that the means justifies the ends.

The arguments for prohibition

People who use illegal drugs know the risks they are taking. People have to take responsibility for their own actions. Some reform options, like decriminalisation, might make matters worse. It would do nothing to undermine the illicit market while encouraging more widespread use.

How would legalisation work?

Crucial to the debate on legalisation are the issues around the practicalities of one situation over another. On the one hand, making drugs legal, and so more available, will result in possibly more use and therefore more harmful side effects – at great cost to society as a whole. On the other hand, removing or significantly undermining the illegal market could raise drug-related revenues for the government. The main arguments for and against are presented here.

Arguments for making legalisation work

Legalisation would transfer huge revenues to the government by way of taxation as happens now with tobacco, while at the same time wiping out the illicit market and all the problems it creates. Regulating the markets will assure quality and remove the risk of receiving dodgy or even dangerous goods. Savings created by ending enforcement of the law are best spent on harm minimisation campaigns, on health, and on helping those who most need it, such as drug addicts.

Arguments against legalisation working

How realistic is it to imagine that drug syndicates would just give up trading in a commodity that currently nets them millions of pounds? Also, cannabis, unlike tobacco, will grow anywhere, so there is every chance that the illicit market would continue to supply cannabis as the licit product would be highly taxed. Even today, otherwise legal products are counterfeited or adulterated and sold on the black market – legalising them will not eradicate this. The main questions around legalisation have not been fully addressed: What drugs? Who is going to have access to what? How do you regulate? Finally, the legal drugs cause the greatest harm and cost to society, by legalising other drugs, how do we know they will not cause equal harm?

Notes

UK Advisory Committee on Drug Dependence (1968) *Cannabis,* London: HMSO

World Health Organization (1997) *Cannabis: a health perspective and research agenda,* Geneva: WHO

Further reading

Cave J and Godfrey C, *Economics of addiction and drugs*, Department of Trade and Industry, Foresight, 2005

Drug Futures 2025: Horizon Scan, Office of Science and Technology *http://www. foresight.gov.uk/Previous_Projects/Brain_Science_Addiction_and_Drugs/Reports_ and_Publications/ScienceReviews/Economics.pdf*
There are many misconceptions about the consumption and control of illicit drugs, including that: drug users are unresponsive to price; controlling licit substance use may encourage young people to switch to illegal drugs; availability controls are

likely to be more effective than measures to reduce demand. Economics provides both theories and empirical evidence to explore factors influencing current drug use, the costs to society of the harm they create and the cost-effectiveness of different policy options.

Edwards G, *Matters of substance. Drugs: is legalization the right answer or the wrong question*, Penguin, 2005, ISBN 014100309X
This book presents a radical approach to the much-debated question of drug control. Arguing for a consideration of all drugs, from Valium to crack cocaine, as more than their chemical structures, the author expands the idea that the effect of a drug is just as dependent on the social setting and psychology of the individual.

Husak D and de Marneffe P, *The legalization of drugs*, Cambridge University Press, 2005, ISBN 0521546869
This book presents two philosophical views on the legalisation of drugs. One author argues in favour of drug decriminalisation, by clarifying the meaning of crucial terms, such as legalise, decriminalise and drugs, and by identifying standards for assessing alternative drug policies. The other argues against legalisation, demonstrating why drug prohibition is necessary to protect young people from self-destructive drug use.

Kallen S A (ed.), *Legalizing drugs*, Greenhaven, 2006, ISBN 0737724099
This book explores mandatory minimum sentencing, public safety, medical cannabis through a collection of articles presenting opinions on both sides of the issue.

Miron J A, *Drug war crimes: the consequences of prohibition*, Independent Institute, 2004, ISBN 0945999909
Each year the US government spends over $30 billion on the drug war and arrests 1.5 million US citizens on drug-related charges. There are now nearly half a million Americans imprisoned for drug offences. In this book, the author offers an analysis of the costs, benefits and consequences of drug prohibition. He also examines various alternatives to drug prohibition and identifies the most effective solution.

Steel A, 'Regaining control: a critique of drug legalisation policies', *Drugs and Alcohol Today*, 6(1), 2006, p 19–23
Global drug control is coming under increasing criticism. Failures to stop or even reduce drug use and the increasing power of the black market highlight prohibition. Alan Steel explores the potential benefits of licensing drug sales, using models from alcohol and tobacco licenses. Is the solution a regulated market?

Transform Drugs Policy Foundation, *After the war on drugs: options for control*, 2004, updated 2006 http://www.tdpf.org.uk/Policy_General_AftertheWaronDrugsReport.htm
Report examining the key themes in the drug policy reform debate, detailing how legal regulation of drug markets will operate, and providing a roadmap and time line for reform.

US Department of Justice, *Speaking out against drug legalisation*, Drug Enforcement Administration, 2003 http://www.usdoj.gov/dea/demand/speakout/speaking_out-may03.pdf

Websites

Drug Enforcement Agency (US) *http://www.usdoj.gov/dea/index.htm*

DrugScope *www.drugscope.org.uk*

International Harm Reduction Association *http://www.ihra.net/*

Legalise Drugs *http://www.legalisedrugs.co.uk/*

Transform Drugs Policy Foundation *http://www.tdpf.org.uk/*

Urban 75 *http://www.urban75.com/Drugs/index.html*

8 The evolution of UK drugs policy

From: *Drugs – facing facts. The report of the RSA Commission on Illegal Drugs, Communities and Public Policy*, RSA, 2007

Drugs policy in Britain has historically had two facets: a health-centred approach to the health harms resulting from drug misuse and a drive against drug-related offending through the criminal justice system. Each approach has always been seen as important but has at different times been given different priorities. At present, for all the money that has recently gone into providing treatment, the criminal justice approach is firmly in the ascendant.

When drug misuse first started to be conceived of as a problem for British society in the mid-19th century, it was defined as a threat to health and therefore as a medical issue. By the turn of the 20th century the newly emerged medical profession was asserting its authority to define and treat addiction as a disease, and the Pharmaceutical Society was claiming the right to be the sole legal supplier of drugs.

However, drug use in the meantime had also begun to be framed as a criminal justice problem. At the outbreak of war in 1914, British policy on drugs became the responsibility of the Privy Council Office as, in the absence of a Ministry of Health (not created until 1919), no other department was willing to take on the responsibility. Two years later, in the middle of the First World War, an interdepartmental meeting in June 1916 agreed that the problems of drugs misuse were most appropriately viewed as 'police matters'. They reached this conclusion in the wake of public concerns over the rumoured use of cocaine by troops and munitions workers. The regulations promulgated under the Defence of the Realm Act of 1914 introduced a definition of 'harmful' substances (primarily cocaine and opium) and criminalized their unauthorized supply and possession. The new definition brought drugs within the sphere of the Home Office because it was the department responsible for the Defence of the Realm Act, and made it, in effect, the lead ministry in terms of policy, though doctors still retained practical control in terms of treatment.

In the early 1920s the penal approach to drugs control gained ground in the UK. A clause in the Treaty of Versailles of 1919 had required signatories to legislate for their internal drugs problems. The Dangerous Drugs Act 1920 authorized the 'Secretary of State' – in practice the Home Secretary – to regulate the manufacture, sale, distribution and possession of dangerous drugs. The drugs to which the Act applied could be extended in future by an Order in Council when such drugs were considered 'likely to be productive, if improperly used, of ill effects ... analogous to those produced by morphine or cocaine'. The Dangerous Drugs Regulations of 1921 provided for a licensing and regulatory framework to implement the provisions of the Dangerous Drugs Act, limiting the supply, prescription and possession of dangerous drugs to doctors, dentists or vets. This was the first statutory expression of special privileges given to doctors in relation to dangerous drugs.

Two years later the Dangerous Drugs Amendment Act 1923 imposed heavier penalties for drug offences and gave the police increased powers of search. The heavier penalties and new powers were partly in response to a changed public − or at least press − mood. The 'vice' conception of drug use dominated the newspaper reports of the period, with stories of 'peddlers' and 'dope fiends' (Stimson and Oppenheimer 1982). There was concern about high-profile celebrity deaths and drugs were increasingly associated with foreigners.

The stringency of the Dangerous Drugs Amendment Act was also partly driven by the Home Office's desire to follow the model of America's 1914 Harrison Act, which treated drugs as a criminal issue and restricted the powers of doctors to prescribe them. However, the new British Act left the medical profession more freedom of action than did the Harrison Act, allowing any doctor to dispense opiates 'so far as may be necessary for the exercise of his profession'. A regulation proposed by the Home Office in 1922 that doctors should not be permitted to prescribe a controlled drug for their own use was withdrawn following objections from the British Medical Association. The Home Office nevertheless remained broadly opposed to the prescribing of 'maintenance' doses of dangerous addictive drugs on the grounds that 'abrupt withdrawal from drug dependence was possible and that any other form of treatment was improper'.[1]

To set out what constituted legitimate prescribing practice, the new Ministry of Health set up a committee under Sir Humphrey Rolleston, President of the Royal College of Physicians. The committee's report in 1926 not surprisingly found in favour of retaining significant medical input into the problem of substance misuse. The Dangerous Drugs Regulations of the same year reasserted the 'disease' model

---

1 Contemporary document cited in an historical overview of drug policy carried out in the course of the Shipman Inquiry. *Shipman Inquiry, Fourth Report − The Regulation of Controlled Drugs in the Community*, 2004, p 46

of addiction and confirmed that prescribing heroin and morphine to addicts was a legitimate medical treatment. These regulations established what was subsequently labelled the 'British system' under which addicts could receive a regular supply of heroin or morphine in order to maintain or gradually to reduce their use without their doctors being liable to prosecution. 'The legacy of Rolleston was to create a dual approach to substance use and misuse,' one observer has written:

> 'On the one hand the police retained the power to prosecute unauthorized use, supply and possession, thus criminalizing drug users not authorized by the medical profession. On the other hand, the medical professions retained the right to diagnose, define and treat addiction. In this way a dual approach developed, with substance misusers being defined as either criminal or sick depending on the arm of the British system with which they came into contact.' (Barton 2003)

The Rolleston Report had declared that drug use was a problem to be solved and not a sin to be punished, and between the 1920s and the early 1950s the dominant approach to the problem was indeed a medical approach, with doctors prescribing to a small number of individual addicts, many of them doctors themselves (Berridge 1999). But such prescribing always took place within the existing criminal framework; and in the late 1950s and early 1960s the situation changed. Instead of the largely middle-class, middle-aged and professional therapeutic opium users of the interwar years, there emerged a far larger group of much younger users taking drugs – primarily cannabis and amphetamines – for pleasure.

These developments prompted a wave of legislation to deal with the rising numbers of users and the wider range of drugs used in new cultural settings. In 1964 the Dangerous Drugs Act made the cultivation of cannabis illegal, and the Drugs (Prevention of Misuse) Act 1964 brought amphetamines within controls. As for opiates and cocaine, there had for some years been concern that a small number of doctors had been prescribing irresponsibly, with the result that excess quantities of heroin and morphine had been leaking onto the illegal market. In 1965 the second report of the Brain Committee recommended that this leakage should, if possible, be brought under control.[2] The report led to the passage of the Dangerous Drugs

_____

2 Set up initially in 1958 by the Department of Health and Social Security at the instigation of the Home Office, to re-examine the Rolleston Committee's decision to allow doctors to prescribe heroin and morphine to drug addicts.

Act 1967. Regulations under the new Act stipulated that doctors now had to be specially licensed by the Home Secretary in order to prescribe heroin or cocaine and that the names of addicts had to be notified to the Chief Medical Officer at the Home Office (not, notice, to any official of the Ministry of Health).

Under the 1967 Act specialist drug dependency units or clinics were established to handle prescribing. Originally offering injectable heroin on a maintenance basis, they increasingly came to offer oral methadone on a reducing basis. In general, according to Professor Gerry Stimson, drugs treatment was taken out of the hands of the GP at this point and given, for the most part, to psychiatrists. 'This "psychiatrization" of the problem fitted well with the growth of psychiatry as a specialism in the 1960s' (Stimson and Lart 2005). Doctors were still the experts on medical problems caused by the use of drugs, but from now on there would be more and more use of the criminal law to achieve, among other things, public health gains.

The Misuse of Drugs Act 1971 and the National Drug Strategy

In 1971 the Misuse of Drugs Act established the approach to drugs and the misuse of drugs that still prevails. The Act introduced a classification system for illegal drugs (only), in a hierarchy that was intended, at least, to be drawn up by reference to the harms, largely medical, that each substance causes. The Act also enshrined in law a clear distinction between the supply and the possession of drugs, and it set up the Advisory Council on the Misuse of Drugs as a source of independent advice on the risk of harmful effects 'sufficient to constitute a social problem' that might be caused by the misuse of drugs. The term 'controlled drugs' now replaced 'dangerous drugs' in all relevant domestic legislation.

Although much of the 1971 Act was couched in medical language, the 1980s were largely dominated by an enforcement approach in response to a sharp rise in drug-related crime (partly as a result of the restrictions on GPs' ability to prescribe) and also in response to a very rapid spread in the use of drugs. At one end of the spectrum, there was a marked growth in injecting heroin use. At the other, there emerged a new culture of recreational drug use, with the rise of 'dance' drugs – mostly ecstasy and amphetamines – involving a much wider range of people than in the past. The amounts of imported drugs rose steeply, and policy increasingly focused on supply reduction.

At the same time public health concerns over HIV/AIDS and a serious AIDS epidemic among injecting drug users in Scotland obliged policy makers to take seriously the need to reduce the medical harms caused by drugs. That an important role in drugs policy was still claimed for doctors was evidenced by a series of directives from the Department of Health, most notably *Treatment and Rehabilitation* in 1982 and the 1984 *Guidelines of Good Clinical Practice in the Treatment of Drug Misuse* (to be followed in 1991 with *Drug Misuse and Dependence Guidelines on Clinical Management,* updated in 1999). Through these directives the Department of Health exerted pressure on doctors to involve themselves in treating and controlling problematic drug use.

By this time the drugs policy community could be seen as composed of two sometimes competing elements (Barton 2003). Supply and dealing were the undisputed territory of the criminal justice system, but where drug use was concerned both law and medicine were laying claim to the same constituency of drug users. The Home Office retained overall control of policy, which was developed within a criminal justice framework; but the medical profession continued to stake its claims to have some input. In the 1980s, in the absence of a comprehensive government drugs strategy, there was little cooperation: the police and Customs worked to enforce the law, and doctors treated those users who happened to come to their attention. But the need for collaboration was becoming increasingly obvious. In 1994 a Department of Health report entitled *Across the Divide* called for joint working. The following year the Major government set up the Central Drugs Coordination Unit and a ministerial sub-committee of the Cabinet on the misuse of drugs. They were headed by the Lord President of the Council, thus locating the Central Drugs Coordination Unit in the Privy Council Office.

The Unit was the first body to attempt to coordinate drugs policy under national leadership. Its 1995 strategy document, *Tackling Drugs Together,* defined drug misuse as a major social problem, giving it a prominence that it has never since lost. *Tackling Drugs Together* looked at the drugs problem through the prism of law and order but also acknowledged the importance of reducing demand through treatment, as well as through education and prevention; and it gave explicit recognition to the concept of harm reduction. By creating a broader definition of 'harm', to include harms to the community as well as harms to the individual, it created a policy umbrella under which the law-and-order and medical approaches could combine, even if the resources were still going primarily into the criminal justice system and into efforts at supply reduction.

This combined approach was largely continued by the Blair government in the ten-year drugs strategy that it launched in the 1998 document *Tackling Drugs to Build a Better Britain*. The latter was issued from the Cabinet Office, which now incorporated the Central Drugs Coordination Unit, headed by Britain's first drugs 'czar', former Chief Constable Keith Hellawell. The strategy's most prominent feature was its central focus on drug-related crime and its insistence that health services and the criminal justice system should combine to combat it. One observer has characterized the document as calling for 'a strange strategic alliance... between law enforcement and the call for greater access to treatment... Treatment was thus re-conceptualized as an intervention which might lead to reduction of criminal behaviour' (Strang and Gossop 2005).'

The ground had been prepared for an alliance of this sort by the 1991 Criminal Justice Act, which gave courts the power to impose drugs treatment – 'coerced treatment' – as part of a sentence. In the absence of clear guidelines to sentencers or information on the availability of treatment, the courts had so far rarely used this power, but the post-1997 government liked it and in the 1998 Crime and Disorder Act introduced Drugs Treatment and Testing Orders (DTTOs) as a further step towards coerced treatment. DTTOs (since replaced by Drug Rehabilitation Requirements that work in a similar way)[3] require a high degree of collaboration between law-enforcement and health agencies. They require police to catch offenders, drug workers to assess their need for treatment and then to provide it, probation officers to ensure compliance with the Order and courts to monitor progress. Nevertheless, they are essentially criminal-justice led. (In a further development of this linkage between treatment and the criminal justice system, the Criminal Justice Interventions Programme, later renamed the Drug Interventions Programme, would be introduced in 2003.)

The government's criminal justice approach to drugs, as part of its general emphasis on law and order, was made even clearer in June 2001 when, as part of a major reorganization of departmental responsibilities, the Central Drugs Coordination Unit (now known as the Anti-Drugs Coordination Unit) was relocated to the Home Office. The announcement from the Prime Minister's Office read:

---

3 DTTOs are still available in Scotland and there are currently no plans to legislate for their removal. The closest equivalent in Scotland to Drug Rehabilitation Requirements is the attaching of Specific Conditions to probation orders, requiring offenders to attend drug treatment or education programmes.

'The Prime Minister has made a number of major changes to the machinery of government. Taken together, they will ensure a much sharper focus on the Government's priorities... The Home Office will be streamlined, losing a number of functions which are not central to its work, to allow it to focus on tackling crime, reform of the criminal justice system and asylum. As part of this, the UK Anti-Drugs Co-ordination Unit will transfer into the Home Office from the Cabinet Office.'

A little later, the drugs czar was sidelined, being given only a part-time advisory role, and the Home Office openly assumed the lead in the drugs strategy.[4] A similar move was made in Scotland in 2005 when lead responsibility for drugs policy was transferred from the Health Department to the Justice Department. In Wales, however, responsibility rests with the Minister for Social Justice and Regeneration and in Northern Ireland with the Department of Health, Social Services and Public Safety.

The evolution of British drugs policy in the twentieth century is a story of constant efforts by successive governments to use the law, the criminal justice system and the medical profession to prevent the use of controlled drugs and limit the harm that they do. Drugs policy has rarely been a subject of party-political contestation. Both Conservative and Labour parties have adopted an approach that treats drug use as first and foremost a matter for the criminal justice system, with prevention and treatment as subsidiary concerns.

Despite this consistent emphasis on crime, however, the international drugs trade has advanced and developed faster than all the efforts at enforcement and it has proved necessary to introduce new legislation at regular intervals, with the governments of both major parties showing themselves ready to add to the growing body of drugs laws. On the face of it, the large volume of new legislation and the frequent reorganizations of the government agencies dealing with drugs suggest that governments themselves have not believed that existing approaches were proving particularly successful.

---

4 Keith Hellawell resigned a year later in protest at the downgrading of cannabis to Class C and the relaunching of the drugs strategy, which he described as 'a re-spinning of the issue to appear as if something has been done'. *Guardian*, 10 July 2002.

The objectives of policy

Current drugs policy displays many of the tensions of the past. The demands of the criminal justice system compete, in funding terms at least, with the demands of public health, and the demands of social care are often overlooked. The principal objective of policy makers, in our view, should be the search for a better equilibrium between these demands, one which acknowledges that they could more profitably be seen as complementary.

Between 2001 and 2006 the National Drug Strategy was taken forward in England by the Drug Strategy Directorate in the Home Office.[5] The most recent version of the strategy is the *Updated Drug Strategy 2002*. Its overall objective is 'reducing the harm that drugs cause to society – communities, individuals and their families'. This objective is anchored in a philosophy of prohibition. The opening paragraph of the summary of the strategy states: 'We have no intention of legalising any illicit drug. All controlled drugs are dangerous and nobody should take them.'

Scotland, Wales and Northern Ireland are bound by the Misuse of Drugs Act 1971, but within that common legal framework most aspects of drugs policy – notably health and criminal justice – are devolved to their respective administrations. Each has put in place a drug or substance misuse strategy tailored to the particular circumstances of the country. The Scottish and Welsh strategies place particular emphasis on the need for joint working: *Tackling Drugs in Scotland: Action in Partnership* and *Tackling Substance Misuse in Wales: A Partnership Approach*. Northern Ireland had a five-year strategy along much the same lines – *Drugs Strategy for Northern Ireland* – which ran from 1999 to 2004. It has recently been updated in the *New Strategic Direction for Alcohol and Drugs 2006–2011*.

The drug strategy's main objectives

The four strands of the English drug strategy as currently set out on the Home Office's 'Tackling Drugs, Changing Lives' website are:
- reducing the supply of illegal drugs;
- preventing young people from becoming drug misusers;
- reducing drug-related crime; and
- reducing the use of drugs through increased participation in treatment programmes.

---

5 The Directorate was renamed the Crime and Drug Strategy Directorate in 2006.

These strands coincide broadly with the three objectives set out in the Public Service Agreement addressed specifically towards 'Action on Illegal Drugs' in 2000. The first target for 'action on illegal drugs' was to *reduce the harm* caused by illegal drugs (as measured by the Drug Harm Index encompassing measures of the availability of Class A drugs and drug-related crime) including substantially increasing the number of drug misusing offenders entering treatment through the criminal justice system.[6] The second target was to *increase the participation* of problem drug users in drug treatment programmes by 100 per cent by 2008 and increase year on year the proportion of users successfully sustaining or completing treatment programmes. The third target was to *reduce the use of* Class A drugs and the frequent use of any illicit drug among all young people under the age of 25, especially by the most vulnerable young people.

Drugs and the Public Service Agreements

Public Service Agreements (PSAs) were introduced in 1998 as part of the Comprehensive Spending Review process and will be reviewed as part of the 2007 Comprehensive Spending Review. They represent public commitments by government departments to the Treasury to meet certain targets in the delivery of public services in return for 'additional investment'. Each Agreement specifies an overall aim, a set of objectives and a set of targets and sets out explicitly which minister is accountable for the delivery of the targets. The 2000 Comprehensive Spending Review set out Public Service Agreements for every government department and added some extra agreements to address 'cross-cutting issues', of which illegal drugs was one.

The objectives of the English drug strategy have until now been generally reflected in the strategies of the devolved administrations and have remained broadly the same since the strategy was first formulated in 1998. There have, however, been some interesting changes in emphasis. In the original version of the English strategy, for example, there was a strand related specifically to minimizing the

6 The Drug Harm Index is a matrix developed for the Home Office within which the harms that individuals and society suffer due to drug-related crime, the health impacts arising from drug abuse, and the impact of drug use and dealing on communities are calculated.

impact of drug misuse on communities. That has now disappeared.[7] The *New Strategic Direction* set out by Northern Ireland also shows signs of rather different policy priorities.

The strengths of current policy

Britain's drug strategy over the past dozen years – since the Major government's 1995 document *Tackling Drugs Together* – is remarkable for having actually been a coordinated effort deserving of the name 'strategy'. Mike Trace, at one stage deputy drugs czar in the Blair government and one of the Labour strategy's architects, explains:

> 'Until the mid-1990s nobody had made a serious attempt to bring together all the complex strands of how drugs affect a western society and bring together all the issues of how you link up your education work to your treatment work, how you link up your social inclusion policy to your drugs policy, how you link the supply-side efforts with the demand-side efforts... The UK drug strategy of 1998 was the most sophisticated attempt to bring all those strands together, identify what the overarching objectives were and bring all of that morass of activities together into a government programme... My claims for its value are mainly in terms of giving people a structure by which to consider some very complex issues rather than its outcome success'.[8]

The drug strategy has achieved a considerable amount. It has embodied an important distinction between different types of drug use by explicitly focusing on problematic use of Class A drugs (even if, as we shall see, the law itself does not adequately distinguish the relative harmfulness of drugs within the present classification). Over the years the strategy has also made growing, if discreet, acknowledgement of the importance of minimizing harm from drug use as well as preventing or ending it. It has introduced drugs education into the school curriculum. Since 2001, it has funnelled unprecedented amounts of money into

---

7 The four original aims as set out in *Tackling Drugs to Build a Better Britain* (1998) were: 'to help young people resist drug misuse in order to achieve their full potential in society; to protect our communities from drug-related anti-social and criminal behaviour; to enable people with drug problems to overcome them and live healthy and crime-free lives; to stifle the availability of illegal drugs on our streets.'
8 Evidence to the Home Affairs Committee, 11 December 2001

drug services. The drug treatment workforce has been almost doubled and the number of drug users in treatment has increased – by more than 50 per cent, according to the Home Office – with shorter waiting times for the remainder. Drugs have become a much higher governmental priority.

Raising the profile of drugs issues has had the invaluable effects of seizing the attention of the public, focusing the efforts of policy makers and making it possible in consequence to channel funding into the area of drugs treatment. However, isolating a single 'drugs strategy' may inadvertently have helped to foster the impression that there is a single 'drugs problem', and this is misleading.

The drug strategy's weaknesses

It is clear that a multitude of problems arises out of drug use, especially problematic drug use. Problematic drug use is a health problem, because problematic users do serious damage to their own health. Drug use that is currently non-problematic can become so. The association between drug use and acquisitive crime inevitably means that drugs constitute a criminal justice problem. Not least, problematic drug use points to problems in the fields of education, housing, employment and social care. A strategy that confronts all these various problems as though they constituted a single problem – and is based on a wholly unrealistic rhetoric – is bound to be flawed.

More specifically, the current strategy suffers from defects of presentation, balance and priorities. Four weaknesses stand out. First, the strategy's objectives are not clearly or candidly stated. The logic of the harms-prevention strand in its approach conflicts with the logic of a largely prohibitionist rhetoric.

Second, the strategy gives undue emphasis to the relationship of drug use to crime at the expense of the relationship of drug use to health. The strategy is cast first and foremost as a campaign against crime. It acknowledges the health damage and the misery endured by people who have problems with drugs but, both implicitly and explicitly, it treats these as being of less importance than the damage done to others by drug-related crimes and other anti-social behaviour. The strategy identifies its objective as 'reducing the harm that drugs cause', but its view of harm is a hierarchical one, with the harms cause by crime coming at the top. The overall ethos of the current drugs strategy is one of law enforcement and crime prevention rather than one concerned at least as much with education, public health, the health of individuals, social support and social cohesion.

The tendency to accord priority to the imperatives of the criminal justice system is most obvious in the Drug Interventions Programme. The primary aim of the programme is to reduce drug-related crime by coercing into treatment Class A drug users who have committed offences like theft and burglary. It has the effect of securing treatment for offenders far more quickly than for drug users who have committed no crime other than possessing the drug itself. To some extent, the health strand of drugs policy has been hijacked by the criminal justice strand, with the criminal justice system used to force an entry into the treatment system.

Third, the prioritizing of the criminal justice strand of the strategy and the positioning of the Home Office as the agency leading the drugs strategy have created a climate in which it is almost impossible to focus, in addition, on reducing other drug-related harms without looking soft and unconcerned with crime. The constant association of drugs with crime creates a stigma that clings to all drug users, even those who have not committed other crimes, and it undercuts efforts to minimise the harms that problematic users do to themselves. It continues the demonization of individual drugs and the individual drug user rather than projecting drug use as a problem to be solved in communities and by communities.

Fourth, the drugs strategy does not include alcohol or tobacco. This undermines its credibility and its effectiveness.

To summarise, current drugs policy lacks integrity in both senses of the word: honesty and cohesion. There is a gap between the prohibitionist rhetoric produced for public consumption – 'All controlled drugs are dangerous and no one should take them' – and, within the detail of the strategy, indications of a subtler and more realistic approach, aimed at reducing harm. It is as if the government is trying to do good by stealth but, precisely because it feels it has to do good by stealth, it is not doing as much good as it could. Unable to acknowledge all of its objectives, it is condemned to pursue policies that certainly appear, and sometimes are, confused and contradictory.

Drugs policy needs internal consistency, with equal weight being given to health imperatives and criminal justice imperatives and to the needs of drug-using offenders and non-offenders alike. Drugs policy must have some distinct identity of its own, with the problems related specifically to drugs recognized for what they are. But at the same time drugs policy needs to be part of a greater whole. Many of the worst problems surrounding drug use grow out of, and contribute to, other social problems – deprivation, family breakdown, unemployment, educational failure and social exclusion. To such social problems, the current strategy, with its emphasis on the criminal justice system, offers neither quick fixes nor slow ones.

References

Barton A (2003) *Illicit drugs: use and control*, London: Routledge

Berridge V (1999) *Opium and the people: opiate use and drug control policy in nineteenth and early twentieth century England*, London: Free Association Books, p 269

Stimson G and Oppenheimer E (1982) *Heroin addiction: treatment and control in Britain*, London: Tavistock

Stimson G and Lart R (2005) 'The relation ship between the state and local practice in the development of national policy on drugs between 1920 and 1990', in Strang J and Gossop M (eds), *Heroin addiction and the British System*, Vol. 1

Strang J and Gossop M (2005) 'The "British System" of drug policy: extraordinary individual freedom, but to what end?' in Strang J and Gossop M (eds), *Heroin addiction and the British System*, Vol. 2, Routledge, p 215

9 Drug and alcohol treatment

From: *Essential guide to drugs and alcohol*, Harry Shapiro, DrugScope, 2007

Getting advice and treatment

If someone needs help with a drug problem, there are various routes into advice and treatment available in the UK. Users can access these services either through the health and welfare system (eg via a drugs advice service or GP referral) or through the criminal justice system. The National Treatment Agency (NTA) introduced a Models of Care framework in 2002 (updated in 2006) to ensure there is consistency and equity in the provision of drug services across England. This framework provides a tier of types of drug treatment services, classified in a way that is easy to understand. The framework also means that individuals can choose from a range of services available to them and they can move through the tiers according to their needs.

Tiers of drug treatment provisions

Tier	Type	Service
1	Non- specific (general)	General practitioners (general medical services) Probation Housing
2	Open access	Advice and information Drop-in service Harm reduction services
3	Community services	Community drug teams Drug dependency units Day treatment
4a	Specialist services (residential)	Inpatient Residential rehabilitation
4b	Highly specialist (non-substance misuse)	Liver units Forensic services

Tiers of alcohol treatment provision

The Models of Care framework for adult alcohol misusers (MoCAM) outlines a four-tiered framework of provision similar to that for drug treatment but with the emphasis on the level of interventions for alcohol misuse rather than referring to the provider organisations.

Tier	Intervention and setting
1	Alcohol-related information and advice; screening; simple brief interventions and referral. Interventions can be delivered in a range of settings where the main focus is not alcohol treatment, for example: primary healthcare services; A&E departments; the prison service; homelessness services.
2	Alcohol-specific open access, non-care-planned interventions (eg alcohol specific information, advice and support). Provision may be delivered by specialist alcohol services; antenatal clinics; acute hospitals (eg A&E and liver units); psychiatric services.
3	Interventions: community-based, structured, care-planned alcohol treatment. Interventions are normally delivered in specialised alcohol treatment services, within their own premises or by outreach (eg home visits).
4	Interventions: alcohol specialist inpatient treatment and residential rehabilitation.

Health and welfare system

The tier system can be misleading, because one agency may provide more than one tier of service. Hence, services are described below as they are popularly known.

GPs

Problem drug users invariably experience physical and psychological difficulties, and in most cases, the main source of primary care will be their local doctor. GPs can refer patients to treatment services, as well as provide general medical services, promote harm minimisation and participate in an overall treatment regime in partnership with the local drug dependency unit or community drug team in an arrangement known as 'shared care'.

Street agencies

Street agencies provide advice, sterile needles and syringes, counselling, supervised detoxification and other therapies, such as yoga and acupuncture. Usually they are open only during normal working hours, but appointments are not necessary.

Drug dependency units (DDUs)

DDUs are usually located in, or adjacent to, hospitals. They will see users without a referral, but not without an appointment. There are waiting lists, but these have come down in most areas in recent years. DDUs provide counselling, detoxification, substitute prescribing and other related therapies.

Community drug teams (CDTs)

They offer similar multidisciplinary services as DDUs, and, as their name suggests, they are often located in the community.

Outreach services

Outreach attempts to bring the service to the user by offering individual advice, support and risk-reduction interventions, such as providing clean injecting equipment and condoms to those who would not normally come into contact with services. Outreach also offers peer-type education to encourage lower-risk behaviour.

The service comes in two forms: detached work, where workers go out into the users' own environment such as raves and homes; and institutional work, where the service works on site with other agencies such as health centres and schools. Many of the institutional outreach projects have a close relationship with some agencies and are able to put individuals in touch with appropriate helpers.

Residential services

Residential treatment programmes are used by heavily dependent users who experience ongoing social and psychological problems, such as a disturbed family life and homelessness, and who may engage in persistent criminal activities.

Usually residents must be drug-free on admission, which usually means the entrant has undergone detoxification before entry, although some programmes provide this facility on admission. Programmes usually last three to six months, with some 12-step programmes lasting 12 months. Residential services are usually found in rural settings, often with a large catchment area. At present there are around 2,000 residential places in the UK.

Programmes vary widely in concept and practice, but fall into four main categories:

- **Therapeutic communities**
  They operate a hierarchical structure and residents work their way through it as part of the programme. The structure consists of intense therapy sessions involving all members of the community on an equal basis.
- **Minnesota model**
  Associated with the Alcoholics/Narcotics Anonymous programmes, the Minnesota model offers a 12-step programme towards long-term abstinence. Based on the idea that addiction is a disease, and devised by the Hazelden Hospital in Minnesota, the programme offers spiritual as well as practical guidance. A number of programmes offer detoxification on entry, and many may require a financial contribution from the resident or their family, according to their disposable income.
- **General house**
  As the term implies, these programmes differ from one another in their approach. All provide group and individual support. Participants are encouraged to take an active role in monitoring and shaping their therapy.
- **Christian house**
  The programme may be run by Christian or non-Christian staff, with or without any required religious structure. Where there is a specific religious requirement, non-Christian and gay/lesbian people may not be accepted. Those without a required religious structure, but run by Christian staff, offer group and individual support, and encourage participants to monitor and shape their therapy.

Helplines

There are an increasing number of helplines available to drug users, which offer confidential advice on HIV, alcohol dependence, drug misuse and drug awareness, general information and counselling. The main one for drugs is **Talk to Frank** (0800 776600) which offers free, confidential information and advice 24 hours a day. It is part of the government's overall public information campaign to encourage people to come forward for help. Other helplines include **Drinkline** (0845 601 4357), which offers a similar service for alcohol, and **Release** for legal help and general help with drug issues (0845 450 0215).

Self-help groups

Narcotics Anonymous and **Families Anonymous** provide advice and support to users or their families, and provide a self-help regime, usually a 12-step abstinence model. Other services offer participation in self-help groups and counselling sessions; **ADFAM**, for example, provides information about such groups and supervises counselling (020 7553 7640).

Criminal justice system

In April 2003, the government launched the Criminal Justice Intervention Programme (CJIP), under the banner 'Out of crime and into treatment'. It was later renamed the Drug Interventions Programme (DIP).

DIP builds on existing provisions for referral to treatment, and treatment itself, within the criminal justice system, but adopts more of a case management approach which tries to ensure that offenders with chronic drug problems are cared for through the system and, crucially, into aftercare services covering the following areas:

- police custody
- the courts and probation
- prison
- treatment
- throughcare and aftercare.

The elements of DIP covered:

- enhanced arrest referral of drug-misusing offenders into treatment by drug workers in custody suites. This added a case management element and other 'best practice' to the schemes started by the police in recent years
- drug testing, for cocaine and opiates, for offenders originally charged with 'trigger' offences. This became 'test on arrest' under the Drugs Act 2005
- community sentences with treatment conditions (such as Drug Rehabilitation Requirements) attached – to be more widely used and supported by all agencies to make sure they are effective

- Counselling, Assessment, Referral, Advice and Throughcare (CARAT) service in prisons, including treatment programmes – to be integrated into the way drug-misusing offenders are managed by multi-agency teams.

Some of the DIP elements in more detail are described below.

Police

Arrest referral schemes, introduced in 1996, take advantage of the regular contact made with drug users to encourage them to seek support. This can range from the offer of contact numbers, to getting access to on-site drug workers. Most schemes do not require those being approached to take up treatment, and although take-up rates appear to be low for the whole scheme (around 25% of those approached), those who have accepted treatment appear to benefit from their referral, with proportions reporting heroin- and/or crack cocaine- use halved.

Prisons

One of the key objectives of the prison drug strategy is to make drug services within the system more accessible, reflecting more closely the range of services available on the outside. Prisons, therefore, are required to provide a set standard of care, and reduce the harm caused by drug use.

Available to the user within the system are a range of in-house treatment services, advice, information and harm minimisation provisions. (Currently, clean needles are not provided, although some prisons provide sterilisation facilities.) Prison doctors are able to refer prisoners to services that are provided either in-house or by institutional workers. In the majority of these cases, take-up of treatment is voluntary. However, the introduction of drug treatment orders and mandatory drug testing has meant that prisoners can be required to take up treatment within the system or on probation. Individuals must present themselves for assessment and take up a prescribed treatment regime.

CARATS

The provision of help and throughcare of prisoners is founded in all prisons on the CARATS framework. The scheme provides low-level intervention for prisoners with low to moderate drug problems and aims to:
- identify (problem) drug users as soon as possible

- provide ongoing support and advice while users are in prison
- assess and engage prisoners in appropriate help where needed, in partnership with internal and external agencies
- link various departments and agencies involved in dealing with prisoners, including prison officers, medical staff, psychologists, specialist drug workers and probation officers to create the CARATS team
- provide continuity between treatment in prison and that available on release.

Entrance into a CARATS scheme can occur at any stage of a sentence or remand. Prisoners can self-refer, although most are referred following a reception interview, a medical assessment or a positive mandatory drugs test (regular mandatory tests carried out on inmates to screen for drug use). Care is generally overseen by the prison's drugs strategy co-ordinator. Direct care and care planning is undertaken by an allocated CARATS worker, who will meet, assess and monitor the progress of the prisoner. Probation officers take the lead role in throughcare arrangements.

A new initiative is the Integrated Drug Treatment System (IDTS). The objective of IDTS is to increase the availability and improve the quality of drug treatment within HM Prisons by:

- increasing the range of treatment options available to those in prison, notably substitute prescribing
- integrating clinical and psychological treatment in prison into one system that works to the standards of the NTA's Models of Care and the Treatment Effectiveness Strategy, and that works to one care plan
- integrating prison and community treatment to prevent damaging interruptions either on reception into custody or on release back home.

Probation

The core of probation work is to prevent individuals from re-offending, and part of that work is to minimise the problems caused by drug use. Probation services have good contacts with local health authorities and street agencies and can refer individuals to appropriate services and treatment. They also play an important role in: supervising care and reporting to courts prior to and after sentencing; overseeing the management of care and the participation of the user; and providing information and support in the form of housing and benefits. Throughcare may also be available. The individual has the right to expect, from the prison and probation service, the continuation of treatment by retaining contact with outside agencies and close family, and, importantly, making provision for care and treatment upon release.

Different types of drug treatment

The main types of intervention available within the treatment system in the UK are, briefly, as follows.

Advice and counselling

Intervention can range from individual therapy to counselling, as well as advice in arranging suitable housing, work and benefits. Almost all street agencies and DDUs offer counselling as part of their remit to provide support to problem users.

Opiate (detox) detoxification

The aim of detox is to eliminate the drug, usually heroin, from the body, prior to some form of extended support to help maintain abstinence. Doses of the drug, or a substitute, such as methadone or lofexedine in the case of heroin, are gradually reduced over time, or abruptly stopped, until the user is drug free. Other drugs, including substitute drugs, are often used to alleviate several of the withdrawal symptoms. Treatment continues until symptoms, or drug use, have ceased. Detox programmes can be administered on an inpatient basis, usually in psychiatric units or medical wards, or on a community basis provided on the NHS by drug dependency units (DDU), community drug teams (CDTs), or by private clinics (some of which take NHS clients). Individuals are usually referred to such clinics either by GPs or drug agencies. On completion of detox, support is provided by CDTs, day programmes and outpatient services.

Methadone reduction programmes

Methadone reduction programmes involve the prescribing of methadone to opiate users to control withdrawal symptoms. The aim is to gradually reduce the quantity prescribed until the user experiences no withdrawal complaints and is drug free. The degree of reduction and length of time afforded to achieve abstinence can vary greatly from a few weeks to several months, depending on the requirements of the individual. Motivation is often seen as a key issue in such programmes. Participants are regularly asked to review their progress (eg weekly), while receiving therapy and support as part of a structured methadone programme. Methadone reduction programmes are delivered in a community setting, with care from nursing staff and doctors. Pharmacies are the main suppliers of the drug and often supervise consumption.

Methadone maintenance programmes

The aim of these programme is not to eliminate drug use in the short term, but to stabilise the user by prescribing methadone as a substitute for heroin and other opiates – therefore reducing illicit drug use, the need for criminal activity and the harm caused by injecting. Methadone maintenance programmes are delivered in a community setting and may be structured, as with reduction programmes. The methadone is supplied by either a pharmacy or specialist drug clinics where consumption is usually supervised. As a general rule, more complex users – that is, those with more chaotic lifestyles and problematic use, are treated by drug clinics which provide more support and supervision. Less chaotic users tend to be seen by CDTs, which provide structured and supervised off-site dispensing, while those in a more stable situation will be prescribed methadone by their GP to use, unsupervised, at home. It is not uncommon for a user to be prescribed the drug for several months or years.

Concerns have been raised that increasing amounts of methadone are leaking into the illicit market, often sold to buy heroin. This leakage into the illicit market has, it is thought, led to an increase in the number of methadone-related deaths over the last few years. Guidelines for the prescribing of drugs to problem drug users are provided by the Department of Health and the National Treatment Agency.

However, there is also concern that users are routinely prescribed amounts insufficient for their needs, with the consequence that many seek heroin to boost their existing methadone use.

Subutex

Buprenorphine (marketed as Subutex) is preferred by some doctors and users over methadone. The drug has the benefits of methadone without the sedating effects. The Royal College of General Practitioners issued guidelines on prescribing in 2004 and stated:

- 'Buprenorphine may be better suited to those who wish to cease using heroin completely, as the blockade effects of even moderate dose buprenorphine interfere with the subjective effects of additional heroin use. In contrast, whilst high dose methadone treatment is also well suited to those who wish to stop using heroin, those patients who wish to continue to use heroin may prefer low dose methadone treatment.

- Withdrawal from buprenorphine appears to be easier than from methadone, and as such may be preferred for those considering a detoxification program.
- Buprenorphine is less sedating than methadone. This may be positive or negative for different patients.
- Using buprenorphine alone is safer in overdose.'

Heroin prescribing

Very few doctors are licensed to prescribe heroin to addicts. Currently, only 450 people are prescribed diamorphine, although this number may change as a result of renewed interest in this therapy following trials in Switzerland and the Netherlands. The National Treatment Agency and the Joseph Rowntree Foundation have published reports on heroin prescribing. At the time of writing (2007), heroin prescribing trials are underway in the UK.

Treatment for stimulant drug use

Although legally permissible, the issue of prescribing the drug of choice for amphetamine users is a contentious one. On the one hand, advocates of prescribed amphetamine argue that, in extreme cases, short-term maintenance is effective as a means of rapid stabilisation. On the other hand, GPs and drug agencies highlight the risks associated with continued amphetamine use and its inherent psychological and physical consequences.

Most agencies offer some form of limited amphetamine treatment such as counselling, referral to residential rehabilitation and ameliorative prescribing regimes, alternative therapies such as acupuncture, relapse prevention and stress management techniques with alternative (not substitute) prescriptions – usually antidepressants. Structured day programmes are available.

The lack of specialist care also applies to those dependent on cocaine and crack. However, over the last decade, due to concerns about the increase in crack use, agencies have responded by offering more specialised treatment for this group including counselling, cognitive behavioural therapy, and acupuncture and other complementary therapies. Unlike amphetamine, the prescribing of cocaine to a chronic drug user does require a Home Office licence. Thus, the only drug treatment likely to be offered to this type of user would be antidepressants. There are a number of support groups for female crack users.

Treatment for alcohol

Most treatment for alcohol-related problems includes some form of therapy (eg cognitive behavioural therapy) designed to help alcohol users to change their behaviour or acquire coping skills. Brief interventions, in the form of simple advice lasting a few minutes, can help hazardous and harmful drinkers and may include, for example, information about the effects of alcohol and potential harms and setting targets. More intensive and structured interventions may be required for people with moderate or severe alcohol dependence.

Medication can be prescribed to help with withdrawal symptoms (usually benzodiazepines) and to prevent relapse or help with abstinence. However, these are only recommended in combination with other interventions, such as talking therapies.

Services for young people

Most services are ill-equipped to deal with needs of young people (defined as anyone under the age of 18). Services for young people should operate within the Children Act 1989, which entails partnership work with local Area Child Protection Committees and social services children and families teams, along with other relevant child-focused agencies. The parents or guardians of the young person should also be involved where possible, although treatment may be provided without parental consent in certain situations. Unlike services for adults, treatment services for young people are not able to provide a fully confidential service, as sharing information with social services may be good practice in certain child protection situations. Other young people's services, such as needle exchanges, may not be provided without full assessment and further intervention where possible.

Key policy documents concerning young people and drugs are *Every Child Matters* – www.everychildmatters.gov.uk/ and *Hidden Harms* – drugs.homeoffice.gov.uk/ publication-search/acmd/hidden-harm

10 Drugs and the media

Ross Coomber and Stephen Parkin

Dr Ross Coomber, Reader in Sociology, Faculty of Social Science and Business, School of Law and Social Sciences, University of Plymouth, ross.coomber@plymouth.ac.uk

Stephen Parkin, PhD candidate, Faculty of Social Science and Business, School of Law and Social Sciences, University of Plymouth, stephen.parkin@plymouth.ac.uk

This chapter will briefly review and explore the relationship between drugs and the media. It is not intended to be exhaustive nor does it seek to provide more than an introduction to many of the issues raised.

The relationship between drugs and the media is not a simple one. Messages about drugs are often mixed and contradictory, and people do not receive messages from the media passively, simply accepting the views of journalists and politicians without reference to their own experience and beliefs. This situation is further complicated when we consider the *role* of the media. Is it there to inform, to reflect the views of the population, or to stimulate serious debate? It has also been argued that the media is manipulated into playing up and exaggerating drug issues to move the focus away from other sensitive topics, such as unemployment and poverty (Goode and Ben-Yehuda 1994; Kohn 1987; Edelman 1988). These issues will be considered below.

What type of images of drugs and drug users does the media portray?

'Skunk-addicted schizophrenic fulfils sick fantasy by killing a black woman.' (*Daily Telegraph*, 03.04.07)

'Man injected brother with bad heroin batch.' (*Glasgow Evening Times*, 10.01.06)

'H&M drops Kate [Moss] as she faces police inquiry for drug-taking.' (*The Independent*, 21.09.05)

'Nine years for junkie mum who gave son, nine, heroin.' (*The Daily Mail*, 17.08.06)

Each of these headlines are examples of how the national tabloid and local press commonly build up stories related to drugs and/or drug users. The headlines are powerful and succinct, sticking to the commonly perceived dangers of drugs and what happens if you get mixed up with them. Drug stories are considered by the media to be newsworthy, at least in the sense that they are judged to be of such popular interest that they will attract audiences or readers. But it is not just newspapers and magazines which have a consistent interest. Drug-related themes are also the stuff of many films, documentaries, chat shows, commercials (government health education campaigns), and television soap operas. Overwhelmingly, they tend to present a variation on the images evoked by the headlines above.

It is true, however, that depending on the medium involved (television, magazines, broadsheet newspapers, tabloids) the approach will tend to vary, even if the general message does not. So, for example, reports on an ex-steroid user who committed suicide by running head first into a wall while resident in a psychiatric ward was headlined on the front page of the national tabloid *Today* as 'Steroids Drove Him Mad... then Mr Muscles killed himself.' In the local newspaper, the front page kept up the drug connection with the headline, 'Emotional plea by mother of bodybuilder driven mad by steroid abuse' (*South London Press*, 10.3.95). By contrast, *The Guardian* devoted only a small column to the story headed 'Man Died After Butting Wall', but then uncritically reported that the individual had used steroids and that this had been cited as sufficient cause. In fact, it is by no means certain that the 'quality' broadsheet newspapers are necessarily more reliable, for as Bean (1993, p 61) has pointed out, in relation to reporting around crack cocaine, '*The Observer* had consistently been the source of some of the most dramatic forms of presentation and indeed misinformation, even overtaking some of the tabloids... crack was described as "a highly refined and smokable variant of cocaine, said to be so potent that a single dose can lead to addiction... this drug crack is a killer. And Britain could be its next target in the 1980s".'

Most drug-related stories, like those above, do not try to present the story within a broader context or question its facts but are happy to blame the drug as sole cause. No consideration, for example, was given in these stories to the bodybuilder's previous psychiatric disposition or, in the case of crack, whether the reports were consistent with what we know about addiction and the effects of cocaine in general. Assumptions therefore are made about drug effects and their harmful potential which are neither substantiated nor questioned. It is as though there is an underlying assumption that we already know as much as we need to know about drugs and their effects and about drug users and the things they are capable of doing. This is often taken to its logical conclusion by the common use of drug-user biographies:

> 'I have no doubt cannabis killed my son. It's an evil drug. It took his life away. He was a perfectly happy boy – the life and soul of the party. But his personality changed after he started smoking pot.' (*The Sun, 05.04.07,* quoting a distressed mother about her dead son, aged 22, who had used cannabis and skunk over a five-year period)

or the unquestioned quoting/interviewing of an ex-drug user or someone close to them:

> 'As my life spiraled further and further towards chaos, I was no longer able to care for my son and a daughter I had from a subsequent relationship. I surrendered them to my daughter's family and devoted myself to the round-the-clock miseries of addiction, prostitution and desperation.' (*The Guardian,* 29.04.06, an excerpt from a former crack-addict's autobiography)

or reference to what is often just hearsay and assumption and then reporting it as fact:

> 'Crystal meth has been taken by people who come to the court. I know it's being taken, because everyone on a drug order is tested. A lot of them don't know they are taking it – cocaine is cut with it, skunk is being cut with it, which may be in an attempt to hook people, as it is so addictive.' (*BBC News,* quoting Judge Justin Phillips' court experience of crystal meth, 01.03.2007)

Drug stories can be so useful to reporting that even when the drug connection is tenuous to the main story it is not unusual for the drug aspect to be given undue and often misleading prominence. For example, the story that ran under the heading 'Drugs Kill Def Leppard Rock Idol Steve' (*Today,* 1991), actually reported that the musician died from alcohol poisoning not a drug overdose. Similarly, the headline 'Teenager Kim Armitage died after a cocktail of drink and drugs...' (*Daily Express,* 1995) arguably suggested use of illicit drugs, whereas the drugs in question were in fact 'aspirin with her mother's painkillers'. Messner et al (1993) illustrate how a story about wife battering in two major daily newspapers framed it as a drugs story while largely ignoring the violence aspect.

Some stories carry with them widely held assumptions about street drugs that journalists feel able to cite with impunity, despite almost no evidence: 'Ecstasy has turned to agony for thousands of E users as dealers spike tablets and capsules with heroin, LSD, *rat poison and crushed glass* [emphasis added]' (*Time Out*, 27.10.93). Although firmly believed, even by many drug agency workers and users themselves, the existence of rat poison or crushed glass as adulterants in street drugs is almost unheard of (see Chapter 11).

Statistics provide another potentially misleading source about the drug scene, when 'official statistics are swallowed whole [and] where official/expert (or not so expert) statements are uncritically treated as reality' (Shapiro 1981).

What are media education campaigns?

There are often many factual inaccuracies and distortions in media reporting of drugs. For example, in portraying heroin use, popular media in particular will revert to stereotypical images of the heroin user as being invariably spotty, skinny, ill and deceitful, living a life of unremitting crime and degradation leading to the mortuary slab. This view of heroin use was adopted wholesale by the government's 1985/86 and 1987 drug education campaigns, which used conventional scare tactics in an attempt to prevent young people trying drugs. These tactics are illustrated in the Barnardo's poster campaign of January 2000, which depicted heroin use as a way of shocking people. In asking why a young man injects heroin due to a lack of care early on in his life, the poster shows a baby injecting himself with heroin while sitting in his own faeces in a filthy room. The combination of a young vulnerable baby and drug use is a common tool for eliciting horror, sympathy and abhorrence.

A similar poster campaign was launched in Newcastle by the city's *Evening Chronicle* newspaper in May 2005 as part of its local anti-drugs campaign. This image was designed in conjunction with the parents of a heroin user called John Courtney, aged 21. The poster shows John's dead, half-naked body lying on the floor, clutched in the fetal position, following a fatal heroin overdose. The tragedy of this death was made worse when it was revealed that the deceased had been a promising local football player and was a trainee for Newcastle United Football Club. In an effort to illustrate the futility of drug use and the lost potential of a city's youth, the newspaper included a banner on the poster which read, 'If this picture saves just one life, then it's worth showing.'

These campaigns were deliberate attempts to use the media as a tool for preventing drug use, by communicating the potential horrors of heroin addiction. While not being wrong (in the sense that the images can and do represent the *consequences* of heroin use in many instances), they are unhelpful as a way of understanding much about drug use and addiction.

One obvious consequence of these media campaigns was that media reporting of drugs in the more sensationalist forms already discussed was given added credibility. Interestingly, there was anecdotal evidence that some young people found the emaciated image of the boy in the 1987 'Heroin Screws You Up' poster campaign accompanying the TV adverts rather attractive, and used the poster to decorate their bedrooms. The actual research conducted to evaluate the impact of the campaigns indicated that those who were anti-heroin in the first place had their feelings confirmed by the campaign, but there was nothing to indicate that any sort of scare campaign would actually stop somebody experimenting with the drug.

One unintended effect of scare campaigns, which give such massive prominence and visibility to drugs such as heroin, is that they may actually *increase* experimentation with these drugs. In its 1984 report *Prevention* (pp 35–36), the government's own advisory body, the Advisory Council on the Misuse of Drugs (ACMD) warned, 'Whilst we accept the need, in appropriate circumstances, for education to include factual information about drugs and their effects, we are concerned about measures which deliberately present information in a way which is intended to shock or scare. We believe that educational programmes based on such measures on their own are likely to be ineffective or, at the very worst, positively harmful.' Research elsewhere has supported this fear (Beck 1998; De Haes 1987; Hawthorne 2001; Schaps et al 1981). Thus, for some young people, branding the use of mysterious and dangerous substances as antisocial and deviant may (especially if they have seen peers using these drugs with few of the effects sensationalised by the media) provide a focus and new outlet through which their frustrations may be vented and their resistance demonstrated, while for others it may merely spark their curiosity.

Recent research (Miller 2007) has also examined media reports of 'killer batches' of heroin (ie overdoses connected to heroin with high purity levels) in Australia and questioned whether such stories are valid public health messages, moral panics or a means of inadvertently promoting risk behaviour. Miller concluded that these kinds of media reports were instrumental in encouraging drug users to seek out the supposedly stronger batches of the drugs concerned and subsequently impacted on the levels of risk users were prepared to take. From this study, Miller also concluded that media reports of supposed 'killer batches' of specific drugs have little value as a public health strategy – and may have the opposite effect of promoting increased risks within the population being reported upon.

Why do drug articles sound the same? The language of drug reporting

When it comes to presenting the drug issue to the public there is a common vocabulary, with recurrent metaphors informing the statements and reports not only of the press but also of national and local politicians, medical experts and many others. Two of the most consistent metaphors are the drug 'epidemic' – the disease running unchecked across the land, contaminating all it touches – and the 'war' against drugs, where gung-ho language such as 'fight', 'battle' and 'weeding out dealers and traffickers' (all from one story, *The Scotsman,* 19.06.06) is used to reassure the public that the sternest possible law and order response is in place to deal with the problem.

The notion of an epidemic (for example, as in the *Scotland on Sunday,* 26.11.06, headline 'Quick fix for the heroin epidemic is a counsel of despair') is useful because it evokes an image of contamination that cannot be controlled except by the harshest measures – segregation, incarceration, kill or cure. An epidemic is a public health issue, affecting us all. It is not a problem of individuals, but of communities and society. The metaphor completely removes from the picture the active individual, the circumstances under which initial drug experimentation takes place and the context in which continued use is likely to occur – that is, it de-personalises the problem. Epidemics can also be forecast to achieve all sorts of worrying proportions, and, as we shall see later in relation to crack, be exaggerated out of all proportion to the actual problem.

By using and repeating particular metaphors, some have argued that reality is framed and organised in particular ways, 'For example, framing the issue of drug abuse... by using the "drug war" metaphor implies a strong application of law enforcement and even military intervention to the problem' (McLeod et al 1992), as has happened in the USA (Trebach 1987). In Thailand, during 2003, the Thai Rak Thai Party (translation: Thais Love Thais Party) took this warring metaphor to quite literal extremes in an attempt to rid the country of methamphetamine use and production. During a 12-month period, more than 2,000 (ALRC 2005) alleged users, dealers and their families were shot by police in extra-judicial killings that shocked governments and human rights organisations throughout the world.

On the other hand, an emphasis on addiction as a health problem rather than a social one may frame the issue differently and consequently lead to a helpful response instead of a criminal justice one. There was evidence of both these approaches in the UK during the mid-1980s. Concern over the rising number of young heroin addicts (seen as victims who needed help) ran parallel to the more traditional reporting about drug traffickers (seen as 'evil merchants of doom' who needed locking up). Thus the media helped create the climate where substantial new resources were made available for treatment and rehabilitation, while at the same time re-stating the public demand for a 'war against drugs' directed at traffickers.

What is the impact of media reporting on attitudes to drugs and drug users?

The oldest debates about the press have centred around its ability to influence people's thinking and attitudes. This debate remains relevant to the drug issue. If most media portrayals of drugs tend to reproduce existing drug mythologies, fail to contextualise drug issues more broadly, and sensationalise much of the experience of drug use in society, then we need to consider how important this is to how drug use is generally understood and dealt with.

However, trying to determine the impact of the press on attitudes to particular issues is far from easy. Certainly, the aptly named 'hypodermic syringe model' – which has it that audiences are directly and predictably influenced by the media, information being pumped into the body of the population and absorbed – is inappropriate in this case. On the other hand, many surveys about drugs show that most people's main source of information about drugs is the popular media (Coomber et al 2000; Coggans 1991).

Most media output is intended to be informative or entertaining. Research that has attempted to find out how much the media can inform and educate, and therefore alter or even reinforce existing beliefs, has shown that media effects are complex. Different status, class, gender and cultural groups receive information differently and do different things with it (Anderson 1997, 2002; Morley 1980; Tichenor et al 1970; Cantril 1940). Despite this complexity, there are a number of areas where media influence appears able to have impacts that are relevant to our discussion.

First, and most obviously, the general public is unusually dependent on the media for information about any new phenomenon (Katz and Lazarsfeld 1955; Glover 1984). An example of this, the emergence of HIV/AIDS in the early 1980s led to all sorts of negative images and press sensationalism ('gay plague'), providing false messages and information that proved difficult to dislodge, even from some healthcare workers years after more reliable information was available. This also indicates that initial and fearful images may, in some cases, be relatively resistant to future alternative messages.

Second, it is hardly surprising that existing views and attitudes are easily reinforced, particularly because of the cumulative exposure to similar images in newspapers, television, books and films going back decades. What is significant is that alternative messages, although they occasionally surface, are comfortably countered by the weight of messages that reinforce existing perceptions. This is particularly true when combined with a topic or subject upon which individuals are almost entirely reliant on the media for their information. Finally, the language and metaphors used by the media may help frame the way a problem is seen and help set the agenda for how it should be dealt with.

What are moral panics?

One further recurrent theme around drugs and the media is that of the 'moral panic' or the media-led drug scare. In this scenario, the media is able to create a scare through the reporting of drug-related concerns disproportionately to the actual seriousness of the problem. Scares may originate from an increase in Customs and Excise drug seizures or the arrival of a 'new' drug. The theory of the moral panic was originally developed by Stan Cohen (1972) in relation to fears around violence between mods and rockers in the 1960s. Cohen sought to explain how a relatively small and isolated social problem (a clash of the two groups in a seaside town over a bank holiday weekend) was exaggerated in the media to something more. The stories were spiced up with the negative imagery of leather jackets and motorbike gangs, suggesting that the seriousness of the incident was actually related to the type of individual involved, and the fear that such behaviour and fashions among the young would become a broad threat to society as a whole.

The consequences of a moral panic are that it creates an amplification spiral, with the police, courts, government and the general public becoming less tolerant of the behaviour depicted. Similar styles, fashions and images often get sucked into the vortex and an isolated incident becomes more broadly defined. This results in the creation of new social controls (eg, laws, restrictions) constructed as a response to the problem as conceived. Explicit in most theories of moral panic is the idea that the focus of the panic (the group involved) serves to identify folk-devils (eg, junkies) who are then scapegoated as examples of what is wrong with society and who provide a target onto which general fears and anxieties may be pinned.

The crack cocaine scare of the late 1980s occurred during an ongoing anti-drugs (predominately anti-heroin) campaign, and resulted in what Bean (1993, p 59) described as a drug scare without parallel in all those that have 'beset the British drug scene over the last 25 years'. This was despite the fact that little evidence was available of any significant increase in use in Britain. The scare elicited overstatement from all quarters – neither the quality press, television news nor tabloids were immune. Bean (1993) similarly suggested that the crack scare in Britain was media-*led*, based on speculative assumptions about instant addiction, a ready and existing demand, and the notion that problems which emerge in the USA have a strong likelihood of surfacing here. The epidemic never happened and the National Task Force set up to outmanoeuvre and deal with the expected problem was disbanded two-and-a-half years later through relative inactivity. It was, however, indicative of what the media could do with a drug issue. US drug enforcement agents forecast a crack explosion in Britain and hyped the drug as having previously unseen powers. The media chose not to question the reliability of these predictions but to accept them unconditionally. The situation in Britain in 2007 is that crack does have a significant presence in areas of traditional drug use, such as deprived inner-city areas, and does cause many problems. However, the dire predictions about the end of British society as we know it have thankfully not been proved correct – although the emergence of crystal meth (methamphetamine) on current UK drug scenes has provided similar specualtion concerning further societal breakdown and widespread addiction by those that use it. As such, it would appear that yesteryear's crack is this year's crystal meth.

The impact of panics on public attitudes is borne out by research. Reeves and Campbell (1994) relate how in the USA in the mid-1980s the media-led crack scare helped produce a jump in public opinion on drugs as the nation's most important problem from 2% to 13% over the five-month period of mass coverage. Beckett (1994) has described how public fears and anxieties over crime and drugs are often transformed by panics led and constructed by the media, and others have described similar media-inspired drug scares elsewhere, especially in the US (Goode and Ben-Yehuda 1994; Trebach 1987; Reinerman and Levine 1989).

Why does the media present such images?

So far, we have looked at the type of drug-related images presented in the media and considered how useful they are as a means of understanding drug use. We then considered the effects of these representations and found that, although effects as such are difficult to measure, there are circumstances where they are more likely to occur, such as when new information becomes available. We also have to recognise that in general, the media (or at least the *news* media) is aware that it can influence attitudes and behaviour and accordingly tries to reflect that responsibility in the manner of its information provision. We then have to ask *why* does the news media report drugs in the way that it does? At the very least, there appear to be three interrelated factors that may partly explain how and why such reporting has come to pass: the construction of 'the dope fiend', the importance of the human-interest story, and the view that the media acts as a mirror of society.

The dope fiend

For much of the 19th century there was little concern over the very common use of opium and it was taken widely as a form of self-medication for a wide range of ailments. From the 1830s, a number of factors came together that fundamentally altered public perceptions of opium and the type of person who used it. Fears were soon raised about the displacement of alcohol by opium among the working classes and its use for stimulation rather than for medication. Such use was considered as a societal threat despite little or no evidence to support this belief (Berridge and Edwards 1987).

These fears later coincided with, and were bolstered by, the claims of the emerging medical and pharmaceutical professions that opium was too dangerous a drug to be available for self-medication and that there should be controls (medical and pharmaceutical, of course) over its use. This came about because of genuine concerns over the rise in the number of infant poisonings, but opium and other drugs also became the battleground over which doctors and pharmacists fought for control of the prescription of drugs.

There was also a much more unpleasant concern – that of a perceived threat to society from outside – ie, xenophobia. From the 1860s, interest grew in the numerically small but highly-concentrated and visible Chinese immigrant population in London. And as far as the media of the time was concerned, wherever there was a 'Chinaman' (an archaic term that has *always* been used in a derogatory manner), there was an 'opium den'. Literature was riddled with the drug and its effects, from Dickens's *Mystery of Edwin Drood* (1870) to Oscar Wilde's *Picture of Dorian Gray* (1891) and Conan Doyle's Sherlock Holmes stories. Opium smoking was depicted in these books 'in a manner soon accepted as reality... "fantastic postures on ragged mattresses. The twisted limbs, the gaping mouths, the staring lustreless eyes"... Not all writers were so obviously hostile; yet from the 1870s an increasing tone of racial and cultural hostility was discernible' (Berridge and Edwards 1987, p 197). Opium was blamed for the failure of missionaries to convert the Chinese to Christianity, and the use of opium for pleasure became linked to depravity and weakness. The ever-present Victorian fear of 'racial contamination' was only heightened by the newly-perceived fear of opium.

Similar issues had also emerged in the USA in the 1870s, where there was a much larger Chinese population. Kohn (1992, p 2) noted that, 'Variations on this scene set the tone of the British drug panic of the 1920s, firing on the potent juxtaposition of young white women, "men of colour" [the term was current], sex and drugs. If the ultimate menace of drugs had to be summarised in a single proposition, it would be that they facilitated the seduction of young white women by men of other races.' Parssinen (1983) reports that between 1910 and 1930 'In newspapers, fiction and films, the public was deluged with a mass of fact and opinion about drugs. The perception of danger expressed in... the previous four decades, gave way to near hysteria' (p 115). In the USA, other racist images of black, Mexican and Chinese people were being spread by zealots such as Hamilton Wright who propagated stories about black cocaine users who, once intoxicated, raped white women and could only be halted by a hail of bullets (Musto 1987). In England, headlines demonstrated similar fears: 'White Girls "Hypnotised" by Yellow Men', 'The Lure of the Yellow Man – English Girls' Moral Suicide – Fatal Fascination' (Kohn 1992, p 3). With the First World War furnishing reporters with the opportunity to combine drug scare stories with those of alien conspiracies and spies (Kohn 1992), the construction of the drug fiend and the powers of dope were as firmly entrenched as the troops in France.

In the USA in the 1930s, it was the turn of other drugs to be demonised. Harry Anslinger, head of the newly-formed Narcotics Bureau, saw drug use as deplorable and degenerate but, more importantly, needed a 'good drug scare' to keep funds coming in from the US Congress. Anslinger's descriptions of the effects of cannabis seem astounding to us now, but as Gossop (1993) observes they also satisfied a need: 'The smallest dose, he told his eager audience, was likely to cause fits of raving madness, sexual debauchery, violence and crime.' So-called scientific evidence such as this, presented by a highly placed US official, did much to create the negative view of drugs (even comparatively benign ones like cannabis) which was taken by the media. At times, the descriptions of addicts read like science fiction, but these descriptions came from law courts (Wisotsky 1991), public officials and doctors, not from Martians. In the decades that followed, the connection between drugs and 'others' (foreigners) or 'outsiders' (deviants) was continuously reinforced (Bean 1974) and often acted as a catalyst for action against drug users.

The dope fiend had been born, and once such reporting was underway (and it would have been deemed proper and responsible to inform the public of such evils), the familiar media stereotypes became set in stone. These stereotypes then became increasingly reliant on the framework employed in the reporting of human interest stories and the problems attendant in that reporting.

Human interest stories

Curran et al (1980, p 306) have argued that human interest stories are a type showing that life is 'strongly governed by luck, fate, and chance [and] shares common universal experiences: birth, love, death, accident, illness, and, crucially, the experience of consuming'. They seek to reach the maximum audience through appealing to the lowest common denominator; they 'cross the barriers of sex, class and age, appealing almost equally to all types of reader' (p 301). This, they argue, is true of the so-called quality papers as well as the tabloids. A similar approach can be seen even in highly regarded news programmes, such as News at Ten, which recently introduced an 'And finally...' section into its broadcasting. This explicitly attempts to end a normal broadcast of doom and gloom (unemployment, civil wars, famines, etc) with a happy, light-hearted human interest story. Typical human interest stories are looking to hook the audience, with a certain amount of professional licence applied to the material and its presentation. Curran et al argue that commercial pressures since the early 1920s have led to a particular style of news reporting that needs to attract attention and appeal. Drug stories are only one of many topics (along with sex, crime, scandal and dead donkeys) which are considered to do both. Drug issues fit neatly into the human interest story formula, even (as we have seen) turning stories which may have little saleable interest into drug stories in an effort to spice them up and increase audiences.

Whose media is it anyway?

The six-million dollar question has to be 'who controls the media' – whose views does it reflect? Sometimes the answer is easy. In present day North Korea the media is controlled by a 'Stalinist model of an authoritarian communist state to create the world's deepest information void' (Committee to Protect Journalists (CPJ) 2006) in which social problems are thought to be under-reported and where access by foreign journalists in strictly controlled. Similarly, a military junta in Burma controls all media and any 'anti-government sentiment' (such as listening to radio broadcasts from other countries) is subject to harsh penalties and imprisonment. Similar forms of media control also currently exist in Libya, Syria, Belarus and Cuba (CPJ 2006). But in democratic societies like Britain and the US, the debate continues over whether media output is independent, supportive of capitalist ideas, and/or influenced and manipulated by government or media tycoons. The debate is too lengthy and contorted to repeat here but one aspect, the idea of the media as mirror, is important.

In relation to a subject like drugs, this would suggest that for the most part the media provides us with images and perspectives which are in line with reasoned public and authoritative thinking, and is therefore acting responsibly in the public interest. And indeed, much of what the media is itself fed – in the form of press releases, public comment, and government campaigns – contain images that are not inconsistent with what the media then passes on to us. In this sense, the media may be said to be providing legitimate and responsible images and, rather than trying to agitate and challenge what is a general consensus on drugs, merely reflects what people already believe. If this is true (and it undoubtedly is in part) then – when combined with the reporting style of the human interest story and the dope fiend stereotype – we can begin to understand why so many drug stories take the form they do and why they continue to do so.

We might also note that recent research has shown that the UK print media has no quality control mechanisms regarding the reporting of drug-related issues (Coomber et al 2000) and that there is a belief in the industry that good journalistic practice will ensure that reporting on drugs is objective and well researched. Unfortunately, given the tenor of much media reporting and its common failure to engage with scientific research even on the most basic of issues such as drug-related risk, mortality, the nature of addiction and drug effects in general, we need to strongly question the efficacy of journalistic practice in this regard.

Conclusions

Obviously there are many dangers and problems associated with drug use, but the media consistently represents them in ways which distort and fail to adequately contextualise them. This in turn often results in misleading and uninformative images and text.

Why should this matter? Shouldn't people have the worst possible image of drugs? Putting aside the ethical issue of misleading the public, one of the main problems with scare tactics is the impact they have on drug users and the way they may be treated by family, police, the courts and employers. It may, for example, prevent them and their families seeking help because of the stigma attached to drug use.

At present, the relationship between drugs and the media is not a good one and is a simplistic one, cast in black and white terms. If the role of the media is in any sense to live up to the ideal, where 'access to relevant information affecting the public good is widely available, where discussion is free... [and where] the media facilitates this process by providing an arena of public debate' (Curran 1991), then, in regard to drugs, there is plenty of room for improvement.

References

Advisory Council on the Misuse of Drugs (ACMD) (1984) *Prevention*, London: HMSO

ALRC (2005) *Civil and political rights, including the questions of: disappearances and summary executions*, Asian Legal Resource Centre (ALRC), United Nations. Available at: http://www.alrc.net/doc/doc/chr61/pdf/44-ALRC-11d-Mass_extrajudicial-killings_in_Thailand.pdf

Anderson A (1997) *Media, culture and environment*, London: Routledge

Anderson A (2002) 'The media politics of oil spills', *Spill Science and Technology Bulletin*, 7, 1–2, pp 7–15

Bean P (1974) *The social control of drugs*, London: Martin Robertson

Bean P (1993) 'Cocaine and crack: the promotion of an epidemic', in Bean P (ed.) *Cocaine and crack: supply and use*, London: Macmillan

Beck J (1998) '100 Years of "Just Say No" versus "Just Say Know": re-evaluating drug education goals for the coming century', *Evaluation Review*, 22, 1, pp 15–45

Beckett K (1994) 'Setting the public agenda: "street crime" and drug use in American politics', *Social Problems*, 41, 3, pp 425–47

Berridge V and Edwards G (1987) *Opium and the people*, London: Yale University Press

Cantril H (1940) *The invasion from Mars: a study in the psychology of panic*, Princeton: Princeton University Press

Coggans N, Shenan D, Henderson M and Danes J B (1991) *National evaluation of drug education in Scotland*, London: ISDD

Cohen S (1972) *Folk devils and moral panics: the creation of the mods and rockers*, London: MacGibbon & Kee

Committee to Protect Journalists (CPJ) (2006) *North Korea tops CPJ list of '10 most censored countries': special report.* Available at: http://www.cpj.org/censored/index.html

Coomber R, Morris C and Dunn L (2000) 'How the media do drugs: quality control and the reporting of drug issues in the UK print media', *International Journal of Drug Policy* (in press)

Curran J (1991) 'Mass media and democracy: a reappraisal', in Curran J and Gurevitch M, *Mass media and society*, London: Edward Arnold

Curran J, Douglas A and Whannel G (1980) 'The political economy of the human-interest story', in Smith A (ed.) *Newspapers and democracy: international essays on a changing medium*, Cambridge, Massachusetts: Massachusetts Institute of Technology Press

De Haes W (1987) 'Looking for effective drug education programmes: fifteen years exploration of the effects of different drug education programmes', *Health Education Research*, 2, 4, pp 433–38

Edelman M (1988) *Constructing the political spectacle*, Chicago: University of Chicago Press

Glover D (1984) *The sociology of the mass media,* Lancs: Causeway Books

Goode E and Ben-Yehuda N (1994) *Moral panics: the construction of deviance,* Cambridge, Massachusetts: Blackwell

Gossop M (1993) *Living with drugs,* 3rd Edition, Aldershot: Ashgate

Hawthorne G (2001) 'Drug education: myth and reality', *Drug and Alcohol Review,* 20, 1, pp 111–19

Katz E and Lazarsfeld P (1955) *Personal influence,* New York: The Free Press

Kohn M (1987) *Narcomania: on heroin,* London: Faber and Faber

Kohn M (1992) *Dope girls: the birth of the British underground,* London: Lawrence & Wishart

McLeod J M, Kosicki G M and Pan Z (1992) 'On understanding and misunderstanding media effects', in Curran J and Gurevitch M, *Mass media and society,* Guildford: Edward Arnold

Messner M A (1993) 'Outside the frame: newspaper coverage of the Sugar Ray Leonard wife abuse story', *Sociology of Sport,* 10, 2, June, pp 119–34

Miller P (2007) 'Media reports of heroin overdose spates: public health messages, moral panics or risk advertisements?', *Critical Public Health,* 17, 2, pp 113–21

Morley D (1980) *The 'nationwide' audience,* London: British Film Institute

Musto D (1987) *The American disease: origins of narcotic control,* 2nd edition, Oxford: Oxford University Press

Parssinen T M (1983) *Secret passions, secret remedies: narcotic drugs in British society* 1820–1930, Manchester: Manchester University Press

Reinerman C and Levine H G (1995) 'The crack attack: politics and media in America's latest drug scare 1986–1982', in Best J (ed.) *Images of issues: typifying contemporary social problems,* New York: Aldine Press

Reeves J L and Campbell R (1994) *Cracked coverage: television news, the anti-cocaine crusade, and the Reagan legacy,* Durham: Duke University Press

Schaps E, DiBartolo R, Moskowitz J, Palley C S and Churgin S (1981) 'A review of 127 drug abuse prevention programme evaluations', *Journal of Drug Issues*, pp 17–43

Shapiro H (1981) 'Press review July 1980 – May 1981', *DrugLink*, Summer 1981

Trebach A S (1987) *The great drug war: and radical proposals which could make America safe again*, New York: Macmillan

Tichenor P J, Donohue G A and Olien C N (1970) 'Mass media flow and differential growth in knowledge', *Public Opinion Quarterly*, 34, pp 159–70

Wisotsky S (1991) 'Not thinking like a lawyer: the case of drugs in the courts', in *Notre Dame Journal of Law, Ethic and Public Policy.* 5 (3)

11 Drug myths

Ross Coomber and Stephen Parkin

Dr Ross Coomber, Reader in Sociology, Faculty of Social Science and Business, School of Law and Social Sciences, University of Plymouth, ross.coomber@plymouth.ac.uk
Stephen Parkin, PhD candidate, Faculty of Social Science and Business, School of Law and Social Sciences, University of Plymouth, stephen.parkin@plymouth.ac.uk

A myth is a popular belief which has limited use as a way of understanding the subject on which it is focused. While there are often elements of truth in all myths, in the main it could be said that they are based on stereotypical and simplistic images that have their roots in ignorance and which attribute particular characteristics to things and people that are neither supported nor substantiated by much more than hearsay. Furthermore, there are more often than not consequences (some good, some bad) for those on whom they focus.

Drug myths fit this description quite well. If drug users are classified as degenerate rather than in need of help, they will be treated in ways appropriate to degenerates. They may be subject to harsh criminal laws instead of liberal ones; they may be feared and castigated by their friends, neighbours and community instead of accepted or supported; and they may be scapegoated because of what they do and who they are. In short, when drugs are demonised, the same invariably happens to those people who use them.

There are many myths about drugs. Some, like 'once an addict always an addict', have been covered elsewhere. Below, we outline a few of the hardier myths about the misuse of drugs.

What are the differences between hard and soft drugs?

The terms 'hard' and 'soft' suggest the inherent dangers of using a particular drug. A hard drug is associated with a variety of potential dangers ranging from helpless addiction to mindless violence. Heroin and cocaine are considered to be hard drugs.

Drugs such as cannabis, ecstasy and amphetamines are generally considered to be soft drugs because the effects are considered to be comparatively less intoxicating, less likely to lead to addiction and less likely to be dangerous for the user in general. Sounds simple enough, doesn't it? And that's the problem – not only is it too simple a way of categorising drugs but, in the light of some basic information about the drug scene as a whole, it does not stand up to much scrutiny.

Extrapolating the hard/soft argument, legal drugs such as alcohol, tobacco and paracetamol, which are available in any corner shop, must be softer than the 'softest' illicit drug, otherwise they wouldn't be so widely available. Yet the dangers of misusing these drugs are well documented. Although paracetamol is an effective painkiller, legislation was introduced in 1998 to limit the amount of paracetamol (and related drugs) that could be bought over the counter and it was sold in smaller 'blister packs' to help reduce the number of fatal overdoses (Greene et al 2006). Despite these measures, the Office for National Statistics (2007) reported over 1,400 paracetamol-related deaths in 2005. The prescribing of over-the-counter tranquillisers often results in unwanted side effects and may lead to some form of dependence in over a third of prescribing cases (Gabe and Williams 1986). Research has suggested that significant numbers of hospital prescriptions result in a 'major toxic reaction' to the medicine prescribed (Gossop 1993, p 49).

Tobacco alone is believed to be responsible for 106,000 premature deaths in Britain annually (Department of Health 2004), as well as significantly contributing to thousands of cases of heart disease, thrombosis and cancer. Alcohol is said to have caused over 4,000 liver-related deaths in England and Wales during 2005, with over one million other people considered dependent on alcohol (Drink and Drug News 2007). Alcohol, like tobacco, is also associated with serious health problems for many thousands more. Using the rationale of hard/soft drugs outlined at the beginning, these drugs would have to be designated as hard, yet the hard/soft distinction is never applied to them in the general debate about drugs.

Risk of death is one of the benchmarks by which we label a drug as dangerous, but the number of deaths attributed to *illicit* drugs is far less than commonly thought. Even allowing for the fact that there are far fewer users of heroin than alcohol or tobacco, a smaller proportion of heroin users are likely to die from their drug of choice than the proportion of smokers and drinkers who will die from their drug of choice. Granted, there is a far greater risk of overdosing on heroin than alcohol, and dependence is likely to take hold far more quickly than alcohol or tobacco do. However, in terms of toxicity, heroin, unlike alcohol or tobacco, does not damage major organs of the body such as the heart, liver or brain, and tolerance to huge doses can be built up where even decades of use result in no discernible physical damage from the drug itself. (A regular and reliable supply of heroin may be taken with relatively little impact on the user. It is when supply is interrupted that problems are likely to be encountered.) The main dangers (dependence or overdose apart) relate to *how* the drug is taken. Thus the use of dirty or contaminated needles presents dangers as great as the drug itself.

The historical and cultural context in which drug use takes place also influences the hard/soft distinction. There was a time in the 1960s and '70s in the USA, for example, when cocaine was viewed as a relatively benign drug which caused few problems. The advent of crack cocaine (ie 'crack') radically changed this perspective (Reinarman and Levine 1997).

By contrast, cannabis in the 1950s was associated with numerous harmful attributes, including powerful addictive properties, violence-inducing tendencies and the likelihood of producing both moral and physical degeneration. These views contributed to cannabis being originally classified as a Class B drug. Today, these views have very little credibility. Undoubtedly, cannabis would have been considered a hard drug in the 1950s, whereas in the 21st century it is generally seen as a soft one – so much so that it was controversially downgraded from a Class B to Class C drug in 2004. The advent of a new Prime Minister and Home Secretary in 2007 has seen a re-evaluation of the health risks attached to cannabis – particularly those linking the drug to mental illness – and a tabling of the possibility that the reclassification of cannabis could be reversed. A sober reflection on the status of cannabis, however, reveals that the risks attached to cannabis use still fall a long way short of the kind of beliefs that surrounded it and helped place it originally as a Class B drug.

Another problem with the oppositional separation into hard and soft is that it may conjure up an image of soft drugs as harmless. *All* drugs have some level of danger attached to their use. Ecstasy use has been associated with a number of deaths in recent years (EMCDDA 2006), mainly related to heatstroke when combined with long periods of intense dancing. Amphetamine use can lead to a range of problems (tiredness, delusions, paranoia, psychosis, addiction) depending on the regularity and severity of use. Amphetamine is considered a soft drug, yet its effects are similar to those of cocaine. Cannabis smoke appears to be more damaging than cigarette smoke in relation to respiratory complaints and diseases, while an inexperienced LSD user may suffer distressing psychological effects from a trip. Solvents, barely considered by many to even count as a soft drug, in reality kill substantially more young people in the 7–19 age group than all the other substances put together (Taylor et al 1994; Home Office Statistical Bulletin 1993). In fact, between 1971 and 2004, a total of 1,347 people in this age range died as a result of volatile substance abuse (Field-Smith et al 2006).

Finally, the categorisation of drugs into soft and hard is often a reflection of what is also a politically expedient approach to understanding drugs. Historically, groups lobbying for the legalisation or the decriminalisation of cannabis have sought to distinguish the drug from harder ones, by claiming cannabis to be a drug with few attendant problems compared to the severity of harm caused by drugs like heroin. Similarly, the anti-drug lobby constructs an image of illicit drugs, whereby soft drugs are shown to be no better than hard drugs because they seduce the user to seek the stronger, more intense experiences promised by their more dangerous relatives.

Do soft drugs lead to hard drugs?

Another reason why certain illicit drugs are sometimes referred to as soft or hard relates to the long-held belief that experimentation with or regular use of certain drugs (particularly cannabis) will lead – as sure as night follows day – to the use of harder drugs. The theory goes that the user is exposed to drug-taking, is seduced by its pleasures and moves on to bigger and better things. It is in this way that drugs such as cannabis and amphetamines are seen as being gateway or stepping-stone drugs. However, the relationship and transition between different drugs is not quite as simple as this.

While studies consistently show that nearly all heroin addicts have used cannabis, it is also clear that only a small minority of cannabis users will move on to hard drug use. If this were not true, then there would be many more heroin users given the millions who have ever tried cannabis (perhaps eight million people in Britain alone). The findings of a government survey published in 1993 stated that, although 96 per cent of people who'd used opiates in the past year had also taken cannabis, only 7 per cent of cannabis users had taken opiates (Leitner et al 1993, p 203). This trend of poly-drug use among opiate users and mono-drug use by cannabis users may also be seen in more recent studies of lifetime substance use among different samples of drug users. For example, in a study of over 100 long-term heroin users in Scotland, Shewan and Dalgarno (2005) found that 100% of their sample had a lifetime experience of cannabis use. In contrast to this, a study of over 400 long-term cannabis users found that 'although cannabis was drug of first choice, there was consumption of other drugs, in some cases historical, but relatively few individuals saw other drugs as important, with the exceptions of alcohol and tobacco' (Coggans et al 2004, p 303). Similarly, an international study of cannabis use by MacCoun and Reuter (2001) found that 'just 2% of cannabis users [in Holland] had used heroin more than 25 times' (p 127).

Although it is true that cannabis use is the most common first *illegal* drug to be used, most cannabis users have already experimented with tobacco and alcohol, both of which have significant psychoactive and physiological effects. In fact, many heavy cannabis users never try drugs such as heroin, and often exhibit the same negative prejudices and accept some of the stereotypes about heroin users as members of the non-drug-using population. Similar views have been found among users of ecstasy, who typically viewed heroin and heroin users very negatively (McElrath and McEvoy 2001; Rodner 2005)

Gossop (1993, p 103) makes the point that, ironically, the number of cannabis users who experiment with other drugs may be swollen by the simple fact that in order to get hold of cannabis, users have to mix with dealers who may supply other drugs and are tempted to experiment with them much more than if the current controls on cannabis did not make this association necessary. This may be true of those accessing cannabis in older age groups, but emerging evidence suggests that young people tend to access through friends and friends of friends, through family and other peers who are mostly selling only cannabis (Coomber and Turnbull 2007; Parker et al 1998).

That said, there clearly are cannabis users who do move on to heroin. There are also social drinkers who go on to become alcoholics (and, come to think of it, people who learn sport at school who go on to win Olympic medals). The point, however, is that there is nothing inevitable about this progression. There is nothing inherent in cannabis, or a glass of wine, or a run round a football field which propels people up (or down) an inevitable slope.

Who is pushing drugs at the school gate?

One of the most common and hardy drug myths is that of the evil pusher at the school gates or some other opportunist place (the ice cream van is another favourite) enticing vulnerable young children into drug use in order to increase their sales. There is little, if indeed any, evidence to support such a view. In reality, there are a number of amalgamated myths that help construct this particular picture.

One such long-standing myth is that the dealer will provide free samples in order to hook the child, and that once hooked the child will bring a new and regular income. There are a couple of problems with this scenario (Coomber 2006):

- Most schoolchildren do not have a regular and sufficient income to actually become dependent on drugs, which can be a lengthy and expensive process.
- Pushing drugs onto schoolchildren would also present an unreasonable risk to the seller. Parents and teachers would soon learn of such a character and act accordingly.

Although there is little research on drug dealing in schools, it is likely that where drugs are available in school, it will be one of the students who has access to them and is either dealing to make a bit of cash or selling their own excess to friends (Coomber and Turnbull 2007).

There has always been a fear of the unscrupulous and degenerate character preying on the weakest for their own gain. The fact that the archetypal pusher is not found or caught rarely disproves to believers that he did not exist in the first place. Unfortunately for the mythmakers, initial and early drug use has little to do with pushers as they are conventionally portrayed. Initial provision of an illicit drug is nearly always from within the peer group (friends and acquaintances) or the family (an older brother or sister). It is unlikely that unknown pushers would have much success enticing people into drug use, as they are not equipped with the security of the peer/kin group which gives the drug credibility and desirability, and provides a setting in which it can be taken and learned about, thereby providing a context in which second, third and continuing use can occur.

This persistent mythology sets up parents and children to resist temptation from evil strangers, but this can divert attention from the settings where experimentation is most likely to occur. Friends, friends of friends, relatives and neighbours are not drug fiends, but they are more likely to be the source of drug experimentation than a menacing figure in shadow and shades.

Is addiction inevitable?

The notion that certain drugs have the power to make individuals immediately crave them and compel them towards more use and inevitable addiction is yet another drug fallacy. Recently, we have heard much about the powers of crack cocaine to produce instant addiction. This is not the first time a drug has been given such a press. Heroin is another drug to which such powers are often attributed: an American book was titled *It's so good don't even try it once* (Smith and Gay 1972). Currently, methamphetamine (or 'crystal-meth') is a drug that is causing great concern in the British media and drug services as a result of its supposed 'super-addictiveness' that is considered to be 'ten times stronger than other amphetamines' (Campbell 2007). So great are these fears and concerns about the introduction of crystal meth to the UK that in January 2007 the Association for Chief Police Officers put the country's police forces on high alert about this substance, as it was found some drug users believed they had been taking crack cocaine, when in fact they had been consuming crystal meth (Taylor 2007).

In reality, the process of becoming dependent on drugs such as heroin, for example, is quite lengthy and relies on a number of factors related to personal circumstances (Coomber and Sutton 2006). Most people who try it for the first time are physically sick and won't bother again. Others will try it a few times and then decide heroin isn't for them. If people continue taking the drug, tolerance builds up so that there is a need for higher and more frequent doses to get the same effect. If people got to the point where they were using the drug on a daily basis and then suddenly stopped using it, they would experience the classic heroin withdrawal symptoms. This would mean their body had become physically dependent on heroin and they would feel ill if they stopped using. To feel normal they would need to take more heroin. Even then, it can take many months for someone to reach the point where they are so hooked on heroin both physically and psychologically that it completely dominates their life (Coomber and Sutton 2006; Bennett 1986; Kaplan 1983).

The effects of smoking crack cocaine are very different from those of smoking or injecting heroin, but many of the lessons are the same. Dependence on any drug does not occur solely because of the drug's effects. Although crack cocaine provides a quick and intense euphoria and dependence *may* occur more quickly than to cocaine powder, to become addicted to crack (a psychological addiction in this case) an individual has to be dedicated to the daily ritual of obtaining money for drugs, arranging to buy them, use them, come down from the effects and start all over again. Crack is one of the more recent drugs to be labelled 'instantly addictive', but there is enough research evidence to show that many people do not enjoy the crack experience and fail to repeat it, while others can 'take it or leave it', primarily because to acquire a 'crack habit' means finding hundreds of pounds every week (Ditton and Hammersley 1994; Miller 1991; Newcombe and Matthews 1989; Reinarman and Levine 1997). The association with instant addiction and this particular drug may say more about the type of user *most visible* in the US experience. Research into freebase cocaine users and some crack users suggests that many are, in fact, more involved in heavy and multiple drug use than other users. Thus the scare over the powers of crack may have been exacerbated by the *visibility* of existing heavy drug users using a new drug (crack) to excess, and apparently demonstrating its ability to hook quickly and easily those people already heavily involved in a drug-using lifestyle (Bourgois 2003).

Is withdrawal that bad?

A common myth about heroin dependence is that the pain of withdrawal is unbearable and even life threatening. This is probably a major reason why many heroin users are scared of giving up the drug, and it also helps reinforce the notion that heroin is a drug which enslaves users forever, or at least until they die. Abrupt withdrawal from some drugs such as alcohol, barbiturates and tranquillizers can be highly dangerous, but for many users the effects of withdrawing from heroin are similar to a very bad dose of flu – not very pleasant, but hardly life threatening.

Of course, physically withdrawing from the drug so it is no longer in the body is only the beginning of the process of coming off drugs. As one musician said many years ago about heroin, 'They can get it out of your body, but they can't get it out of your mind.' Although this is an exaggeration, it is true that rehabilitation is a long process involving major changes of attitude, motivation, lifestyle and so on, so that drugs are no longer the central feature of a person's life.

Are drugs adulterated?

There is a widespread notion that dangerous adulteration adds considerably to the risks of illicit drug use. It's often implied that users play a kind of pharmacological Russian roulette. In fact, the risks from dangerous cutting agents (see below) are negligible.

It is commonly believed by the general public, accepted by drug users and health professionals, and reported by the media, that street drugs such as heroin are adulterated (cut) with dangerous substances (cutting agents), eg brick dust, rat poison, ground-up light bulb glass, chalk and scouring powders such as Vim and Ajax among others (Coomber 1997a, 1997b, 1999a and 2006). Actual examination of drugs indicates that far less cutting takes place than is generally thought to be the case (Coomber 1997c, 1999b). Such beliefs were exemplified in a 'health alert' notification circulated by the police to various health agencies in the south-west of England during 2006. This 'evidence based' alert was concerned with notifying drug injectors and service personnel of the need to be aware of a batch of heroin that was believed to contain cement, and that had been responsible for several local drug-related deaths. Subsequent toxicological reports of those that had died from this heroin, however, found no evidence of cement in their bodies – and that all had died of genuine drug overdoses (Plymouth Drug and Alcohol Team 2006).

With heroin, what cutting does take place is predominately carried out before importation and with substances that often enhance, not diminish, the drug's effect. Adulteration is by and large not due to the haphazard desperation of a 'strung-out junkie', or the routine dilution of the drug as it makes its way through the chain of distribution.

What is in street drugs?

Forensic analysis of street drugs does not find any of the substances listed above. In heroin, the most common cutting agents in the late 1990s were caffeine and paracetamol. Comprehensive analysis of heroin samples by the US Drug Enforcement Administration (DEA) since 1990 reveals numerous sugars, prescription drugs (primarily paracetamol), opium alkaloids and occasionally salts. None of the dangerous cutting agents commonly claimed and feared have been found. In Europe, sugars are less likely to be found in heroin. But, here as well, dangerous cutting agents are not found.

One survey of heroin street seizures from around the UK found that nearly 50% of the 228 samples tested did not contain any adulterants at all (Coomber 1997c). This indicates that the cutting of street drugs is far from a predictable outcome of passing through the chain of distribution. Analysis by the US DEA of US heroin (from Mexico) found that in some major cities, even where the selling is gang controlled, buying adulterated heroin may be difficult.

There are a number of reasons why less cutting takes place than is normally assumed (Coomber 1997d). Dealers usually resort to safer methods of increasing profit from drug sales, such as selling smaller amounts for proportionately more money. A related method is selling short measures. A dealer may make 30 single gram wraps from an ounce instead of the standard 28 (Coomber 1997b, 1997d). These methods result in additional profit but do not contaminate the sample (which they usually assume has already been cut). There is no additional danger beyond that entailed in the drug itself.

Risk in drug selling is perceived as a two-way street. Dealers fear reprisal if they were thought to be selling bad drugs. Also, it is not unusual for them to want to protect a reputation for selling good-quality drugs. There is also a reasonable concern that they do not want to harm others (Coomber 1997b, 1997d). Drug dealers are generally not chemists or otherwise knowledgeable about what is a healthy or dangerous cutting substance. The result is that the cutting of street drugs by dealers or desperate addicts is neither systematic nor predictable.

Why is cutting presumed?

Given there is almost no forensic evidence to suggest that dangerous cutting agents are put into street drugs, why is the belief in it so strong? Even drug dealers believe that other dealers do it.

The question is worth asking because there seems to be little concrete evidence to support the notion, even from drug users. The residue left after preparing injected and/or inhaled drugs shows no evidence of unusual insoluble cutting agents, or other indications of adulteration with dangerous substances (Coomber, unpublished)

If adulterants are not found in the residue, then where? Users often believe they can tell when a drug they have taken contains something other than the primary drug (Coomber and Maher 2006; McElrath and McEvoy 2001). In one research sample, 37 of 319 previously taken ecstasy samples were believed by those users to have contained heroin (Forsyth 1995). Similarly, in McElrath and McEvoy's (2001) study of ecstasy users in Northern Ireland, they found that certain individuals believed they may develop an addiction to heroin through using ecstasy that they believed had been adulterated with this drug. Heroin has never been found in ecstasy tablets and as such it is very unlikely that an addiction to it would result from using such pills.

In another sample, cocaine users provided the researcher with cocaine they believed to be adulterated with amphetamine: something they and many others believed to be a common cutting agent of cocaine. No amphetamine was found in these samples and forensic analysis almost never finds amphetamine in cocaine (Cohen 1989).

Is LSD often contaminated with strychnine?

LSD users often believe the stomach ache that sometimes accompanies use of this drug comes from strychnine in the original solution. One user told me this was well known. Strychnine is not found in LSD.

When a user has an adverse reaction to a drug it is not uncommon to blame dangerous cutting agents. This line of thought is particularly evident among peers when the individual concerned is an experienced user. It is also the first line of thought for authorities such as the police when responding to a tragedy such as the death of Leah Betts in 1995. Leah Betts was a British schoolgirl who took an ecstasy tablet as part of her 18th birthday celebrations and later failed to come out of a coma. Her subsequent death became the centre of media attention and anti-drug campaigns during 1995–96. However, analysis of the ecstasy she had taken did not reveal anything but the drug and toxicological reports into her death concluded that she died of water intoxication as a result of her use of ecstasy (ie she drank too much water in an attempt to remain hydrated).

Adverse reactions

In cases of overdose and other adverse reactions to drugs such as heroin, where samples are analysed nothing unusual is generally found. Purity can sometimes be very high, but this is also not common. Blood tests of those who end up in hospital do not show poisons other than the drug in question.

More reasoned explanations of why adverse reactions occur relate to build-up overdose. The individual consumes more than normal over a period of time, without realising it. This also partly explains why such events can happen to only one user in a group, where all had been using the same sample.

A usual factor in adverse reactions is drug mixing, most commonly with alcohol. One research paper suggested that most events recorded as heroin overdoses are in fact nothing of the sort (Darke and Zador 1996). Similarly, Forsyth's (2001) comparative study of toxicology and newspaper reports of Scottish drug deaths found that the media tended to give disproportionate attention to atypical fatalities. Namely, those deaths that involved young people (particularly females) who had been using stimulant drugs (especially ecstasy) tended to receive the most media attention. However, what the newspapers under-reported in such deaths (but what *was* contained within the toxicology reports of the same deaths) was the evidence relating to the use of several different substances that may have caused a fatality. In this way, Forsyth states, the media can present a distorted view on the effects of particular drugs (such as ecstasy), particularly when such drugs may have been mixed with other substances leading to tragic consequences.

A third contributing factor to adverse reactions is inappropriate co-activity. With ecstasy, this would be over-exertion without periodic rehydration or chilling-out, or over-rehydration – ie drinking too much water.

Belief without evidence

If users cannot in reality tell whether a drug is cut with particular substances or not and do not find suspicious residue in their drugs post-preparation, why do they assume dangerous cutting practices are to blame for ill health or overdose? In the absence of concrete evidence, it is difficult to know exactly how a belief system such as this arises. It is almost unquestioned and believed even by those who are supposed to do it – the dealers. There are three primary issues:

- the development of images of the dope fiend at the end of the last century and up to the present day
- certain common drug myths that reinforce each other, each proving the truth of the other
- the clandestine nature of drug supply (Coomber 1997e).

Drugs like heroin and cocaine have long had the reputation of transforming users into moral degenerates. Over 50 years ago, the dope fiend was associated with the capability to carry out the most heinous of crimes. '... [he] becomes a moral degenerate, liar, thief, etc, because of the direct influence of the drug' (Lindesmith 1941).

The heroin campaigns of the 1980s presented similar images of moral degeneracy brought about by addiction (Rhodes 1990). Media images of pushers targeting the young at school gates and street corners depict drug dealers as willing to hook the most vulnerable members of society to ensure a steady custom (Coomber 2006).

Drug transformation

The supposed transformative powers of drugs are important for understanding how dangerous adulteration could be believed. Knowingly putting dangerous substances, such as strychnine, ground glass or scouring powders, into drugs that you are to sell is clearly an act of premeditated violence or of diminished responsibility. Both fit into the broad spectrum of beliefs about how this practice occurs, but neither makes any real sense.

Even strung-out junkies who don't care what they put into the drugs they sell in order to dilute them (diminished responsibility/morally degenerate), would find it is easier to grab sugar off the shelf, or buy glucose or lactose (both cheap) than to find strychnine or spend time grinding down a brick, a light bulb or chalk.

A number of drug myths, when considered in isolation, do not hold up to scrutiny. There is little or no evidence for the pusher at the street corner/school gate preying on children and giving away free samples. Such pushers are not found, though stories of them are common, and drugs like heroin do not become addictive quickly enough to make this a viable economic activity (Kaplan 1983; Coomber and Sutton 2006). When combined with the assumption of dangerous adulteration they gain plausibility. Thus, the evil drug dealer, likely to prey on the young, becomes credible because of the widely accepted existence of dangerous drug adulteration.

The chain of assumption runs: dangerous drug adulteration occurs because the transformative powers of drugs degenerate the moral faculties of drug dealers (turns them into dope fiends and junkies) and make it possible or, in times of desperation, likely. Of course, only crazy or evil individuals would cut the drugs they sell with dangerous substances and to such individuals, pushing drugs on the vulnerable would give little concern.

But dangerous drug adulteration does not occur. Rather than showing no regard for their customers, dealers are often concerned not to harm them (Coomber 1997b). A more considered view of who and what the drug dealer is must now be undertaken. Without the underlying assumptions relating to dangerous adulteration, other drug myths are left with little or no foundation.

Buyer beware

To these concerns must be added the context in which drug selling takes place. Mistrust of retailers by consumers is common even in licit buying and selling. A second-hand car may have been patched-up, written-off or stolen. The 'pure' orange juice or the '100 per cent beef' product we buy may be something quite different. Concern about being cheated or ripped-off is part of everyday life, so we should not be surprised when such fears and anxieties are magnified in an illicit and clandestine market.

To some extent, consumers of drugs may even invest in the danger of the illicit market place. Drug use is generally a fairly mundane activity. Convincing yourself that there is a possible danger in every hit, beyond that of the drug, arguably makes it a little bit more interesting.

Common assumptions about dangerous drug adulteration are, by and large, mistaken. Dangerous cutting agents do not represent significant risk to drug users. Drugs are not cut with any substance routinely or haphazardly down through the chain of distribution.

In fact, the contaminants found in heroin for smoking, such as caffeine or paracetamol, often increase the amount of heroin available rather than reducing the quality of the drug.

By emphasising imaginary risks of dangerous cutting agents, the media and other authorities divert attention from the real risks of the drugs and the inappropriate activities that may accompany their use. They also reproduce unhelpful stereotypes about drugs, addiction and those who sell drugs.

References

Bennett T (1986) 'A decision-making approach to opioid addiction', in Cornish D B and Clarke R V (eds) *The reasoning criminal: rational choice perspectives in offending*, New York: Springer-Verlag

Bourgois P L (2003) *In search of respect: selling crack in El Barrio*, Cambridge: Cambridge University Press

Campbell C (2007) 'Crystal meth: Middle England's new crack cocaine?', *Daily Mail*, 8 January 2007. Available at: http://www.dailymail.co.uk/pages/live/articles/news/news.html?in_article_id=427170&in_page_id=1770

Cohen P (1989) *Cocaine use in Amsterdam – in non-deviant sub-cultures*, Amsterdam: University of Amsterdam Press

Coggans N, Dalgarno P, Johnson L and Shewan D (2004) 'Long-term heavy cannabis use: implications for health education', *Drugs: Education, Prevention and Policy*, 11, 4, 299–313

Coomber R (1997a) 'Vim in the veins – fantasy or fact: the adulteration of illicit drugs', *Addiction Research*, 5(3), p 195–212

Coomber R (1997b) 'The adulteration of drugs: what dealers do, what dealers think', *Addiction Research* 5(4), p 297–306

Coomber R (1997c) 'How often does the adulteration/dilution of heroin actually occur: an analysis of 228 street samples across the UK (1995–1996) and discussion of monitoring policy', *International Journal of Drug Policy*, 8(4), p 178–86.

Coomber R (1997d) 'Dangerous drug adulteration – an international survey of drug dealers using the internet and the world wide web (www)', *International Journal of Drug Policy*, 8(2), p 18–28

Coomber R (1997e) 'Adulteration of drugs: the discovery of a myth', *Contemporary Drug Problems*: 24(2), p 239–71

Coomber R (1999a) 'Lay perceptions and beliefs about the adulteration of illicit drugs in 1990s: a student sample', *Addiction Research* 7(4) p 323–38

Coomber R (1999b) 'The cutting of heroin in the United States in the 1990s', *Journal of Drug Issues*, Winter 1999, pp 17–36

Coomber R (2006) *Pusher myths: resituating the drug dealer*, London: Free Association Press

Coomber R (Unpublished) 'Post-preparation residue: a contribution to beliefs in the dangerous adulteration of street drugs?', Unpublished research

Coomber R and Maher L (2006) 'Street level drug market activity at two of Australia's primary dealing areas: consideration of organization, cutting practices and violence', *Journal of Drug Issues*, p 719–54

Coomber R and Sutton C (2006) 'How quick to heroin dependence?', *Drug and Alcohol Review*, 25 (4), p 463–71

Coomber R and Turnbull P (2007) 'Arenas of drug transaction: Adolescent cannabis transactions in England – "social supply" ', *Journal of Drug Issues*, 37(4), pp 845–66

Darke S and Zador D (1996) 'Fatal heroin overdose: a review', *Addiction*, 91(12), p 1765–72

Drink and Drug News (2007) 'Safe, sensible, social... and effective?', *Drink and Drug News*, 18 June 2007. Also available at www.drinkanddrugnews.net (last accessed 24 June 2007)

Department of Health (2004) *Tobacco and borders: death made cheaper*, London: Department of Health. Available at: http://www. dh.gov.uk/en/Policyandguidance/Healthandsocialcaretopics/Tobacco/ Tobaccogeneralinformation/DH_4126403 (last accessed 23 June 2007)

Ditton J and Hammersley R (1994) 'The typical cocaine user: how our blinkered vision of the cocaine user has created the myth of cocaine's irresistibility', *DrugLink*, 9, 6, pp 11–14

EMCDDA (2006) *The state of the drugs problem in Europe. Annual report 2006*, Lisbon: European Monitoring Centre for Drugs and Drug Addiction

Field-Smith M E, Butland B K, Ramsey J D and Anderson H K (2006) *Trends in death associated with abuse of volatile substances*, London: St George's, University of London. Available at www.vsareport.org (last accessed 23 June 2007)

Forsyth A J M (1995) 'Ecstasy and illegal drug design: a new concept in drug use', *International Journal of Drug Policy*, 6(3) pp 193–209

Forsyth A J M (2001) 'Distorted? A quantitative exploration of drug fatality reports in the popular press', *International Journal of Drug Policy* 12, pp 435–53

Gabe J and Williams P (eds) (1986) *Tranquillisers: social, psychological and clinical perspectives*, London: Tavistock

Gossop M (1993) *Living with drugs* (3rd edition), Cambridge: Arena

Greene S L, Dargan P I, Leman P and Jones A L (2006) 'Paracetamol availability and recent changes in paracetamol poisoning: is the 1998 legislation limiting availability of paracetamol being followed?' *Postgraduate Medical Journal*, 82, pp 520–3

Home Office Statistical Bulletin (1993) *Statistics of drug addicts notified to the Home Office, United Kingdom 1992*, Issue 15/93, 27 May

Kaplan J (1983) *The hardest drug: heroin and public policy*, Chicago: University of Chicago Press

Leitner M, Shapland J and Wiles P (1993) *Drug usage and drugs prevention*, London: The Stationery Office

Lindesmith A R (1941) 'Dope fiend mythology', *Journal of Criminal Law and Criminology.* 32, pp 199–208

MacCoun R and Reuter R (2001) 'Evaluating alternative cannabis regimes', *British Journal of Psychiatry*, 178, pp 123–8. Available at: http://bjp.rcpsych.org/cgi/reprint/178/2/123

McElrath K and McEvoy K (2001) 'Heroin as evil: ecstasy users' perceptions about heroin', *Drugs: Education, Prevention and Policy* 8 (2), pp 177–89

Miller R M (1991) *The case for legalising drugs*, Westport: Praeger

Newcombe R and Matthews L (1989) 'Crack in Liverpool', *DrugLink*, September/October, p 16

Office for National Statistics (2007) *Deaths related to drug poisoning, England and Wales, 2005*, London: Office for National Statistics. Available at: http://www.statistics.gov.uk/statbase/Product.asp?vlnk=11695 (last accessed 23 June 2007)

Parker H, Measham F and Aldridge J (1998) *Illegal leisure: normalization of adolescent recreational drug use*, London: Routledge

Plymouth Drug and Alcohol Team (2006) Personal communication via e-mail

Reinarman C and Levine H G (997) *Crack in America: demon drugs and social justice*, Berkeley: University of California Press

Rhodes T (1990) 'The politics of anti-drugs campaigns', *DrugLink* 5(3), p 16–18

Rodner S (2005) ' "I'm not a drug abuser, I am a drug user": a discourse analysis of 44 drug users' construction of identity', *Addiction Research and Theory* 13 (4), pp 333–46

Shewan D and Dalgarno P (2005) 'Evidence for controlled heroin use? Low levels of negative health and social outcomes among non-treatment heroin users in Glasgow (Scotland)', *British Journal of Health Psychology*, 10, pp 33–48

Smith D E and Gay G (1972) *It's so good don't even try it once: heroin in perspective*, New York: Prentice-Hall

Taylor M (2007) 'Police issue warning on spread of crystal meth', *The Guardian*, 25 January 2007. Available at: http://www.guardian.co.uk/drugs/Story/0,,1997972,00.html

Taylor J C, Norman C L, Bland J M, Anderson H R and Ramsey J D (1994) *Trends in deaths associated with abuse of volatile substances* 1971–1992, Report No 7, London: St George's Hospital Medical School

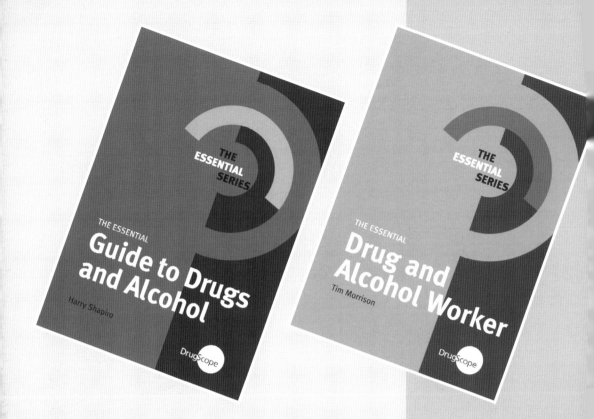

THE
ESSENTIAL
SERIES